The Viennese Pastry Cookbook

The Viennese Pastry Cookbook

Lilly Joss Reich

Biscuit Books, Inc.
Newton, Massachusetts

All pastries that appear on the cover were prepared by the author.

Cover photograph by Otto Fenn
Drawings by Rosalie Schmidt

Reprinted by arrangement with Scribner, An Imprint of Simon & Schuster Inc.
First Biscuit Books Edition, 1996

Biscuit Books, Inc.
P. O. Box 610159
Newton, Massachusetts 02161

ISBN 0-9643600-5-5 (previously 0-02-010110-4, paper)

Printed and bound in the United States of America

00 99 98 97 96   5 4 3 2 1

Library of Congress Cataloging-in-Publication Data
Reich, Lilly Joss.
        The Viennese pastry cookbook / Lilly Joss Reich. — 1st Biscuit
Books ed.
            p.   cm.
        Reprint. Originally published: New York: Macmillan, 1978.
        Includes index.
        ISBN 0-9643600-5-5
        1. Pastry—Austria—Vienna. 2. Cookery, Austrian.   I. Title.
TX773.R34   1996
641.8'65'0943613—dc20   96-35934
                                                              CIP

To My Mother

*Most of all I want to thank my husband
for helping me with my "upside down" English,
and for sampling all my pastries
without ever getting tired of his "chore."*

TABLE OF EQUIVALENTS

SOLID MEASURES

1 cup finely ground almonds	2 oz.	55 gr.
1 cup slivered almonds	4 oz.	113 gr.
1 cup sliced almonds	4 oz.	113 gr.
1 cup apricot jam	10 oz.	285 gr.
1 bar sweet butter	4 oz.	113 gr.
1 cup bread crumbs	3½ oz.	100 gr.
1½ cups (generous) dry beans, cooked, whole	9 oz.	260 gr.
1 cup cooked, riced chestnuts	3½ oz.	100 gr.
1 lb. unpeeled fresh chestnuts	16 oz.	453 gr.
1 bar or square chocolate	1 oz.	30 gr.
½ cup cornstarch	2 oz.	55 gr.
1 cup currants	5 oz.	142 gr.
1 cup uncooked farina	6 oz.	170 gr.
1 cup flour	4½ oz.	125 gr.
1 cup sifted flour	4 oz.	113 gr.
1 cup finely ground hazelnuts	2 oz.	113 gr.
¼ cup finely chopped lemon peel	1 oz.	30 gr.
1 cup ground poppyseeds	2 oz.	55 gr.
⅓ cup potato flour	2 oz.	55 gr.
½ lb. pot cheese	8 oz.	226 gr.
1 cup blond raisins	5 oz.	142 gr.
1 cup prune butter (lekvar)	10 oz.	285 gr.
1 cup confectioner's sugar	4 oz.	113 gr.
1 cup very fine sugar	8 oz.	227 gr.
1 cup granulated sugar	8 oz.	227 gr.
½ cup finely chopped walnuts	2 oz.	55 gr.
1 cup finely ground walnuts	2 oz.	55 gr.
1 oz. fresh yeast	1 oz.	30 gr.

LIQUID MEASURES

1 cup	½ pint	¼ liter

TEMPERATURES

	Fahrenheit	Centigrade
Degrees	300 (F)	149 (C)
	325 (F)	163 (C)
	350 (F)	177 (C)
	375 (F)	190 (C)
	400 (F)	205 (C)

Contents

Some of the special features of this book are:

pastries with flour;
pastries without flour;
pastries with almonds, hazelnuts, walnuts, coconuts or pignolia;
pastries with chocolate;
pastries with cheese;
pastries with fresh or canned fruit;
pastries with yeast;
pastries with chestnuts;
pastries with puff paste;
pastries with egg white;
pastries with poppy seeds;
pastries with dry beans;
pastries with farina.

Some of the desserts served hot from top of stove are:
Bohemian Dalken;
Fresh Fruit Dumplings, made with cheese dough, potato dough or puff
    paste dough;
Fruit Fritters;
Pot Cheese Desserts;
Yeast Dumplings.

And some of the desserts served hot baked in oven are:
Farina Dumplings;
Omelet;
Rice Pudding;
Salzburger Nockerl;
Yeast Buns with Wine Chaudeau.

Introduction

Baking is an art that unfortunately seems to be almost lost. Baking can be simple and relaxing, but it is also a challenge. It can spur your imagination and be a source of great satisfaction.

My reason for writing this "unconventional" book is twofold. First, I want to help to restore the art of baking to its rightful place in the modern kitchen; second, I want to convince housewives, working women, and sophisticated (or, at the very least, quite experienced) hostesses that home-baked cakes and desserts are still the very best.

I do not claim to be a professional pastry cook. But none of us have to consider ourselves amateurs simply because we are not professionals. I have always had the good fortune to have the enthusiasm that the really dedicated "nonprofessional" can bring to any hobby. The professional can become jaded after a time; he is doing the job for money. But we do it because we love it. Does that mean that we are less skilled? Quite possibly not. And our enthusiasm always guarantees that special ingredient without which no recipe will really work—love.

For me it began a short time back—only eight years ago. Until then I had never baked a cake in my life! Actually, of course, since my early childhood in Vienna, I had been surrounded by the most lavish pastries, an endless list of different kinds of desserts, hot and cold. In our house baking was a daily event. To buy a cake in a store (even in Vienna, at

Demel's, perhaps the world's greatest institution devoted to the enjoyment of pastry) was unthinkable.

Every day there was some sort of home-baked dessert on the dinner table, and on Sunday mornings a Kugelhupf, Kipferl, or Buchteln—mostly made of yeast dough—could be found on the breakfast table.

But in Vienna desserts are not reserved to meal times only. There is also the afternoon *Jause*, a great Austrian tradition, a most enjoyable and relaxing event for the Viennese.

For women the *Jause* offers a beautiful opportunity to escape from their daily dull routine. They meet in small or large groups in someone's home or in one of the many coffeehouses Vienna is famous for, to play bridge or just for a *"klatsch"* over a cup of coffee, with or without *Schlag* (whipped cream), or a cup of hot chocolate served, of course, with their favorite pastry.

The *Jause* tradition is also very deeply implanted in the souls of Viennese men. You will find them alone, sitting in corners in coffee houses, buried behind a newspaper or magazine—dozens of newspapers and magazines are at their disposal, hanging from racks along the wall—or seated at the window, more interested in watching the pretty Viennese girls pass by than in reading the latest news.

At other tables you will find lovers, married couples, businessmen, and artists. But no matter what they want to discuss, from domestic to love affairs, from politics to business, there is nothing, but nothing, that cannot be accomplished or settled over a cup of coffee—and cake.

The peak of activity comes at Christmastime—Weihnachtszeit! The festivities start in the kitchen. The speciality of our house in Vienna was the famous Striezel (Christmas Stollen). They were baked by the dozens, since everyone from the maid to the superintendent, from the mailman to the garbage collector, would not only receive a Christmas present, but also a never-to-be-forgotten Striezel.

At that time of year all other cooking was cut to the barest minimum and everyone was obliged to help with the baking. My sister and I, small as we were, had to peel almonds, crack nuts, prepare raisins, and help to fetch and carry.

Once the yeast dough was mixed and prepared, it was left to rise overnight. At around six o'clock on the following morning every room of the house would be filled with the delicious aroma that indicated the baking had started. We made three sizes of these traditional Christmas loaves—large ones for the family, medium-sized ones for gifts, and tiny ones to decorate our Christmas tree.

Then came the most difficult time for us children since we were no longer allowed in the kitchen. As a rule it was not hard to keep us out of it, but on this special day it was quite a job because we wanted to see with our own eyes how our tiny Striezel were getting along. Nothing was more important than the success of the baked goods. The kitchen window and the door had to be kept closed to allow a slow and even cooling-off period; a draft or a whiff of cold air could make the Striezel droop or—God forbid—"glitschig," so the Striezel, and also Mother's reputation, had to be well protected.

Fortunately, you don't have to burden yourself with those precautions any longer. Very little of Mother's theory stands up today. Of course, with my yeast cakes I am more cautious than with others, but not overprotective. I just let them cool off the normal way—put them in a kitchen corner or on top of the refrigerator to keep them out of any draft or a sudden sharp temperature drop.

The Striezel was by no means the end of the baking activities for the holidays.

Next came the day for making cookies, which was impatiently awaited by us children since we were asked to help to cut out the dough with forms in different shapes. But when it came to making Vanille Kipferl (Vanilla Crescents), Mürber Teig (Short Dough), Nussbusserl (Nut Kisses), or Pfeffernüsse (Peppernuts) *by hand*, nobody had any use for us any longer and back we went to our room (but not without having smuggled some dough out with us so we could bake for our own "children," our dolls).

The next day found us again in the kitchen: a torte was to be baked and no matter how often that happened, it was always a delight for us because we were allowed to lick the batter from the bowl, the wooden spoons, and from the other gadgets.

The short resting period between Christmas and the New Year came to an end on New Year's Eve when the world famous Sylvester Krapfen (Doughnuts) had to be made. It was a must. According to an old European saying, eaten at midnight they will bring you luck, and who doesn't wish for good luck in the New Year! Besides, eating Sylvester Krapfen at midnight is no hardship, especially with a glass of champagne to toast the New Year. But they taste equally delicious with coffee or tea. They are made of yeast dough and filled with apricot jam and, most important, have to be light, fluffy, and golden brown.

As long as we are talking about yeast dough, I may as well admit that it is a little more tricky to work with than other dough; I know that many people don't mind baking but refuse to tackle anything made with yeast. Just try to put a little more love into it and you will be surprised with your success; once successful you will become better and better with experience, and once you've gotten the feeling for it and "mastered" yeast, you may consider yourself proudly a *real* pastry cook.

At least that was my mother's opinion. In her eyes, as in the eyes of any Viennese homemaker, you had obtained your "master's degree" if you were able to make first a yeast cake and secondly Knödel (Dumplings) or vice versa since it is hard to say which plays the more important role in the making of Austrian desserts.

Mother wouldn't have dreamed of hiring a cook without first testing her on those two desserts; only if she passed the test was she hired. The paradox of it was that Mother always baked everything herself, but even so the new cook had to go through that rigid examination—just in case.

When we came to America, Mother continued her cooking and baking, but without the assistance of a cook or maid.

Then I lost my mother. What she hadn't been able to achieve in all those years finally came about: I developed a true interest in baking and decided to follow in her footsteps in spite of the fact that my baking experiences up to then amounted to no more than grinding and peeling nuts or apples, turning the batter, and whipping the egg whites.

Perhaps another reason for my sudden interest in baking was that I had married and my husband was used to Mother's superior pastries—I couldn't let him down, could I?

Fortunately, Mother left two thick notebooks with recipes, but all of them were written in what I call "telegram style," enumerating only the weight of the different ingredients with few other explanations—she didn't need any since she was a baker by instinct. If I asked her how she did something, watching her mix the various ingredients, she would answer me: "You have to have a feeling for it."

She certainly had it. She was taught by her mother and grandmother, educated from her early youth to become an exemplary housewife. That was not *my* goal. I wanted to become a photographer, and my interest in the profession I had chosen didn't leave me much time for culinary adventures until, when Mother was no longer there, I had to enter the kitchen on my own.

I soon discovered that here in the New World—now overpopulated with the frozen, the fully prepared, the ready mixed, and the half-baked—the magic word is *homemade*. No longer are my guests refusing desserts on the grounds of some diet, with a devastating "No, thanks, I don't eat sweets," which hurts the hardworking hostess and spoils her evening. On the contrary, all principles are now thrown overboard. Calories are

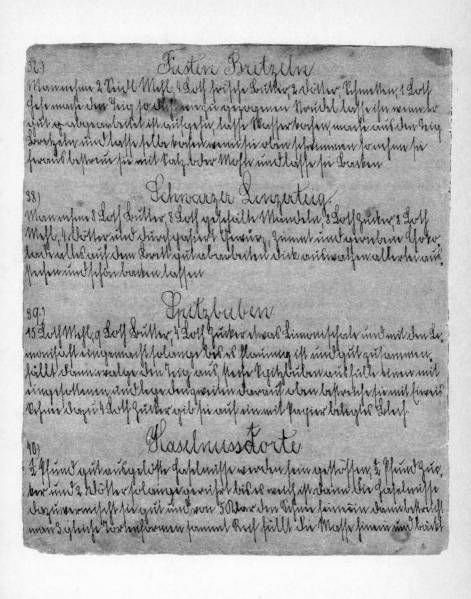

37) Fasten Bretzeln

Man nehme 2 Pfund Mehl, 4 Loth frische Butter, 2 Dotter, Schmalzer, 1 Loth Zucker macht den Teig so ... ...

38) Schwarzer Linzerteig

Man nehme 8 Loth Butter, 8 Loth geschälte Mandeln, 8 Loth Zucker, 8 Loth Mehl, 4 Dotter und durchgehacktes Gewürz, Zimmet und geriebene Chokoladi alles mit dem Teich gut abarbeiten dick ... ...

39) Spitzbuben

15 Loth Mehl, 9 Loth Butter, 4 Loth Zucker etwas Limonischali und mit dem Limonisaft ... ... bis es flaumig ist und gut zusammen fällt ... ... Schnee dazu 4 Loth Zucker ... ...

40) Haselnuss Torte

½ Pfund gut ... ... Haselnüsse werden fein gestoßen, ½ Pfund Zucker und 2 Dotter so lange ... ... die Haselnüsse dazu ... ... von 5 ... ...

forgotten. Ten out of a dozen guests will timidly ask for a second help-ing; the other two will want to take some home.

What a wonderful feeling it is to know that you have conquered the —so often exaggerated—calorie fear of baked desserts and made your guests forget their "special diets," even if for only one meal.

Yes, *homemade* is the magic key. Real homemade makes all the dif-ference.

Being a working woman with limited time for the kitchen, I did my baking mostly in the evening. Slowly but surely I saw my way through the recipes, and the more successful I was, the more courageous I be-came—experimenting, rewriting recipes, learning to make the various pastries. I never changed much in the basic recipes, but I added a little bit here or took away a little bit there until they turned out to my fullest satisfaction. No hour of the day is too early or too late for me quickly to make a cake.

Before we came to America, we had moved from Vienna to Paris and it became our second home. We lived there until the fall of Paris in 1940 when we had to leave in a hurry. I want to tell you how I saved the two old notebooks with recipes—some coming from my grandmother and great-grandmother, I presume, since in some recipes the measurement "*Loth*" was used, which is so old it was abolished during the reign of Napoleon. Some were written in the handwriting of my mother as a very, very young girl, while others were written later and some still later as the change in her handwriting revealed.

Those notebooks were saved thanks to an American friend who let us transfer our valuables to her safe-deposit box a few days before the Germans reached Paris. On the spur of the moment I also put the two notebooks with the old recipes in it. Until this day I don't know why I did it, since I left behind possessions that at the time meant much more to us. Despite my precautions, not counting that the United States would enter the war, the enemy, of course, cleaned out the safes of all the Americans, but left items behind which they considered of no importance, among them my two notebooks with recipes, their pages faded and yellow with age.

I consider this a good omen, and since I don't have children of my own, I thought to pass on some of these precious recipes of an old country to the future generations of the New World.

Tips and Techniques

Ingredients

LET's get ready to bake!

The first step, which is of vital importance to your baking success, is to read every recipe carefully from beginning to end before you start.

Next, assemble all utensils and indicated ingredients so you won't have to look for them in the midst of preparations, just when the batter is rising or your dough is about to enter the oven.

It is essential to weigh, grind, grate, clarify butter, sift, and blanch *before* the baking starts.

When all these preliminary steps have been taken, you will feel at ease and much more secure in what you are doing—especially if you are still an inexperienced baker.

EGGS

Egg is the king of the ingredients. With few rare exceptions, the rule is: no eggs, no cake. Consequently, eggs represent a most important part of the baking process.

Yolks give flavor, color, and texture, and they bind. Egg whites, well beaten—best done at room temperature—will contain a lot of air that is beaten into them and therefore become a dependable leavening agent, bringing lightness to your cakes and tortes.

I am sure you often have egg whites left over from your baking or from binding a sauce or a Zabaglione. This happens in every kitchen. Of course, you can freeze the egg whites and wait for another occasion to use them, but I think there is more fun in trying a new creation. So take my suggestion and use them to bake some of the many fine tortes and cookies that can be made from egg whites.

The recipes in this book are all based on *large* eggs—not medium, not extra large.

Lightly beaten egg white: Beat with a fork until the egg white starts to get lightly foamy.

BUTTER

I strongly feel that there is no substitute for butter. Nothing, but nothing, can replace fresh sweet butter in fine quality pastries. However, if for health or dietary reasons you must avoid butter or flour, there are many recipes in this book that call for neither.

These recipes are based on unsalted butter. If only salted is available, you should use *lightly* salted butter and omit the salt listed in the recipe. Not only has salted butter a much greater water consistency, but nothing is more unpleasant than a pronounced salty taste in sweet pastries.

If the recipe calls for butter to be *cut* into ingredients, I prefer to use a knife rather than a pastry blender. I have learned by experience that a blender softens the butter to such a degree that later, when butter and ingredients have to be kneaded by hand, the butter becomes too soft and easily turns oily. Then much more flour must be used, which will change the character of the particular recipe: the pastry will harden and the lightness will be lost.

To clarify butter: Place butter in a saucepan over low heat. When melted, pour off clear yellow liquid and discard any milky substance and sediment. Not only should clarified butter be used whenever the recipe calls for it, but I would like to suggest that you use it at all opportunities, since the great advantage of clarified butter is that it will keep for a long, long time and when cooked at temperatures below 400° will not burn.

SUGAR

Does sugar need an introduction? Everybody knows it is the base that makes cakes so appealing. But we must also keep in mind that oversweetening pastries can be downright unpleasant and create the opposite result from that desired.

In my baking I use three different kinds of sugar: granulated, verifine (or superfine), and confectioners' sugar.

Sugar gives taste and texture; in icing it is the basic ingredient. Confectioners' sugar, simply dusted over your pastry, not only looks decorative but is also appetizing.

FLOUR

When it comes to flour, I don't burden myself with many different kinds. What is most important to me is that the flour be of first quality and dry. I use all-purpose flour with excellent results.

Flour is by no means a necessary ingredient in every pastry. As you will see when you read these recipes, many are made without flour, instead calling for ground nuts or, no less intriguing and incredibly good, ground chestnuts, poppyseeds, dry beans, farina, and, last but not least, chocolate.

All these ingredients will give the necessary body to your pastries and not only successfully replace the flour, but also create a pastry that will be out of the ordinary.

Nuts, from almonds to pistachios, belong to the wonders of nature. Blanched or unblanched, ground, sliced, slivered, or crushed—not only can they be used as decoration, but as ingredients they bring a distinctive taste to your pastries and tortes.

The full extent of the distinct flavor of nuts is brought out when they are used in place of flour. In Mocha Almond Torte, Meringue Torte, Walnut Torte, or in small pastries like Nut Kisses, Pignolia Crescents, and Almond Bows—to name a few from a long list—you have an exquisite composition of ingredients: whole eggs or only egg whites, sugar, and ground nuts. Besides, these pastries take only a short time to prepare.

It seems to me that in home baking the many possibilities for the uses of this fruit specimen—the nut—have not been taken advantage of.

In both specialty stores and supermarkets you will find all kinds of prepared nuts, from blanched to slivered, which will ease your work, but ground nuts can be found only in specialty stores. For that reason a nut grinder, small or large, is a must, but even a mouli grinder will do. Nut grinders are relatively inexpensive, and I favor those with interchangeable drums; they will not only grind all kinds of nuts, but also grate orange peels, shred coconuts, etc. Nut grinders with interchangeable drums are European imports, and you can buy them in specialty and in many department and hardware stores.

You may ask, why can't an electric blender do the work? It can, but with a completely different result. With a nut grinder you obtain a flaky, sawdust-like consistency, pleasantly soft and dry, but with a blender it will be grainy and not as fine and dry as it should be. This same grainy consistency will be found in preground nuts (bought in specialty stores).

In this book, all the pastries made with nuts are made with home-ground nuts that have been ground with a regular nut grinder or a mouli grinder. I use a regular nut grinder, but with a mouli grinder you will obtain the same sawdust-like consistency that I favor; however, you will have to regrind chunks of nuts that fall through.

There will be a slight difference in the personality, taste, and texture of the pastries if made with preground or blender-ground nuts. And since I want you to enjoy the pastries in the most authentic form, I can't overemphasize the fact that you will achieve the best results if you grind the nuts yourself.

To blanch and toast hazelnuts: Place nuts in a frying or baking pan into a 350° F. oven for about 10 minutes. Stir from time to time. When brown skin starts to darken and cracks slightly, transfer nuts to a kitchen towel and rub against a hard surface—on the kitchen table or between your hands—to remove skin from the nuts. It does not matter if hazelnuts don't get clean of all skin. If not sufficiently toasted, return skinless nuts to pan and toast once more until golden brown.

To blanch almonds and pistachios: Place in boiling water. Let boil for one or two minutes. Slip skin off by pressing almond or pistachio between thumb and fingers. Blanching pistachios is completely optional since, when ground, the thin brown skin is barely noticeable. Allow to dry, preferably one to two days before grinding.

To toast almonds: Cut blanched almonds into coarse pieces. Place in frying pan and stir or shake over low flame until lightly browned.

To split almonds: It is best to split almonds when they are freshly blanched.

To prepare coconut: Here are two ways to open a fresh coconut. Take your choice.

First method: Pierce the eyes (three small, smooth dots at one end of coconut) with a sharp, pointed instrument and drain off milky liquid. Place coconut in oven (350° F.) for about 15 minutes.

The shell will crack. Remove shell by tapping with a mallet all around until it is evenly cracked. Pare off brown skin and grate white "meat."

Second method: Proceed as above, but instead of placing coconut into oven, tap hard brown shell firmly and evenly with mallet all around until shell cracks. Remove shell. With a pointed knife separate white meat from hard brown shell. Peel off brown skin before shredding. Before using, let shreds dry for a few hours.

Note: Many people think the white liquid, coconut milk, is a delicious drink. Try it!

CHESTNUTS

You may be acquainted with such fairly well-known dishes as Chestnut Purée, Marron Glacé, and Chestnut Montblanc, but chestnut pastries have not yet found their way into many American kitchens. That is my reason for giving you as many as five equally delicious recipes for pastries made of chestnuts.

Contrary to generally expressed opinions, chestnut pastries are not heavy or difficult to digest.

You will have no trouble peeling fresh chestnuts, if you cook them for 15–20 minutes, without incisions, then simply take them out of the hot water (peeling them one by one, so that the remaining chestnuts will stay hot).

Chestnuts are only difficult to peel when cold or lukewarm.

CHOCOLATE

What a blessing that chocolate exists! Everybody likes it, and for that reason it is in great demand. Chocolate gives flavor, aroma, and color to your pastry. It can be used melted or grated.

Rightly or wrongly, many foreign chocolates are still considered superior to the domestic ones, but you will be able to find some excellent semisweet baking chocolates—originally from Belgium and Holland but now manufactured according to the original recipes in the United States—in the food sections of department stores and specialty candy stores. You will also find big block chunks of fine quality chocolate in specialty stores. Last but not least, I also recommend a more modestly priced chocolate that comes from Puerto Rico and is available in most food markets.

(One bar or one square as used in this book is equal to one ounce of chocolate.)

SPICES

What is so intriguing in spices? The exotic flavors maybe? It is hard to say. Aroma? Perhaps. Whatever the reason, spices will provide your palate with new and interesting tastes.

Spices should never be used to the extent that they overpower your pastry; their flavor should be present but should stay modestly in the background. In most cases a pinch is enough, except, of course, in spiced cookies. In those cookies spices are the masters and ought to be present as distinctive flavors.

VANILLA BEANS

A vanilla bean resembles a long, dark brown stringbean. On looking at it, nobody would ever suspect what a powerful but pleasant aroma this little dark bean has. And its flavor will serve you in many different ways. If a recipe calls for fresh vanilla bean, nothing can replace its natural flavor.

To buy: Watch for the plump bean with a full belly. The fuller its body, the more "meat" (grains) it contains.

To keep: Vanilla beans are sold in pairs, in narrow glass tubes. When tubes are kept tightly closed, the beans will stay fresh and moist and conserve their flavor. If purchased singly, the bean should be kept in a tightly closed jar in the company of a few dried raisins to prevent the vanilla bean from drying out.

To use: Split bean open lengthwise. With a pointed knife scrape out only as much of the soft, black meat (grains) as the recipe calls for. Blend into batter, cream filling, heavy cream, or sugar as required. Save the empty vanilla shell for making vanilla sugar.

To make vanilla sugar: Place the shell of a vanilla bean into an airtight jar filled with sugar (granulated, verifine, or confectioners'). After the sugar is well flavored, which will take a few weeks, you can use the bean again to cook with—for flavoring rice pudding, vanilla sauce and cream, and any kind of custard.

You must admit it is quite an outstanding little bean to serve so many purposes with its flavor.

No artificial vanilla flavoring should ever come near your cake.

Now that I have come to the end of these explanations that I hope you find helpful, I would like to advise you on how to keep your baked goods as fresh as possible for a long time without freezing. It is not necessary to freeze pastry if you plan to serve it within about ten days to two weeks. Keep it in a dry, cool place or in a refrigerator.

Some pastries are best eaten fresh, but many more are not harmed by storing—well wrapped, of course. They will have time to mellow, and this process, strangely enough, improves them. But to keep pastry from becoming stale, it is essential at all times to protect it by proper wrapping. Foil and plastic wrap do a fine job.

Baking Equipment

There is no reason to get discouraged if you are not the proud owner of the latest kitchen gadgets. I admit they are helpful, but not absolutely necessary.

Of course, it is nice to have a big electric beater, but a small electric hand mixer serves the same purpose, and there is nothing wrong with the old-fashioned rotary, hand eggbeater, and even a wooden spoon for stirring by hand will do nicely. Don't forget: the end result is what counts.

OVEN

Learn to know your oven. Each one works differently. Know its weaknesses and faults.

I was often told that the success of my baking must be due to my first-class oven, when actually I had an old, worn-out one, but I knew it so well that everything I baked turned out all right. When I couldn't bear the looks of it any longer, I decided to buy a new oven. That was a big decision to make. Should it be an expensive, moderately priced, or inexpensive one? After long and careful consideration, I decided to buy an inexpensive oven for one important reason: to prove to myself and everybody else that an inexpensive oven can work as well as a higher priced one as long as it is well insulated so that the heat is evenly distributed and will not escape. But I had to learn to know my oven.

You can rarely depend on your oven's thermostat. In most cases, if anything goes wrong, it is not the fault of the oven but the thermostat, which might be off to a certain degree and give an entirely wrong temperature. Therefore you ought to have an oven thermometer. It is a precious little instrument that should not be missing in your oven. It will enable you to doublecheck the temperature, which will save you from many unpleasant experiences.

ESSENTIAL BASIC EQUIPMENT

Springform pan with interchangeable bottom

Baking pan with removable bottom

Square baking pan

Tube pan or, even better, tinned ring mold

Jelly-roll pan, 11 x 17 inches

Gugelhupf form (Turk's head mold)

Assorted cooky cutters

Mixing bowls

Flour sifter

Measuring cups and spoons

Rolling pin

Wooden spoons, slotted and round

Nut or mouli grinder

Food mill

Rotary egg beater

Grater (shredder)

Strainer, fine meshed

Spatulas, rubber and metal

Pastry bags with assorted tubes

Pastry brush

Cake tester

Cooky jar

Pastry rack

Oven thermometer

I consider the above list indispensable. Gradually you should add to your equipment according to your needs, depending on the selection of pastries you expect to bake.

ADDITIONAL EQUIPMENT, NICE TO HAVE

Electric mixer or portable electric hand mixer

Wooden pastry board

Baking pan, 10 x 16 x 2 inches

Cooky pan or sheet, 11 x 17 inches

Decorating comb

Pastry wheel with plain blade

Chocolate curler

Set of biscuit cutters

Baking pan with scalloped edges and removable bottom (for fruit tortes)

Flan rings, oblong and round

Tartlet tins

Biscuit form with round bottom, or muffin form

Food chopper (glass container)

Double boiler

EQUIPMENT FOR DESSERTS SERVED HOT

Steam pudding mold, fluted, 1½–2
    quarts
One or two large kettles
Two 10- or 12-inch frying pans
7- or 8-inch frying or omelet pan
Dalken form with 4 or 6 cavities or a
    Danish cake pan or egg poacher
    with 4 or 6 cavities

Roasting pan, large
Wooden spoon, plain, flat, round
Slotted wooden spoon
Colander
Ladles, 1 and 2 inch

SUBSTITUTE EQUIPMENT

EQUIPMENT	SUBSTITUTE
Flour sifter	Fine meshed strainer or sieve
Pastry board	Table, covered with pastry cloth
Pastry rack	Grill from oven or rotisserie
Mixing bowls	Saucepans of different sizes
Round biscuit form	Muffin form
Sugar duster	Fine meshed strainer or sieve
Double boiler	Two pans; top pan should not touch water when inserted in bottom pan
Pastry wheel with plain blade	Straight blade knife
Decorating comb	Fork
Biscuit cutters	Tops of assorted glasses, from small brandy to water glass
Chocolate curler	Vegetable peeler or butter scraper
Cake tester	Toothpick
Metal spatula	Knife with wide blade
Cooky cutter, round, ¾ inch	Thimble
Pastry brush	Small paper napkin, firmly rolled
Electric mixer	Wooden spoon or rotary egg beater
Ladle, 1 inch	Ice cream scoop, ¾ filled, or serving spoon
Square cooky cutter	Diamond-shaped cooky cutter, bent into a square

A Few Helpful Suggestions

Adapt your baking to the season.

During spring and summer use fresh fruit in your tortes and cakes. During warm weather your guests will find a fruitcake more enjoyable than a chocolate cake.

Avoid serving the same dessert to the same guests over and over again if they praised it the first time. You don't want your guests to think you can bake only one kind of cake. Use your imagination. If you are using the same dough, change the shape of the cake and change the icing. Besides, every main dish demands a different dessert. If a heavy main dish is served, a light dessert is required. Needless to say, you cannot serve a soufflé as an hors d'oeuvre and a yeast dumpling as dessert. I would also not serve a fruit torte at the end of the meal if I served fruit at the beginning.

Most tortes, coffee and tea pastries—with the exception of some yeast cakes—can be made several days in advance. In fact, most of them, especially those with a filling, seem to improve with time. Leave only the frosting for the day of the serving to make the dessert look its best.

To keep your homemade cake fresh for days or even weeks, put it back into the original baking form and wrap it in foil. Of course, you can wrap it in foil without putting it back into the baking form if you need to use the form.

Assemble all the ingredients you will need and grind or cut and measure them *before* you start to bake. This will save you time and make baking much easier for you.

My motto: the simpler the better. This applies not only to the ingredients I use, but also to the decorating of my cakes.

Don't put a freshly baked or still hot cake into the refrigerator.

Avoid cutting, filling, or icing a cake that is still warm. The filling or icing will soak in and ruin the cake.

Don't forget to butter and flour your baking form when a recipe calls for it. Always remove excess flour from baking pan.

Keep candied orange or lemon peels in a glass jar; put parchment or wax paper under metal cover that has small holes punched into it: the air will keep the jar odor free.

When a recipe calls for stiffly beaten egg whites, the surest way to judge whether they are beaten enough is slowly to turn the bowl that contains them upside down. If the egg white is not beaten enough, it will start to slide out. If it is ready, it will stay in the bowl even if it is turned upside down.

It is easier to whip heavy cream that is one to two days old.

When the recipe calls for it, flour should always be sifted *before* measuring.

Always start with the smallest indicated amount of flour the recipe calls for. Add additional flour only if necessary.

All recipes in this book are based on large eggs, not medium, not extra large.

Rum or liqueur can be replaced in most cases with lemon juice or vanilla extract.

Egg yolks can be stored by gliding them gently into a bowl or cup of cold water. Keep covered and refrigerated. When needed, carefully remove each yolk with a spoon.

If egg whites do not get stiff quickly, add a pinch of salt and it will be a cinch to beat them.

If top of torte turns out uneven, reverse torte and use bottom, or level top by removing the uneven part with a sharp knife.

If pot cheese is unavailable, it can be replaced by farmer's cheese or cottage cheese. Cottage cheese must be strained through a cheesecloth to remove excess water, in which case you have to buy a slightly larger quantity to make up for the loss of weight.

If a pastry tube does not fit into the pastry bag, cut off tip of bag to enlarge opening.

Keep pantry and refrigerator always well stocked with the most basic baking ingredients like butter, sugar, eggs, flour, yeast, nuts, chocolate, etc., so you will have everything ready if a rainy, snowy, or stormy day keeps you indoors. The best baking days are thus provided by nature herself.

1. Small Pastries

Introduction

Some of the most festive and enjoyable members of the extensive pastry family are the small coffee and tea pastries. You might call them the nephews and nieces of tortes and cakes.

At a tea party or a coffee *klatsch*, when a slice of Gugelhupf or a piece of cake would be too filling Cones Filled with Whipped Cream (*Skarnitzel, Gefüllt*), Nut Kisses (*Nussbusserl*), Hazelnut Bars (*Haselnuss Stangerl*), Vanilla Crescents (*Vanille Kipferl*), or Rolled Almond Wafers (*Gerollte Mandelscheiben*), to mention just a few, will do the trick.

These pastries will also be appreciated after a heavy meal when there is only room left for a light dessert, and they go very well with chocolate mousse, lemon cream, Zabaglione, Jello, ice cream, and stewed fruit.

ALMOND CONES WITH WHIPPED CREAM	*Mandelskarnitzel mit Schlagobers*
ALMOND ENVELOPES	*Mandelmaultaschen*
ALMOND HAZELNUT STICKS	*Mandel-Haselnuss Stangen*
ALMOND ROUNDS	*Mandelkrapferl*

ALMOND SUGAR PRETZEL	*Mandel Zucker Bretzel*
ANISE CHOCOLATE CRESCENTS	*Anis Schokoladen Kipferl*
ANISE CRESCENTS	*Anis Kipferl*
CHOCOLATE BUTTER COOKIES	*Schokoladen Butter Keks*
COCONUT MACAROONS	*Kokosnuss Makronen*
CONES FILLED WITH WHIPPED CREAM	*Skarnitzel (Gefüllt)*
EASTER COOKIES	*Osterbäckerei*
GINGER COOKIES	*Ingwer Bäckerei*
HAZELNUT APRICOT BARS (SHORT DOUGH)	*Haselnuss Marmeladen Stangerl (Mürber Teig)*
HAZELNUT CRESCENTS	*Haselnuss Kipferl*
HUSSAR ROUNDS	*Husaren Krapferl*
ISCHLER COOKIES	*Ischler Plätzchen*
POT CHEESE CRESCENTS	*Topfenkipferl*
RASCALS	*Spitzbuben*
ROLLED ALMOND WAFERS	*Gerollte Mandelscheiben*
SHORT DOUGH HAZELNUT BARS	*Mürbe Haselnuss Stangerl*
SPONGE DOUGH ROUNDS	*Biskuitteig Plätzchen*
VANILLA CRESCENTS	*Vanille Kipferl*
VANILLA WAFERS	*Vanille Plätzchen*
VIENNESE POCKETS	*Wiener Tascherln*
WALNUT FILLED COOKIES	*Nuss Krapferl*
WALNUT SLICES (FILLED)	*Walnuss Scheibchen (Gefüllt)*
WOOD SHAVINGS	*Hobelspäne*

ALMOND CONES WITH WHIPPED CREAM

20–24 pieces

4 egg whites
⅓ cup sugar (generous)
1¾ cups finely ground blanched
   almonds

1 Tbs. sifted flour (generous)
Chocolate Icing
1 cup heavy cream, whipped
1–3 tsps. confectioners' sugar

11 x 17-inch baking pan or cooky sheet

Beat egg whites until stiff. Add sugar and almonds. Stir mixture by hand for a minute or two. Fold in flour. Drop teaspoons of mixture on a well-buttered, lightly floured baking pan or cooky sheet, leaving ample space in between, about 6 to a baking pan. Keep remaining batter refrigerated.

With the back of a spoon flatten each mound into thin rounds about 3½-inches in diameter.

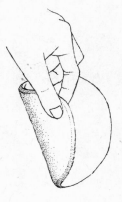

Place in oven (400° F.) and bake for 6–8 minutes until edges are starting to brown. The rounds should be firm but still soft; they harden as they cool. (Watch them carefully—they burn easily.)

With a table knife or a spatula, loosen rounds with one sharp stroke. Shape them immediately into cones. Place them seam side down to prevent uncurling. If some of the rounds harden before you have shaped them, return pan to oven for a few seconds. Repeat until whole batch is shaped. Let cool.

Before filling cones with whipped cream, dip tip of open end into chocolate icing. Place on pastry rack. Refrigerate. When icing is firm, fill cones with lightly sweetened whipped cream. Keep refrigerated until serving.

Cones can be baked days in advance, if kept in a tightly closed tin box before being iced and filled.

Note: You may also choose to leave the plain round wafers as they are instead of turning them into cones. They will save you time and work and are just as tasty.

ALMOND ENVELOPES

The whole secret in preparing this delicate butter dough is speed.
Keep butter and hands cool and work quickly. Avoid preparing this
pastry on a hot day to prevent the butter in the dough from getting
too soft and oily. Your effort will be well rewarded.

14–16 pieces

1 cup flour	**FILLING:**
1 pinch salt	1½ cups finely ground blanched
1 bar sweet butter, cold	almonds
1 Tbs. sugar (optional)	⅓ cup sugar
2 egg yolks	1 egg yolk
1 egg white	2 egg whites
	1 tsp. cognac or rum

11 x 17-inch baking pan

Place flour and salt on pastry board. Cut in butter and then, with
fingers, work these ingredients quickly into coarse crumbs. Make a
well in center and add sugar and egg yolks. With a table knife, fold
ingredients over yolks. First blend quickly with fingertips, then
knead by hand into a smooth dough.

Form a ball and wrap in wax paper. Refrigerate for 2–3 hours.
Dough should be cold but have a spreadable consistency. Divide
dough in half and keep one part refrigerated.

With a floured rolling pin on a floured board roll dough into a
rectangular piece about ⅛ inch thick, turning dough over from time
to time, reflouring board and rolling pin. Trim edges straight. Cut
into strips 4 inches wide and the strips into 4-inch squares. Save and
keep scraps refrigerated.

Place a teaspoon of filling on each square. With the help of a
knife lift corners and very lightly fold two pairs of opposite corners
over, slightly overlapping in center. With a spatula transfer gently

to baking pan. Refrigerate. Proceed same way with remainder of refrigerated dough.

Brush tops with lightly beaten egg white.

Bake in preheated oven (400° F.) for 12–15 minutes until golden brown. Let cool on baking pan. Remove with care since envelopes have the tendency to break easily.

Before serving, dust with confectioners' sugar.

Filling: Combine blanched, ground almonds with sugar. Fold egg yolk into beaten egg whites and gradually blend in almond mixture. Spoon 1 teaspoon of cognac or rum into mixture. Combine.

You can replace the cognac or rum with ½ egg white (beaten) or ½ teaspoon vanilla extract.

ALMOND HAZELNUT STICKS

About 36 single or 18 double pieces

1¼ cups finely ground hazelnuts
1½ cups finely ground almonds
3 egg whites
¾ cup sugar

¼ cup sifted flour (scant)
¼ cup apricot, strawberry, or
    currant jam
Chocolate Icing

10 x 16 x 2-inch baking pan

Combine ground hazelnuts and almonds.

Beat egg whites and sugar until foamy. Add nuts. Blend. Dust flour into mixture. Fold together.

Fill a pastry bag, fitted with a ¾-inch-wide pastry tube, or a cooky press with a ¾-inch-wide, ¼-inch-high opening, tip 32. On a generously buttered 10 × 16 × 2-inch baking pan with a smooth surface, press out sticks 3 inches long.

Bake in preheated oven (325° F.) for 10–15 minutes, until firm, but still soft inside. When slightly cooled, remove gently with spatula.

When completely cool, coat one end of all sticks with chocolate icing. Place on wire rack. Refrigerate.

When icing is firm, spread bottoms of half the sticks with jam of your choice. Top each with a second stick so that chocolate ends are on opposite sides. Keep refrigerated.

Iced sticks (use either chocolate or punch icing) can also be served singly.

Note: The hazelnuts and the almonds make a tasty combination, as you will find out.

ALMOND ROUNDS

Almond Rounds are prepared in a very interesting way.

First make a mixture of egg whites, sugar, and ground almonds. When baked, this resembles a macaroon in texture and taste, except it is baked in one sheet, then finely grated to be used as a binding. A very refined binding it is.

The use of an already baked binding occurs in many other recipes that call for ground zwieback and graham crackers or bread crumbs, but in this recipe the macaroon mixture makes the difference.

Next, blend this binding into a second mixture and proceed to complete these very delicious Almond Rounds.

24–26 pieces

FIRST MIXTURE:
1 egg white
⅔ cup sugar
2 cups finely ground blanched
almonds

SECOND MIXTURE:
½ bar sweet butter, soft
2 egg yolks
⅓ cup flour (generous)
Punch Icing
Apricot jam or sweet or sour
cherry preserves

7 x 11-inch baking pan
10 x 16-inch baking pan

First Mixture: Beat egg white until stiff. Fold in sugar and ground almonds until well blended. Spread mixture evenly on a buttered 7 × 11-inch (approx.) baking pan. Preheat oven to 300° F. Bake for about 15 minutes until brown and crisp. When completely cool, grate or grind baked almond sheet to fine crumbs.

Second Mixture: Beat butter and egg yolks until smooth. Combine with flour. Fold in grated almond crumbs and blend well. Break off small pieces of dough and roll between the palms of your hands into little balls, about 1 inch in diameter. Place on buttered 10 × 16-inch baking pan. Make a small depression in center of each ball.

Bake in preheated oven (350° F.) for 20–30 minutes until golden brown. Cool.

Garnish: Spread punch icing over top. Refrigerate. After icing has set, decorate each round with a dab of apricot jam, or, if you prefer, you can place a whole cherry from preserve in center of each round. If you use both alternately, the rounds will look very attractive.

ALMOND SUGAR PRETZEL

MANDEL ZUCKER BRETZEL

About 20 pieces

1 cup flour
¾ bar sweet butter, cold
Rind of 1 lemon, grated
¼ cup sugar (scant)

¾ cup finely ground blanched
  almonds
1 egg yolk
1 egg white
Crystal (harlequin) sugar, white

11 x 17-inch baking pan

Place flour on pastry board and with a knife cut butter into it. Crumble ingredients between your fingers into coarse pieces. Add grated lemon rind, sugar, ground almonds, and egg yolk. Combine. Blend and quickly knead into a smooth dough. Form a ball, wrap in wax paper, and refrigerate for a short time.

Divide dough and keep one half refrigerated. Roll other half between your hands or on pastry board into a short roll 1½ inches thick. Cut roll into half-inch slices. On a pastry board, lightly roll each piece into a roll about ¼ inch thick and 9 inches long, tapering off slightly on both ends.

To form pretzel, lift both ends, make them cross in center by pressing ends lightly against top of roll.

Transfer gently to baking pan. Repeat all steps with refrigerated half of dough.

Brush with lightly beaten egg white and sprinkle with crystal (harlequin) sugar.

To sprinkle sugar evenly over pretzels, place sugar into a wax paper or aluminum foil cone, cut tip off, and let sugar drop over pretzels.

Place in preheated oven (350° F.) for about 20 minutes until lightly colored. Remove when cool.

Pretzels keep very well in an airtight container.

ANISE CHOCOLATE CRESCENTS

About 24 pieces

¼ bar plus 1 Tbs. sweet butter, soft

¼ cup sugar

2 egg yolks

1¼ bars or squares semisweet chocolate, grated

¾ cup flour (generous)

1 egg white

2 Tbs. aniseeds (approx.)

11 x 17-inch baking pan

Beat butter and sugar together until well blended. Add egg yolks and beat until light and creamy. Add grated chocolate and combine thoroughly. Gradually fold flour into mixture. Take a small piece of dough, about ¾ teaspoonful, roll between the palms of your hands into 2½-inch length, and bend into crescent.

Brush crescents with egg white and sprinkle with aniseeds before placing them on 11 × 17-inch baking pan.

Bake in preheated oven (350° F.) for about 15 minutes.

ANISE CRESCENTS

About 24 pieces

¼ bar plus 1 Tbs. sweet butter, soft
¼ cup sugar
2 egg yolks

1 cup flour
2–3 Tbs. aniseeds
1 egg white

11 x 17-inch baking pan

Stir butter and sugar until well blended. Add egg yolks and beat until mixture is light and creamy. Gradually fold in flour and aniseeds. Take about ¾ teaspoonful of dough, roll between the palms of your hands into a 2½-inch length, taper ends off slightly, bend into crescent.

Place on 11 × 17-inch baking pan. Brush crescents with lightly beaten egg white before placing them in preheated oven (350° F). Bake for about 15 minutes until lightly colored.

Note: If you would prefer a milder anise taste; brush crescents with egg white and sprinkle with aniseeds instead of working seeds into dough.

CHOCOLATE BUTTER COOKIES

About 30 cookies

2–2¼ cups flour
4 Tbs. sugar
1¼ bars sweet butter, cold
1 egg yolk
2 bars or squares semisweet
  chocolate, grated

1 Tbs. milk
1 egg white
Raspberry or raspberry-currant jam
2–3 Tbs. coarsely chopped,
  blanched almonds

11 x 17-inch cooky sheet

Combine flour and sugar on pastry board. Make a well in center and cut butter into it. Add egg yolk. Cover ingredients with grated chocolate. Combine. Work quickly, first with fingertips, then kneading by hand into a smooth dough. If dough seems too dry, gradually add milk. Form dough into a ball, wrap in wax paper, and refrigerate for about 30 minutes.

Divide dough into two to three parts and place each part between two sheets of wax paper. With a rolling pin roll dough to about ⅛-inch thickness. Remove top sheet of wax paper. Cut dough out with a plain or fluted round cooky cutter, 2½ inches in diameter, as close to each other as possible. Transfer cookies with a spatula to cooky sheet.

Proceed with remaining dough as above. Save and combine scraps and roll out again.

Brush half of the cookies with egg white and sprinkle centers with chopped almonds for decoration. Leave the other cookies plain.

Bake in preheated oven (325° F.) for about 15 minutes until firm and puffy.

When completely cool, spread plain cookies with jam and sandwich them together with garnished ones.

COCONUT MACAROONS

About 26 pieces

2⅔ cups fresh coconut, peeled
and shredded

1 cup sugar

1 egg white

Juice of ½ medium-sized lemon,
strained

Rind of 1 lemon, grated

3 egg whites

3 Tbs. flour (approx.)

11 x 17-inch baking pan or cooky sheet

Combine coconut, sugar, 1 egg white, lemon rind, and lemon juice in a medium saucepan. Stir over low flame until lukewarm. Remove from fire and cool. Beat remaining egg whites until they form soft peaks. Gradually fold in egg whites to cooled coconut mixture. Add flour and combine gently.

On a generously buttered, lightly floured 11 × 17-inch baking pan, place heaping teaspoons of mixture at 1½-inch intervals.

Bake in preheated oven (275° F.) for about 30 minutes until golden brown.

Note: Directions for how to prepare a fresh coconut are given in the section "Tips and Techniques." Preshredded coconut in cans or packages may be used, but will change the texture of the macaroons considerably. If the coconut is presweetened, omit half the sugar in the recipe.

CONES FILLED WITH WHIPPED CREAM

20–24 pieces

2 whole eggs
⅓ cup verifine sugar
1 Tbs. cold water
¾ cup sifted flour

Chocolate Icing
1 cup heavy cream, whipped
2–3 Tbs. confectioners' sugar

11 x 17-inch baking pan or cooky sheet

Beat whole eggs with sugar until mixture is light and foamy. Gradually add cold water, stirring constantly. Fold sifted flour gently into batter. Drop a teaspoonful on a well-greased baking pan or cooky sheet. With the back of a spoon spread each mound into thin 3 × 3-inch rounds or into about 2½ × 3½-inch oblong forms.

Bake quickly in preheated oven (400° F.) for 3–5 minutes. When cookies are still pale, soft, and lightly browned around edges, remove with spatula and quickly form into cones. If cookies become too firm to turn into cones, return to oven for a few seconds to soften. Bake only 6–8 rounds at a time. (See figure, p. 34.)

Since cones have the tendency to unfold during cooling time, place formed cones seam side down. If they should still unfold, secure each cone with a toothpick as an emergency measure. Remove toothpick when cones are firm.

A few hours before serving, brush tip of open edge with chocolate icing or dip tip of open edge lightly into icing. Place on a wire rack. Refrigerate.

Shortly before serving, fill each cone with lightly sweetened whipped cream. Keep refrigerated until serving.

Of course, you can also use flavored whipped cream, from coffee flavor to crushed strawberries or raspberries. Or you may add grated nuts to the whipped cream.

Note: If cones are kept in an airtight container before filling, they will keep fresh for quite some time.

EASTER COOKIES

42–48 pieces

1 hard-boiled egg yolk, mashed
1 Tbs. lemon juice
2 cups flour (scant)
½ cup sugar (scant)
Rind of 1 lemon, grated
1 bar sweet butter, cold
1 whole egg

½ egg yolk
¾ cup finely ground, blanched almonds
1 whole egg (for brushing tops of cookies)
¼ cup finely chopped, blanched almonds

11 x 17-inch baking pan or cooky sheet

Combine mashed hard-boiled egg yolk thoroughly with lemon juice.

Combine flour and sugar on pastry board; make well in center. Grate lemon rind into well and cut butter into it. Add mashed boiled-egg-yolk mixture, whole egg, half egg yolk, and ground almonds. Combine ingredients quickly. Work by hand into a smooth but firm dough until dough no longer sticks to board or hands. (If necessary, gradually add a little more flour.) Refrigerate for about 30 minutes.

Divide dough. On a lightly floured board, with a floured rolling pin, roll dough out to about ⅛-inch thickness. Cut out dough with a cooky cutter (about 2½ inches long) shaped like an Easter bunny or baby chicken or any other cooky cutter of your choice. Re-use scraps.

Transfer to baking pan. Brush tops with lightly beaten egg and sprinkle with chopped almonds.

Instead of sprinkling chopped almonds over cookies, you can give the bunnies or chickens mouths, eyes, etc., by using small pieces of almonds.

Place in preheated oven (350° F.) for about 15 minutes until golden.

GINGER COOKIES

4–5 dozen

2 whole eggs	Rind of 1 lemon, grated
1 egg yolk	1–1½ Tbs. ground ginger
1 cup sugar	2½–3 cups flour

11 x 17-inch baking pan

Stir whole eggs, egg yolk, and sugar until light and foamy. Add lemon rind, ginger, and flour until dough holds together and no longer sticks to bowl and hands. Cover and refrigerate.

When firm but still pliable, divide into 3–4 parts. While working with one part, keep unused parts refrigerated.

On a lightly floured pastry board, roll each part with a floured rolling pin to about ⅛-inch thickness. Cut out with a fancy cooky cutter of your choice. Place on a lightly buttered baking pan, close together. Let dry for about 1 hour.

In preheated oven (325° F.) bake for 12–15 minutes or until lightly colored. Remove.

Note: Ginger Cookies will turn crisp and stay crisp for a long time. Therefore, if you happen to like ginger, you will have an ideal cooky for tea.

HAZELNUT APRICOT BARS
(Short Dough)

HASELNUSS MARMELADEN
STANGERL (MÜRBER TEIG)

22 bars

1½ cups flour
1 bar less 1 Tbs. sweet butter, cold
¼ cup sugar
2 egg yolks
½ cup apricot jam

HAZELNUT TOPPING:
2 egg whites
½ cup confectioners' sugar
2 cups coarsely ground hazelnuts
2–3 Tbs. lemon juice, strained

7 x 11-inch baking pan

Place flour on pastry board and cut butter into it. Crumble butter and flour between fingers into coarse pieces. Combine with sugar. Make a well and add egg yolks. With a table knife blend ingredients quickly together. Knead into a smooth dough. From time to time scrape off dough sticking to pastry board until it is cleaned of all ingredients. Work into a ball and wrap in wax paper. Refrigerate for about 20 minutes.

Pat dough out by hand to fit pan, or, if you prefer, roll dough out between 2 sheets of wax paper to the desired size. Gently remove top sheet of wax paper. Flip dough over into pan. Remove remaining sheet of wax paper and fit dough into pan. Refrigerate.

While dough is chilling, prepare hazelnut topping.

Spread apricot jam generously over surface of dough with the back of a tablespoon. Spread hazelnut topping evenly over jam.

Place in preheated oven (350° F.) on lowest rack for 10 minutes, remove to center rack for 20–30 minutes longer until golden brown.

While still hot, cut into 1 × 3½-inch pieces.

Hazelnut Topping: Stir egg whites and sugar until foamy. Fold hazelnuts into it and gradually add lemon juice. Combine thoroughly.

HAZELNUT CRESCENTS

About 24 pieces

⅓ cup sugar
1¼ cups finely ground hazelnuts
¼ cup sifted flour
3 egg whites
¼ bar sweet butter (scant), melted

HAZELNUT COCOA FILLING:
¼ bar sweet butter, soft
2 Tbs. verifine sugar (generous)
1 tsp. unsweetened cocoa (scant)
½ cup finely ground hazelnuts

11 x 17-inch baking pan

Mix sugar, hazelnuts, and flour together. Combine ingredients gently with stiffly beaten egg whites and gradually pour in cooled butter. Fold together delicately.

Through a pastry bag, fitted with a No. 5 pastry tube, press small crescents, about 2 inches long, on a buttered 11 × 17-inch baking pan.

Bake for 15–20 minutes in preheated oven (350° F.). The crescents will harden as they cool. When firm and cool, remove from pan with a wide knife or spatula.

Spread hazelnut cocoa filling or apricot jam between two crescents and sandwich together.

Hazelnut Cocoa Filling: Cream butter and sugar until fluffy. Stir cocoa into mixture until well blended. Add hazelnuts and combine well.

HUSSAR ROUNDS

These very simple but really good cookies are listed among my mother's recipes under two different names: *"Husaren Krapferl"* and *"Je länger je besser,"* meaning "the longer the better." This is a very appropriate name, because the longer you keep them, the better they taste. They have the rare virtue of improving with time. Accordingly, bake them in advance and keep in a tightly closed tin box in a cool place.

4–4½ *dozen pieces*

2 *bars sweet butter, soft*
½ *cup sugar (generous)*
Rind of 1 lemon, grated
1 *inch vanilla bean or ½ tsp.*
  vanilla extract
3 *egg yolks*

2¾–3¼ *cups flour*
1 *egg white*
3 *Tbs. coarsely chopped, blanched*
  almonds
2 *Tbs. apricot jam*

11 x 17-*inch baking pan or cooky sheet*

Cream together butter and sugar until smooth. Add grated lemon rind and vanilla. Mix egg yolks alternately with spoons of flour into batter. Work in remaining flour until dough is firm but smooth. Place a small piece of dough in the palm of your hand and roll between palms into a small ball, about 1 inch in diameter.

Place cookies on baking pan, allowing space between cookies. With your finger make a small indentation in center of each cooky. You can bake them plain or brush edges lightly with beaten egg white and top with chopped almonds. Place almonds in a pointed paper cup or a cone of wax paper and cut off tip. This will make it easier for you to garnish the cookies.

Bake in preheated oven (350° F.) for 20–25 minutes or until lightly colored. When cool, place a dab of apricot jam in center.

Serve dusted with confectioners' sugar.

Without the apricot filling, these cookies will keep extremely well in a cool, but unrefrigerated, place.

Note: HUSSAR ROUNDS can also be served plain, omitting jam or almonds. Serve sprinkled with confectioners' sugar.

ISCHLER COOKIES

40–48 pieces

1¼ cups flour (scant)
⅓ cup sugar
2½ cups finely ground hazelnuts or
walnuts

1¼ bars sweet butter, cold
Apricot jam
Chocolate Icing

11 x 17-inch baking pan

Blend flour, sugar, and ground hazelnuts or walnuts on pastry board. Cut cold butter into mixture. Blend with fingertips and work by hand quickly into a smooth, firm dough, with no ingredients left on pastry board. Form dough into a ball, cover, refrigerate until firm but still pliable enough to be rolled out.

Divide dough into two parts. Keep one refrigerated. Between two sheets of wax paper roll one part of dough out to about ¼-inch thickness. From time to time lift wax paper on both sides to allow dough to spread. With a 1½-inch round cooky cutter cut dough into rounds, one close to the other. With a spatula place rounds on an ungreased baking pan. Proceed same way with refrigerated dough. Save scraps, refrigerate, roll out again.

In preheated oven (350° F.) bake cookies for 10–15 minutes until lightly colored. Watch closely to avoid browning. Allow cookies to cool before removing from pan.

Spread half of cookies with a thin coat of apricot jam, sandwich together. Place small dot of chocolate icing in center of each cooky or brush half of top with chocolate icing. Both will look attractive, so why not try both ways?

Note: A small brandy glass can be used as a cooky cutter if you should not have the desired size available.

POT CHEESE CRESCENTS

This is a crescent with an outstanding dough, very close to puff paste dough but made with pot cheese. It has the advantage of being so much quicker to make, easier to handle, and less fragile than puff paste dough.

30–40 pieces

½ lb. pot cheese	¾ cup apricot jam
2 cups flour (scant)	1 whole egg
2 bars sweet butter, cold	

11 x 17-inch baking pan

Put pot cheese through a food mill or strainer or mash with a fork until all lumps have disappeared.

Place flour and pot cheese on pastry board. Cut pieces of butter into it. Quickly mix all ingredients together with a table knife. First with fingertips, then with hands, knead very lightly and quickly into a smooth dough. Add a little more flour if necessary (depending on the dryness of the pot cheese) until dough no longer sticks to board or hands. Wrap, and refrigerate for about 2 hours.

Divide dough into 2 or 3 parts. Keep unused parts refrigerated. On a lightly floured pastry board, with a floured rolling pin roll each part of dough into an oblong piece to less than ⅛-inch thickness. Cut into about 2½-inch strips, then cut each strip into about 2½-inch squares. (Save all trimmings, combine and roll out again.)

Dough is at its best when very thin, but that can almost never be obtained at the first rolling. Therefore roll each square once more into about 3–3½-inch squares.

Place ½–¾ teaspoon of apricot jam on each square. Roll very lightly from one corner to the opposite corner. Bend into a crescent in such a fashion that the overlapping corner faces away from you. Place crescents on ungreased baking pan. Keep refrigerated until remaining dough is formed into crescents.

Brush tops of crescents with lightly beaten egg before placing into preheated oven (350° F.) for about 15 minutes, until golden brown. Remove from pan when hot.

You can serve crescents either cold or slightly heated. Before serving, dust tops with confectioners' sugar.

Reheated they will taste as fresh as on the first day.

RASCALS

24–28 pieces

1⅔–1¾ cups flour
⅓ cup sugar (scant)
1 bar sweet butter

4 egg yolks
¾ cup apricot jam
Lemon Icing

11 x 17-inch baking pan or cooky sheet

Combine flour and sugar on pastry board and make well in center. Cut butter into well and add egg yolks. Work into a smooth dough. If too soft, add a little more flour. Shape dough into a ball. Cover. Refrigerate for at least 1 hour.

Divide dough into two parts and keep one refrigerated. On lightly floured pastry board or between two sheets of wax paper roll each part to about ⅛-inch thickness. With a diamond-shaped 2 × 3½-inch cooky cutter cut dough out. Lift cut-outs carefully with the help of a knife or a spatula and place on a 11 × 17-inch baking pan or cooky sheet. Save scraps, refrigerate until firm, and then roll out again. Proceed same way with remaining part of dough.

Place in preheated oven (325° F.) for 12–15 minutes or until lightly browned.

When cool, spread one half of the cookies thinly with apricot jam and place other cookies on top.

Spread tops with lemon icing.

ROLLED ALMOND WAFERS   GEROLLTE MANDELSCHEIBEN

24–28 pieces

2 egg whites
⅓ cup sugar
⅓ cup sifted flour

3 Tbs. sweet butter, melted
½ cup finely ground, blanched
   almonds

11 x 17-inch baking pan or cooky sheet

Beat egg whites until very stiff. Fold in sugar. Add flour, combine gently but thoroughly, and fold cooled melted butter into mixture. Combine with almonds. Blend.

Drop teaspoons of batter, 3 inches apart, on a generously buttered 11 × 17-inch baking pan or cooky sheet. Spread with back of spoon into very thin 3-inch rounds.

Bake in preheated hot oven (450° F.) for 4–5 minutes or until edges are beginning to brown. Remove at once with a spatula or a pancake turner. Quickly roll each round, jelly-roll style, into shape. If wafers harden before all are shaped, return them to oven for a few more seconds. Cool on wire rack. They harden as they cool.

Before serving, dust lightly with confectioners' sugar.

If you feel very ambitious and happen to like whipped cream, you can fill the Rolled Almond Wafers with it.

Note: I suggest that you bake only 5 or 6 wafers at a time until you master the art of rolling them quickly into shape before they harden.

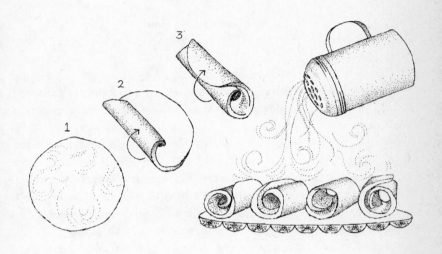

SHORT DOUGH HAZELNUT BARS

24 bars

1⅓ cups flour
⅔ cup sugar (scant)
1¼ bars sweet butter, cold
1 egg yolk

2½ cups blanched, finely ground
  hazelnuts
1 egg white
½–¾ cup thick apricot jam, hot

10 x 16-inch baking pan

Mix flour with sugar on pastry board. Make well in center and cut butter into it. Add egg yolk and ground hazelnuts. Combine ingredients with a table knife. Work dough with fingertips and then knead quickly into a smooth, firm dough until pastry board is clean of all ingredients. Wrap dough in wax paper and refrigerate for a short time.

Cut dough into two parts and return one part to refrigerator.

On a lightly floured pastry board roll other half into a long roll, about 2 inches thick. Transfer to a 10 × 16-inch baking pan. With the edge of your hand form a groove in center all along roll. Refrigerate. Repeat process with remaining dough and place into baking pan.

Brush tops of rolls with lightly beaten egg white and bake in preheated oven (350° F.) for about 25 minutes or until lightly brown. Fill grooves immediately with hot jam. When slightly cool, cut rolls into about ¾-inch-wide bars and allow to cool completely on baking pan.

Before serving, dust lightly with confectioners' sugar.

Note: You can also form several rolls, only 1-inch thick. To form the grooves, use the handle of a wooden spoon, pressing handle down all along the center of rolls. Bake for about 15 minutes until lightly brown. Fill grooves with hot jam. When slightly cool, cut into slices.

SPONGE DOUGH ROUNDS

BISKUITTEIG PLÄTZCHEN

These delicate round cookies are made the same way as Cones Filled with Whipped Cream, but these rounds are not turned into cones.

Perhaps a little less eye-catching, these cookies are very good, very light, and also will save you work.

24 individual pieces
12 sandwiched pieces

2 whole eggs
⅓ cup verifine sugar
1 Tbs. water
¾ cup sifted flour

Chocolate Cream
egg white
Assortment of nuts (for garnish)

11 x 17-inch baking pan

Beat eggs with sugar until mixture is light and foamy. Gradually add cold water, stirring constantly. Fold sifted flour gently into batter. Drop a teaspoonful on a well-greased baking pan or cooky sheet. With the back of a spoon, spread each mound into 3-inch thin rounds or into oblong forms about 2½ × 3½ inches.

Bake quickly in preheated oven (375° F.) for about 3–5 minutes until cookies are lightly browned around edges but still pale. Remove with spatula while still warm.

Allow to cool and then spread rounds with chocolate cream (use recipe of your choice), sandwich together, brush centers lightly with egg white, and garnish with a pecan half, walnut or hazelnut half. Or simply dust rounds with confectioners' sugar.

If you should decide against a filling, leave them as individual rounds. After baking, you may also decorate them with chopped nuts or diced mixed candied fruit, placed in center of each cooky after brushing them lightly with egg white.

VANILLA CRESCENTS

The Kipferl plays an important role in the daily life of an Austrian. In the morning he starts the day with a Kipferl, made from yeast, like a croissant, and it had better be good since his mood for the rest of the day may depend on it.

Crescents are made in all sizes and of all kinds of dough. There are Topfen-Nuss-Mohn and Mandel Kipferl and many others, but a Vanille Kipferl occupies a special place in every Austrian's heart.

50–60 pieces

2 cups flour
¼ cup sugar (generous)
1¾ cups finely ground, blanched almonds

1¾ bars sweet butter, cold
1½–2 cups confectioners' sugar
1½–2 inches vanilla bean

11 x 17-inch baking pan

Mix flour, sugar, and ground almonds on pastry board. Cut in butter. First with fingers, then with hands, knead ingredients together quickly. Shape into a smooth ball. Wrap in wax paper and refrigerate for at least 1 hour.

Place ¾–1 teaspoon of dough between the palms of your hands, roll into about 1½-inch-long roll, tapering off both ends, and shape into small crescent.

Transfer crescents to baking pan, leaving small spaces between them.

Preheat oven to 350° F. Bake for 15–20 minutes, until lightly colored.

While crescents are baking, combine confectioners' sugar with vanilla bean on a sheet of wax paper. Blend well.

When slightly cool, gently put several crescents in prepared sugar–vanilla mixture, cover them with it, and transfer to a plate.

When completely cool, store crescents in an airtight container. If kept in a cool place, they will keep fresh for many weeks—if they last that long!

Note: If vanilla bean is not available, use 2–3 Tbs. concentrated vanilla sugar combined with confectioners' sugar.

VANILLA WAFERS

About 30 pieces

2 whole eggs
⅓ cup sugar

1 Tbs. vanilla sugar or ½ inch
  vanilla bean
½ cup sifted flour

11 x 17-inch baking pan or cooky sheet

Whisk together whole eggs, sugar, and vanilla sugar until just blended. Over low flame beat constantly until a bit warmer than lukewarm. Remove from flame and keep beating until cool and batter starts to thicken. Gradually dust flour into batter, folding gently but thoroughly together, without overmixing.

Place batter by teaspoons on a buttered baking pan with a smooth surface in 1½–2-inch intervals. Spread to about 2½-inch rounds. (If air bubbles appear on surface of cookies, hit pan hard on table to remove them.) Let rest at room temperature for 3–4 hours before baking in preheated oven (275° F.) for about 12 minutes until edges start to brown. Let cool in pan. They will turn very crisp when cool.

Cookies will keep well in airtight container.

They can be served plain or can be sandwiched together, filled with cream or jam of your choice.

VIENNESE POCKETS

About 20 pieces

2 hard-boiled egg yolks, mashed
2 Tbs. lemon juice, strained
1⅓ cups flour
¼ cup sugar (scant)
1 cup finely ground, blanched
almonds

1 bar sweet butter, cold
1 egg white
1 Tbs. water
½ cup apricot jam

11 x 17-inch baking pan

Combine mashed egg yolks thoroughly with lemon juice.

Mix flour, sugar, and ground almonds on pastry board. Make well in center. Cut in butter. Add egg yolk mixture. With a table knife fold flour mixture over ingredients in well. Combine. First blend with fingertips, then knead quickly until dough no longer clings to hands or board. If necessary, add a little more flour. Form dough into ball, wrap in wax paper, and refrigerate.

Divide dough into two parts, keep one refrigerated. Roll each part on a lightly floured board with a floured rolling pin into ⅛-inch thickness. Cut edges straight.

Cut into about 3-inch-wide strips and cut the strips into 3-inch squares. (Save scraps, refrigerate, and roll out again.) Spread a small amount of apricot jam in center of each square. With the help of a table knife lift up one half and fold over to form a triangle. Press edges firmly together. Refrigerate. Brush pockets lightly with egg white beaten with 1 tablespoon of water.

Place in preheated oven (350° F.) for about 30 minutes or until golden brown.

Before serving, dust with confectioners' sugar.

Note: Instead of cutting dough into squares, you can cut it into rounds with a 2½-inch cooky cutter. Spread with jam and fold over. You will not have the authentic shape of Viennese Pockets, but these are equally good and quicker to make.

WALNUT FILLED COOKIES

About 18 pieces

1⅔ cups flour (scant)
1 bar plus 1 Tbs. sweet butter, cold
1 whole egg
¼ cup sugar
Coffee Icing
18 walnut halves or quarters
  (for garnish)

WALNUT FILLING:
½ bar sweet butter, soft
¼ cup verifine sugar
1 cup finely ground walnuts
1 Tbs. rum or 1 Tbs. milk

11 x 17-inch baking pan or cooky sheet

Place flour on pastry board and cut in butter. Between fingertips crumble butter and flour into coarse pieces. Form a mound and make a well in center. Break egg in and add sugar. Combine and knead quickly together until board is clean of all ingredients. Refrigerate.

Divide dough into two parts. On a floured pastry board, with a floured rolling pin, roll each part to less than ¼-inch thickness. With a 2½-inch biscuit cutter, cut out rounds. Place on a lightly floured 11 × 17-inch baking pan.

Bake in preheated oven (350° F.) for 12–15 minutes until lightly colored.

When cool, spread half the rounds with walnut filling, top with plain rounds. Refrigerate.

Shortly before serving, glaze top with coffee icing. When icing starts to get firm, decorate each round with half or one-quarter of a walnut.

Walnut Filling: Stir butter and sugar until fluffy. Blend in walnuts. Add rum or milk and mix thoroughly.

WALNUT SLICES (Filled)

WALNUSS SCHEIBCHEN (GEFÜLLT)

About 12 pieces

1–1¼ cups flour
¼ cup sugar
Rind of 1 lemon, grated
½ bar sweet butter, cold
1 whole egg
1¾ cups finely ground walnuts
White Icing
12 walnut halves or quarters (for garnish)

WALNUT ORANGE FILLING:

¼ cup milk
¼–⅓ cup sugar
1½ cups finely ground walnuts
½ tsp. vanilla extract or ½ inch vanilla bean
¼ cup candied orange peel, grated
1 Tbs. dark rum

11 x 17-inch baking pan

On a pastry board combine flour and sugar. Add lemon rind. Make well in center, cut butter into it, and add egg. Cover with ground nuts. Quickly combine ingredients, first with a table knife, then knead by hand into a smooth dough. Form dough into ball, wrap in wax paper, and refrigerate.

Divide dough in half. Roll each part between two sheets of wax paper into about ⅛-inch thickness. Cut out with a 2 × 3½-inch gingerbread cooky cutter. Place slices close together on baking pan. Combine scraps and roll out again.

Bake in preheated oven (350° F.) for 10–15 minutes until lightly colored.

When completely cool, spread walnut cream between two slices and sandwich together. Spread top with white icing (optional). Place a half or a quarter walnut, lightly brushed with egg white, in center of each slice.

Walnut Orange Filling: Bring milk and sugar to boiling point. Add ground walnuts, stir, then remove from flame. Add vanilla, orange peel, and rum. Blend. Use when completely cool.

Note: Slices can also be served as single pieces.

WOOD SHAVINGS

To form Wood Shavings is partly work, partly play. Probably many of you will say, "Why bother?" since the texture of Wood Shavings is the same as many other sponge dough cookies that are simpler to make. But what attracts me is the most unusual shape. Imagine serving a plate full of these oddly formed cookies with ice cream, Jello, fruit cocktail, and such.

About 30 pieces

2 whole eggs, room temperature   ½ cup sifted flour (scant)
½ cup sugar (scant)

One or two baking pans or cooky sheets

Beat whole eggs and sugar until thick and foamy. Add flour, keep beating. Place batter into a pastry bag fitted with a No. 3 pastry tube. On a lightly buttered baking pan or cooky sheet, press out strips about 6 inches long, leaving ample space between them, as they will expand considerably. Since they must be rolled while still hot, place not more than six strips on pan.

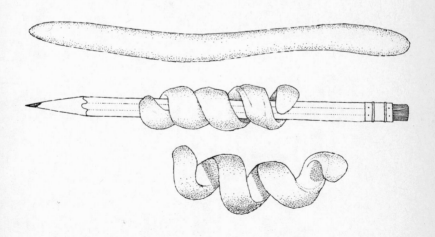

Bake in preheated oven (325° F.) for 5–8 minutes or until lightly colored. Very quickly (speed is essential), while still hot and soft, loosen as many strips as possible from pan. Wrap each strip narrowly around and along a pencil in a spiral. If strips should harden before or while being formed into wood shavings, return them once more to oven.

With a little experience and patience you will master the shaping very quickly; it is not as difficult and time-consuming as it may sound.

Repeat all steps until batter is used up.

Note: Two baking pans or cooky sheets will come in handy since you can prepare a second batch while the first one is in the oven.

2. Small Pastries
Without Flour

Introduction

Nuts, nuts, nuts—used as main ingredient, they are responsible for creating these perfect small pastries. Whether they are walnuts or hazelnuts, almonds or coconuts, they are used to replace the flour. They do an outstanding job, and you will discover that it is not at all necessary to use flour to make pastry.

While these pastries are prepared in different ways, each has its own character.

ALMOND BOWS	*Mandelbögen*
ALMOND MACAROONS	*Mandel Makronen*
CHOCOLATE AMAZONS	*Schokoladen Amazonen*
COCONUT KISSES	*Kokosnuss Busserl*
EASTER ALMOND COOKIES	*Oster Mandel Bäckerei*
EGG WHITE ALMOND DROPS	*Engländer*
HAZELNUT CRESCENTS	*Haselnuss Kipferl*
NUT KISSES	*Nussbusserl*
PINE NUT (PIGNOLIA) CRESCENTS	*Pignolia Nuss Kipferl*

ALMOND BOWS

About 40 pieces

5 egg whites
2 cups sifted confectioners' sugar
1½ cups sliced blanched almonds
   (generous)
3–4 Tbs. lemon juice, strained
Rind of 1½ lemons, grated

5–6 sheets of thin white wafer
   papers (Oblaten), 8 x 11-inches,
   to be cut to desired sizes
   (can be found in many specialty
   stores)

11 x 17-inch baking pan or cooky sheet

Combine stiffly beaten egg whites with sugar in a saucepan. Place over very low flame. Stir vigorously with wooden spoon. When hot, add lemon juice and lemon rind. Keep stirring until mixture becomes thick and sticky. Add almonds. Watch mixture carefully, as it burns easily. Remove from flame when still foamy and keep stirring until slightly cool.

Spread about 1 tablespoon of mixture to less than ¼-inch thickness over wafers 4 inches long and about 1½ inches wide. Place wafers on a baking pan or cooky sheet, leaving small spaces between.

If no wafers are available, place about 1 tablespoon of mixture on a generously buttered 11 × 17-inch baking pan (with smooth surface), spreading mixture to ¼-inch thickness. Leave ample space between pieces since they expand considerably. Keep unused mixture refrigerated.

Place in preheated oven (350° F.) and bake for 10–15 minutes or until golden brown. When still soft, quickly remove with a spatula and bend each piece carefully over rolling pin. (A bottle can also be used.) Cool slightly on rolling pin or bottle to prevent unbending. The bows harden as they cool.

Repeat until all almond bows are formed. If pieces harden too quickly before being removed from pan, return them to oven for a few more seconds to soften.

This sounds more tricky than it is. I am sure you will find it a very rewarding task once you try.

ALMOND MACAROONS

12-14 pieces

2 egg whites
⅓ cup sugar
½ tsp. vanilla sugar or ½ tsp.
vanilla extract

2 cups finely ground, unblanched
almonds
Blanched almonds, split in half

10 x 16 x 2-inch baking pan

Stir egg whites, sugar, and vanilla sugar or extract until foamy. Add ground almonds. Blend until smooth.

Drop teaspoons of mixture, about 2 inches apart, on a buttered 10 × 16 × 2-inch baking pan, shaping them with the help of a second spoon into medium high mounds. Decorate each macaroon with a split almond, pressing almond down lightly.

Preheat oven (300° F.); just before putting in macaroons, reduce to 275° F. and bake for about 20 minutes or until lightly colored and tops are firm. Remove from pan when still hot.

CHOCOLATE AMAZONS

18–20 pieces

2 egg whites
½ cup sugar (scant)
1¾ cups finely ground, unblanched almonds

1 bar or square semisweet chocolate, grated
Blanched almonds, split in half (for garnish)

10 x 16 x 2-inch baking pan

Beat egg whites until very stiff. Fold in sugar. Combine. Add ground almonds and grated chocolate and blend gently but thoroughly.

Drop a teaspoon of mixture onto a well-buttered 10 × 16 × 2-inch baking pan, forming a small mound with the help of a second spoon. It is essential to keep mound high. Decorate by placing one blanched almond half on top of each dome.

Place in preheated oven (300° F.), reduce to 250° F., and bake for about 25 minutes until firm on surface. Leave on baking pan until slightly cool. Remove. Cookies may be slightly soft, but they will harden during cooling time.

COCONUT KISSES

About 30 pieces

3 egg whites
¾ cup verifine sugar (scant)

2¾ cups fresh coconut, peeled and
shredded

10 x 16 x 2-inch baking pan

Beat egg whites until soft peaks form. Gradually, by tablespoons, add about half of sugar. Beat thoroughly after each addition until very stiff and shiny. Fold coconut and remaining sugar delicately into mixture.

On a buttered and lightly heated 10 × 16 ×2-inch baking pan drop heaping teaspoons of mixture in about 1-inch intervals, forming mounds.

In preheated oven (225° F.) bake (it might be better to say "dry") kisses for 1–1¼ hours until pale.

Remove when cool.

See "Tips and Techniques" for directions on how to prepare fresh coconut. If canned shredded coconut is used, omit a quarter cup of sugar and proceed as indicated.

EASTER ALMOND COOKIES

About 20 pieces

1½ cups finely ground, blanched
  almonds
⅓ cup sugar (scant)
1 egg yolk

2 egg whites
1 tsp. rum or cognac or ½ tsp.
  vanilla extract

11 x 17-inch baking pan or cooky sheet

Mix ground almonds with sugar.

Combine egg yolk with well-beaten egg whites. Gradually add almond mixture and fold together well. Add flavoring you prefer and blend.

Drop teaspoons of batter, about 1½ inches apart, on a buttered baking pan.

Bake in preheated oven (400° F.) for about 10 minutes or until golden brown. Let settle for 5 minutes and then loosen cookies with spatula or table knife. Allow cookies to remain on pan until completely cool.

EGG WHITE ALMOND
DROPS

16–18 pieces

4 egg whites
1¼ cups confectioners' sugar

1¼ cups blanched slivered
almonds

10 x 16-inch baking pan

Place egg whites and sugar in top of double boiler. Combine until smooth. Place double boiler over medium flame and whisk or beat egg mixture until thick and sticky. Add almonds. Blend.

Drop a full teaspoon of mixture on a generously buttered, lightly floured 10 × 16-inch baking pan. With the help of a second spoon, form high mounds. Leave 1-inch spaces between cookies.

Bake in preheated slow oven (275° F.) for about 30 minutes until lightly golden. The almond drops will be soft when taken from the oven. They will harden as they cool.

Remove from pan when slightly cool and firm.

Note: When blanched pre-slivered almonds are used, it is advisable to slice them thinner.

HAZELNUT CRESCENTS

About 24 pieces

1 egg white	2 egg whites
⅓ cup verifine sugar	2 Tbs. sugar (generous)
3 cups finely ground, roasted, blanched hazelnuts	Apricot jam or Chocolate Cream

11 x 17-inch cooky sheet or baking pan

Whisk one egg white and ⅓ cup sugar until foamy and combine thoroughly with ground hazelnuts. Beat remaining two egg whites until soft peaks form. Gradually spoon in 2 tablespoons of sugar and beat until very stiff. Fold beaten egg whites into mixture until well blended.

Press small crescents about 2 inches long through a pastry bag, fitted with a No. 5 pastry tube, on a buttered 11 × 17-inch cooky sheet or baking pan.

Place in preheated oven (300° F.) and bake for 15–20 minutes. Remove when slightly firm. The crescents harden as they cool.

When completely cool, spread apricot jam or chocolate cream (use recipe of your choice) between two crescents and sandwich together.

NUT KISSES

20–22 pieces

Rind of 1 lemon, grated
4 cups finely ground walnuts
3 egg whites

¾ cup sugar
1 tsp. ground coffee (not instant)

11 x 17-inch baking pan

Grate lemon rind into ground walnuts.

Beat egg whites until stiff. Gently but thoroughly fold in walnuts with lemon rind and sugar. Blend in ground coffee.

Drop heaping teaspoons of mixture in high mounds at about 1-inch intervals on a generously buttered 11 × 17-inch baking pan.

Bake in preheated oven (350° F.) for about 20 minutes until firm outside but still soft inside.

When slightly cool, loosen nut kisses from pan.

PINE NUT (Pignolia) CRESCENTS

About 20 pieces

2 egg whites
⅔ cup sugar
Rind of 1 lemon, grated

3–3½ cups finely ground, blanched almonds
⅓–½ cup pine nuts (pignolia nuts), unsalted

11 x 17-inch baking pan

Stir egg whites and sugar. Add grated lemon rind and ground almonds. Keep stirring until well blended. If necessary, add more almonds to get a medium-firm paste.

Take ¾–1 teaspoon of paste, roll in the palms of your hands to about 3-inch length and ¾-inch thickness, then roll in pine nuts to cover paste. Turn into crescents.

When fingers or palms of hands become too sticky, wet them lightly before rolling.

Place crescents on a buttered 11 × 17-inch baking pan.

In preheated oven (300° F.) bake for about 20 minutes until lightly golden. Remove from pan when slightly cooled.

3. Tortes

Introduction

What is a torte? A torte is something very special, elegant, with a certain flair. No matter which torte you choose, simple or elaborate, round or square, big or small, it is and will always be the climax of a fine dinner.

If a torte is served with coffee or tea in the afternoon, it will set the mood for cozy hours to follow.

Chocolate Sour Cherry Torte	Schokoladen Weichsel Torte
Chocolate Sponge Torte	Schokoladen Biskuit Torte
Chocolate Torte Without Egg Yolk	Schokoladen Torte ohne Dotter
Christmas Torte	Weihnachtstorte
Date Torte (Short Dough)	Dattel Torte (Mürber Teig)
Dobos Torte	Dobosh Torte
Egg White Torte (Snow Torte)	Eiweiss Torte (Schnee Torte)
Ladyfinger Torte (Champagne Torte)	Biskotten Torte
Layer Nut Torte	Blätter Nusstorte
Linzer Torte	Linzer Torte
Linzer Torte (Stirred)	Linzer Torte (Gerührt)
Linzer Torte (White)	Linzer Torte (Weiss)
Macaroon Torte	Makronen Torte
Maraschino Chocolate Torte	Maraschino Schokoladen Torte
Old Vienna Torte	Alt Wiener Torte
Orange Torte	Orangen Torte
Peach Torte (Canned Fruit) (Hazelnut Short Dough)	Pfirsich Torte (Eingelegtes Obst) (Mürber Haselnuss Teig)
Peach Torte (Fresh Peaches) (Short Dough)	Pfirsich Torte (Frische Pfirsiche) (Mürber Teig)
Pischinger Torte	Pischinger Torte (Oblatten Torte)
Plum Torte (Fresh Fruit) (Short Dough)	Pflaumen Torte (Frische Pflaumen) (Mürber Teig)
Punch Torte (Sponge Butter Dough)	Punsch Torte (Biskuit Butterteig)
Sachertorte	Sachertorte
Sand Torte	Sand Torte
Strawberry Torte (Fresh Strawberries)	Erdbeertorte (Frische Erdbeeren)
Torte with Pot Cheese Filling	Topfentorte
Viennese Walnut Strawberry Torte (Fresh Strawberries)	Wiener Walnuss Erdbeertorte (Frische Erdbeeren)
Walnut Cheese Layer Torte	Dreiblättrige Walnuss Topfentorte

APPLE TORTE (Fresh Apples) (Short Dough)

APFEL TORTE (FRISCHE ÄPFEL) (MÜRBER TEIG)

Follow dough recipe for Apple Cake (Open Faced, Short Dough) on p. 175, omitting egg for brushing.

The ingredients used for Apple Cake will give you two Apple Tortes. If you plan on only one torte, divide dough into two equal parts and freeze or refrigerate one. The following ingredients for filling are for one torte only; double the amounts for two.

6–8 servings

2–3 large apples
⅓ cup blond raisins (approx.)
⅓ cup chopped walnuts or almonds

2–3 Tbs. sugar combined with cinnamon
2–3 Tbs. sweet butter, melted

One or two 9-inch baking pans with removable bottoms

Cut apples into slices slightly thicker than ⅛ inch.

On a lightly floured pastry board with a floured rolling pin, roll dough out to about ¼-inch thickness to fit a 9-inch baking pan. Add ¾ inches all around for border. Place into pan and pat to fit. Even out border. With a fork prick border only, several times all around.

Arrange slices of apples neatly and generously on bottom of pastry shell. Sprinkle first layer with two-thirds of the raisins, nuts, and cinnamon sugar. Cover with second layer of apples, top with remaining ingredients. Spoon butter over torte.

Bake in preheated oven (350° F.) on center rack for about 45 minutes until edges of torte are slightly browned or until test done. Allow to settle for 5–10 minutes. Remove outer ring carefully, leaving torte on removable bottom to cool.

Serve dusted with confectioners' sugar.

APPLE TORTE (Butter Dough)

APFEL TORTE (BUTTERTEIG)

10–12 servings

2¼ cups flour
1½ bars sweet butter, cold
1–2 Tbs. sugar (optional)
2 egg yolks
2 Tbs. white wine
1 Tbs. water
¼ tsp. salt
½ cup Apricot Glaze II

APPLE FILLING:
2 lbs. apples
2–3 Tbs. sugar
Rind of 1 lemon, grated
1 Tbs. rum or lemon juice
¼ cup chopped almonds (approx.)

10 x 2½-inch springform pan

Divide flour into two equal parts. Place one part on pastry board. Cut cold butter into it and cover with remaining flour. Roll with rolling pin into thin leaves. With fingers work into coarse crumbs. Add sugar. Mix.

Make a well in center. Whisk egg yolks combined with wine, water, and salt into well. Mix with knife, then work with fingers until paste holds together. Then knead dough lightly and briefly. Roll dough out, folding it over. Repeat rolling and folding over 2 to 3 times. Finally, work into a ball. Cover. Let dough rest, refrigerated, for about 1 hour.

Keep one-third of dough refrigerated to use for lattice.

Roll two-thirds of dough out to fit a 10 × 2½-inch springform pan, adding 1 inch all around for border. Pat dough well into pan and trim or pat border even. Prick bottom and sides several times with a fork to prevent air pockets and puffiness. Refrigerate if dough becomes too soft.

In preheated oven (350° F.) bake shell until very lightly colored. When it is completely cool, coat bottom of shell generously with apricot glaze, which is best done with the back of a tablespoon. Refrigerate.

While shell is chilling, remove remaining dough from refrigerator and roll on pastry board into 11 rolls of different lengths, about ¼-inch thick, to form lattice.

Top glaze with the prepared apple filling, which can be cooked in advance.

Brush border with egg white. Place 6 rolls across torte in intervals of 1½ inches, securing ends of rolls on border. Place remaining rolls in opposite direction on top, to form a lattice pattern.

Brush rolls with egg white before placing in preheated oven (350° F.) for 30 minutes on lowest rack. Increase temperature to 375° F., place torte on center rack, and bake for another 30 minutes or longer until golden brown.

Apple Filling: Peel and core apples. Cut them into chunks. Place into a pan and add sugar and grated lemon rind. Cover and cook, without water, over low flame for 10–15 minutes. Remove cover and let simmer until excess liquid is absorbed, stirring from time to time.

Cooking time of your apples depends on their quality. Increase or decrease time accordingly.

When cooked, remove from flame. Spoon rum into apples and stir. Let cool. Add chopped almonds.

APRICOT TORTE (Fresh Apricots) (Short Dough)

MARILLEN TORTE (FRISCHE MARILLEN) (MÜRBER TEIG)

Follow dough recipe for Apple Cake (Open Faced, Short Dough) on p. 175, omitting egg for brushing.

The ingredients used for Apple Cake will give you two Apricot Tortes. If you plan on only one torte, divide dough into two equal parts and freeze or refrigerate one. The following ingredients for filling are for one torte only; double the amounts for two.

6–8 servings

2 lbs. fresh apricots, semi-ripe, me-   ½–¾ cup Apricot Glaze II
dium sized (16–20 pieces)

One or two 9-inch baking pans with removable bottoms

Cut apricots in half.

On a lightly floured pastry board, with a floured rolling pin, roll out dough to about ¼-inch thickness to fit a 9-inch baking pan. Add ¾ inch all around for border. Place into pan and pat to fit. Even out border. Prick border only, several times all around, with a fork.

In an unbaked pastry shell arrange apricot halves neatly and closely together. Fill out small empty spaces with pieces cut in half.

Cover with slightly cooled, thick apricot glaze.

Bake in preheated oven (350° F.) for 45–60 minutes until edges of torte are slightly browned or until test done. Allow to settle for 5–10 minutes. Remove outer ring carefully, leaving torte on removable bottom to cool.

Serve dusted generously with confectioners' sugar since apricots can be tart.

Note: To avoid excessive forming of liquid, do not sugar fruit before baking. If liquid should form during baking, carefully pour off and return to oven.

BITTER CHOCOLATE TORTE

10–12 servings

7 bars or squares semisweet chocolate

1 bar sweet butter, soft

4 egg yolks

2 cups finely ground, unblanched almonds

4 egg whites

3 Tbs. sifted flour

¼ cup apricot jam

¼ cup Apricot Glaze II

Chocolate Icing

9 x 1½-inch baking pan with removable bottom

Melt chocolate with ¼ bar of butter in double boiler.

In separate bowl mix remaining butter and egg yolks together until creamy. Gradually add cooled, melted chocolate, blending well after each addition. Stir in ground almonds. Fold together with stiffly beaten egg whites and sifted flour and blend until all white lumps have disappeared. Butter and flour a 9 × 1½-inch baking pan and pour batter into it.

Bake in preheated oven (350° F.) for about 30 minutes until test done. Remove outer ring and let cool.

Same day or next, cut torte into two layers, spread generously with apricot jam, and sandwich together. Coat top with apricot glaze and pour chocolate icing over top and sides.

Serve with sweetened whipped cream.

BLUE DANUBE CHOCOLATE TORTE

10–12 servings

½ bar plus 1 Tbs. sweet butter, soft

⅔ cup sugar (scant)

6 egg yolks, room temperature

4 bars or squares semisweet chocolate

2–3 Tbs. water

6 egg whites

¾ cup sifted flour

1 cup dark sour cherry preserve (Morellos) or 1 cup pitted sour cherries (water packed)

CHOCOLATE CREAM FILLING and FROSTING:

4 bars or squares semisweet chocolate

½ cup water, scant

1 Tbs. flour

2–3 egg yolks

½ inch vanilla bean or ½ tsp. vanilla extract

1 cup heavy cream, whipped

9 x 2½-inch springform pan

Cream together butter and sugar until smooth. Add one egg yolk after another, beating well after each addition until mixture is pale and creamy. Melt chocolate, combined with water, in double boiler over medium flame. When cooled, fold into batter. Mix well. Beat egg whites until stiff but still moist and stir delicately with sifted flour into batter. Mix thoroughly until all white lumps are absorbed. Pour into a well-buttered, lightly floured 9 × 2½-inch springform pan.

Bake in preheated oven (350° F.) for 45–55 minutes or until cake tester inserted in center of cake comes out dry.

When completely cool, preferably the next day, slice torte with a sharp knife into three layers. Spread bottom layer with chocolate cream and top with second layer. Spread chocolate cream and then dark sour cherry preserve or paper-absorbed sour cherries on second layer before placing last layer on top. Save 2 tablespoons of cherries for decoration.

Coat top and sides generously with chocolate cream.

Comb torte with a pastry comb. If not available, draw wide spirals in snail-like design with the handle of a wooden spoon into the chocolate cream, starting from center.

Shortly before serving, garnish center with dark sour cherry preserve or with well-drained sour cherries.

Chocolate Cream: Melt chocolate with water in top of double boiler. Remove from heat. Stir flour into melted chocolate. Combine with egg yolks. Return to double boiler and keep stirring over low flame until thick. Remove from heat. Add vanilla and stir. When cool, blend with whipped cream. Refrigerate before using.

Note: You should be able to find dark sour cherry preserve (Morellos) in specialty or some department stores. But paper-absorbed, pitted sour cherries, extremely well drained, may be used as substitute.

CHOCOLATE MOCHA TORTE (Squares)

For a change you have here a square torte—and a delicious one.

16 servings

¾ bar sweet butter, soft
⅓ cup sugar
4 egg yolks
3 bars or squares semisweet chocolate, grated
1½ cups finely ground, unblanched almonds
½ cup sifted flour
⅛ tsp. baking powder
4 egg whites

Chocolate Icing
¼ cup Apricot Glaze II
8 blanched almonds, split in half

COFFEE CREAM FILLING:
1 tsp. instant coffee (generous)
1 Tbs. hot water
½ bar sweet butter, soft
¼ cup sugar (approx.)
1 egg yolk

8 x 8 x 2-inch square baking pan

Cream butter and sugar well. Gradually add egg yolks and beat until very pale and fluffy. Blend chocolate into mixture and stir until well absorbed. Delicately fold in ground almonds, stiffly beaten (but not dry) egg whites, and flour and baking powder, sifted together. Fold together well until no white lumps show. Pour batter into a buttered, floured, 8 × 8 × 2-inch square baking pan.

Bake in preheated oven (350° F.) for 30–40 minutes until test done or cake shrinks from sides of pan. Let cool.

Next day or the day after, slice cake into two layers. Spread layers with coffee cream and sandwich together. Return to baking pan, cover, and refrigerate for a few hours.

If top of cake is uneven, slice off a piece to make it level. Turn torte upside down, since bottom is smoother than top, and spread thinly with plain apricot glaze.

Cut torte lengthwise into four equal parts, then crosswise into squares. Cover top and sides with chocolate icing. Refrigerate. After icing has set, place a split blanched almond in center of each square. Refrigerate for at least two hours before serving.

Coffee Cream Filling: Combine instant coffee with hot water until smooth.

Place butter and sugar in a small bowl and cream well. Add egg yolk and coffee extract and stir until fluffy.

CHOCOLATE SOUR CHERRY TORTE

SCHOKOLADEN WEICHSEL TORTE

8–10 servings

¾ bar sweet butter, soft
¾ cup sugar
4 egg yolks
4 bars or squares semisweet chocolate, grated

3 Tbs. sifted flour
1 level tsp. baking powder
4 egg whites
1 lb. can pitted, sour red cherries, water packed

9 x 1½-inch baking pan with removable bottom

Cream butter and sugar together and add egg yolks. Beat until very light and creamy. Add grated chocolate and blend until well absorbed. Gently fold in stiffly beaten egg whites, sprinkled with flour and baking powder sifted together, combine until all white lumps have disappeared. Pour batter into a well-greased, floured 9 × 1½-inch baking pan.

Drop well-drained, paper-absorbed sour cherries one by one into batter, covering the whole surface.

Bake in preheated oven (350° F.) for about 45 minutes or until test done. Let cool.

Torte is best served on same day, lightly dusted with confectioners' sugar. For a more decorative effect, dust sugar through a paper doily over top of torte. Gently remove paper doily.

CHOCOLATE SPONGE TORTE

10–12 servings

5 bars or squares semisweet chocolate, melted
3 Tbs. water
6 egg yolks
⅓ cup sugar (generous)
6 egg whites
½ cup sifted flour

CHOCOLATE CREAM FILLING:
1½ bars sweet butter, soft
4 Tbs. verifine sugar
2 egg yolks
2 or 3 bars or squares semisweet chocolate, grated
1 Tbs. instant coffee
2 Tbs. hot water

10 x 2½-inch springform pan

Melt chocolate with three tablespoons of water in double boiler. Cool.

Beat egg yolks and sugar together until very pale and creamy. Gradually add melted, cooled chocolate and blend ingredients well. Gently fold in stiffly beaten egg whites and sifted flour. Pour batter into a well-greased, floured 10 × 2½-inch springform pan.

Place in preheated oven (375° F.). After 10 minutes reduce to 350° F. and bake for about 15 minutes longer, until test done and springy to touch. Allow to settle for 5 minutes, then remove outer ring. Let cool.

When completely cool, cut cake into two layers. Spread bottom layer with chocolate cream and sandwich together. Cover top and sides with cream.

With a pastry comb draw straight lines in horizontal and vertical directions—a simple but attractive decoration. If no pastry comb is available, draw straight lines with the help of a fork.

Chocolate Cream Filling: Prepare chocolate cream several hours before applying. Refrigerate.

Dissolve instant coffee with 2 tablespoons of boiling water.

Blend butter and sugar well. Add egg yolks and stir until very creamy. Stir in grated chocolate, then instant coffee mixture. Beat until fluffy.

CHOCOLATE TORTE WITHOUT EGG YOLK

8–10 servings

½ bar sweet butter, soft
¼ cup sugar
3½ bars or squares semisweet
    chocolate, melted
6 egg whites
⅔ cup sifted flour
¾ cup currant or raspberry and
    currant jelly

PARISIAN CREAM FILLING and FROSTING:

1 cup heavy cream
4 bars or squares semisweet
    chocolate

9 x 1½-inch baking pan with removable bottom

Cream together butter and sugar. Gradually add almost cool, melted chocolate and blend well until smooth. Beat egg whites until stiff. Fold into batter alternately with sifted flour. Mix gently but thoroughly. Pour into a well-buttered, floured 9 × 1½-inch baking pan.

Place in preheated oven (350° F.), then reduce heat to 325° F. Bake for 30–40 minutes or until test done. Let cool.

Cut torte in two layers. Spread one layer with jelly (of your choice), then with Parisian cream. Top with second layer. Decorate by sprinkling torte with confectioners' sugar. Garnish by filling a pastry bag, fitted with a plain pastry tube No. 1 or 2, with jelly of your choice, and drawing a snail-like design, starting in center of torte.

If torte is decorated with jelly, only half of the required amount of Parisian Cream is used.

Parisian Cream: Considered one of the finest creams.

Place heavy cream with small pieces of chocolate over medium low flame. Stir constantly until chocolate dissolves completely, simmers, and starts to thicken. Remove and place pan in cold water, or even better over ice cubes. Stir by hand or beat using only one attachment of electric beater.

Refrigerate for several hours or overnight, and then stir once more until you obtain a very firm cream.

Variation: Torte can also be served with the same filling. Top with second layer, spread Parisian Cream over top and sides, and decorate with stars or rosettes around outer border.

CHRISTMAS TORTE

12–14 servings

5 whole eggs
½ cup sugar
Rind of 1 lemon, grated
1 Tbs. lemon juice
1 cup sifted flour (scant)
¼ cup finely chopped, candied
   lemon peel
½ cup blond raisins
2 Tbs. dark rum
Punch Icing

Angelica
Whole cherries from cherry
   preserve

**WALNUT WHIPPED CREAM
FILLING:**

2 cups heavy cream
3–4 Tbs. confectioners' sugar
2½ cups finely ground walnuts
2–3 Tbs. dark rum

10-inch springform pan

Chop raisins, sprinkle with rum, cover well, and soak overnight. In a saucepan whisk eggs and sugar together. Beat over low flame until a bit warmer than lukewarm. Remove from flame and beat until batter is cool and becomes light, fluffy, and thick, and volume has risen considerably (like a heavy mousse). While beating, add lemon rind, then gradually add lemon juice. Gently but thoroughly fold in flour alternately with lightly floured candied lemon peel and soaked raisins.

Pour batter into a generously buttered 10-inch springform pan and bake in preheated oven (350° F.) for 35–45 minutes until brown and test done. Do not open oven for the first 15 minutes. Let cool in pan.

Next day cut torte into two layers. Spread bottom layer with two-thirds of walnut cream and sandwich together. (Keep remaining cream refrigerated to be used for decoration.)

Return torte to springform and keep well covered and refrigerated for at least 1–2 days before serving.

Several hours before serving, apply punch icing over top of torte. Refrigerate. When firm, spread remaining walnut cream around sides of torte. Refrigerate.

Cut green angelica into thin slices. Arrange on top of torte to form a long narrow stem, a few thin branches, and small leaves with whole or half cherries at ends of branches. If you prefer, decorate with stars, made out of thinly sliced angelica.

Walnut Whipped Cream: Beat heavy cream until it starts to thicken. Gradually add sugar and whip until stiff. Gently fold ground walnuts into whipped cream. Combine with rum.

DATE TORTE (Short Dough)

DATTEL TORTE (MÜRBER TEIG)

10–12 servings

¾ cup flour
¼ cup sugar (scant)
Rind of 1 lemon, grated
½ bar less 1 Tbs. sweet butter, cold
2 egg yolks

DATE FILLING:

1 cup pitted, sliced dates (approx.)
4 egg whites
⅔ cup sugar
1¼ cups slivered blanched almonds
½ inch vanilla bean or ½ tsp. vanilla sugar

9-inch pie pan or 9 x 1½-inch baking pan with removable bottom

Mix flour and sugar on pastry board. Add grated lemon rind. Make well in center, cut butter into it, add egg yolks. With a knife, work flour mixture from all sides toward well. With fingertips, combine ingredients, gradually kneading dough by hands until it no longer sticks to pastry board and all ingredients are worked into a smooth dough. Form into a ball and cover with wax paper. Refrigerate for about 30 minutes.

Between 2 sheets of wax paper roll dough out to fit baking pan, allowing an extra inch to form rim. Pat down into 9-inch pie pan or 9 × 1½-inch baking pan. Cut rim straight. Prick dough, including rim, several times with fork to prevent puffiness.

Bake in preheated oven (350° F.) for 10–15 minutes or until very lightly colored. Do not overbake since torte will be baked once more with the filling.

Spread date filling into cooled pastry shell and bake for 50–60 minutes at 325° F.

Date Filling: Cut pitted dates lengthwise into thin strips. Beat egg whites until firm. Gradually add sugar, beating after each addition until very stiff. Add slivered almonds, vanilla bean, sliced dates, and combine thoroughly with egg whites. If vanilla sugar is used in place of vanilla bean, beat into egg whites with sugar.

DOBOS TORTE

10–12 servings

4 egg yolks
¾ cup sugar
2 Tbs. half & half or milk
1 cup sifted flour (scant)
⅛ tsp. baking powder
4 egg whites

1¼ bars sweet butter
3 egg yolks
½ cup sugar (scant)

CHOCOLATE BUTTERCREAM FILLING (Cooked):
4½ bars or squares semisweet chocolate

CARAMEL ICING:
¾ cup sugar
½ tsp. sweet butter

9-inch layer cake tins (found in specialty stores) or bottoms of springform pans

Stir egg yolks and sugar until light and thick. Gradually spoon in cream and blend well. Sift flour, combined with baking powder, and fold gently but thoroughly into batter with stiffly beaten egg whites.

Six layers have to be baked; if only two or three tins are available, keep unused batter refrigerated.

With a spatula or a table knife spread ½ cup of batter evenly over generously buttered, lightly flour-dusted cake tins. Bake two or three tins at a time in preheated oven (400° F.) for 8–10 minutes or until lightly golden. Remove layers from tins. If tins are to be re-used, remove any crust with paper towel before butter and flour are newly applied.

When all six layers are baked, select the best (that is, the most even) layer for the top and put it aside for caramel icing. Spread each of the five remaining layers evenly with chocolate cream and sandwich together. Save some cream for decorating sides of torte.

Place selected top layer on a buttered tin. Keep a buttered knife or spatula handy. Spread caramel icing over top of layer, working quickly since it hardens very fast. With buttered knife cut lines almost through the icing to mark off sections of the desired size for servings. These lines will serve as the decoration of the torte and also help to make slicing easier.

When caramel icing has set, carefully break off any icing that may have run over the edges. When completely cool, place coated layer gently on top of cream-filled layers. Cover sides with remaining chocolate cream. Refrigerate.

Before serving, comb chocolate cream around torte with pastry comb.

Chocolate Buttercream Filling (Cooked): Melt chocolate until soft. Cool. Cream butter, add cooled chocolate, and blend thoroughly. Beat egg yolks and sugar in double boiler over low flame until thick. When completely cool, gradually spoon chocolate buttercream into it. Beat well after each addition. Refrigerate.

Caramel Icing: Place sugar in a small saucepan over low flame. Stir constantly. When liquid turns golden brown, add butter and blend. Spread caramel icing quickly over pastry.

EGG WHITE TORTE
(Snow Torte)

8–10 servings

¾ bar sweet butter, soft
¼–⅓ cup sugar
½ inch vanilla bean or ½ tsp.
  vanilla extract
1½ cups finely ground blanched
  almonds

⅓ cup sifted flour (generous)
6 egg whites
¼ cup apricot jam
Rum Icing

9 x 1½-inch baking pan with removable bottom

Cream together soft butter and sugar, then stir in vanilla. Fold in ground blanched almonds, sifted flour, and very stiffly beaten (but not dry) egg whites. Blend ingredients together thoroughly. Pour batter into a well-greased, lightly floured 9 × 1½-inch baking pan.

Place in preheated oven (375° F.). After 5 minutes, reduce heat to 325° F. Bake for 20–30 minutes or until lightly colored. Remove outer ring and let cool.

Next day cut into two layers and fill with apricot jam or a jam of your choice. Sandwich layers together.

Cover top and sides with rum icing. Place one candied cherry in center of torte.

LADYFINGER TORTE

(Champagne Torte)

8–10 servings

10–12 ozs. ladyfingers
1 cup strong, black coffee (sweeten
  to taste)
½ cup finely chopped, toasted,
  blanched hazelnuts

COFFEE CREAM FILLING:
1½ bars sweet butter, soft
⅓ cup verifine sugar
2 egg yolks
2–3 Tbs. instant coffee
2 Tbs. hot water

8 x 8 x 2-inch square cake pan or 8 x 1½-inch round baking pan

Line an 8 × 8 × 2-inch square cake pan or an 8 × 1½-inch round baking pan with wax paper, allowing enough overlap all around to cover top of cake.

Moisten each ladyfinger by dipping lightly into strong coffee and place flat, one next to another, to fit bottom of pan, breaking some to fill empty spaces and corners. Cover layer of ladyfingers with coffee cream. Place second layer of moistened ladyfingers crosswise on top of first layer and cover with coffee cream. Continue same way with each layer, leaving the top one uncovered for the time being. (Save remaining coffee cream for decoration.)

Cover torte with wax paper, place a plate on top, and—to press layers down—place a heavy weight onto the plate. Keep in refrigerator (with the weight) at least overnight.

Several hours before serving, turn torte over, decorate top and sides with coffee cream, and sprinkle with finely chopped toasted hazelnuts. Instead of coffee cream you can also use lightly sweetened coffee whipped cream. Refrigerate.

Coffee Cream Filling: Cream together butter and sugar. Add 2 egg yolks and blend. Combine instant coffee with 2 tablespoons hot water. Spoon into mixture and beat until light and very fluffy.

Variations: Each time you choose to make this torte, you can give it a different filling and a different appearance.

For instance: Dip ladyfingers into coffee, but make a chocolate cream filling, topped with lightly sweetened coffee whipped cream.

Another recommended filling: Dip ladyfinger into a mixture of milk and rum, sweetened to taste. Cover each layer with almond or nut filling. Decorate with whipped cream and chopped, toasted, blanched almonds or coarsely chopped nuts.

LAYER NUT TORTE

Blätter Nusstorte, my mother's favorite, is a very "dignified" torte. Although it may not impress you too much when you first take a bite of it, by the second bite you will think, "Not bad at all." At the third you will be convinced that it is one of the finest and tastiest tortes you ever bit into.

It may require a little more work, time, and patience to make, but, considering the result, it certainly is worthwhile.

12–14 servings

2–2¼ cups flour
2 bars sweet butter, cold
⅔ cup sugar
1 whole egg
2½ cups finely ground walnuts
Lemon Icing
Quartered walnuts and one walnut
  half

WALNUT WHIPPED CREAM
  FILLING:
1½ cups heavy cream
3–4 Tbs. confectioners' sugar
1¾ cups finely ground walnuts

9 x 1½-inch baking pans with removable bottoms or 9-inch flan rings

Place flour on pastry board and make well in center. Cut cold butter into well and add sugar and egg. Combine ingredients with a table knife. Add ground nuts and knead quickly and lightly, but thoroughly, into a smooth dough. Work dough into a thick oblong roll, about 8–9 inches long. Wrap in wax paper and refrigerate for about 2 hours.

Divide dough into five equal parts, keeping unused parts refrigerated since dough has a tendency to soften.

Place one part of dough on bottom of your 9 × 1½-inch baking pan and cover with wax paper. Roll dough out to about the size of bottom of baking pan, replace outer ring, and pat dough lightly until it reaches ring. If too soft, refrigerate for a short time.

Bake in preheated oven (325° F.) for about 15 minutes or until lightly colored. Preferably bake two layers in separate baking pans at the same time. Watch carefully because they brown easily. Allow layers to cool for 2–3 minutes before gently transferring them to wire rack. Layers become crisp as they cool and have to be handled with great care since they break easily.

Bake and handle remaining three layers the same way as first two.

Two or three days before serving, spread first layer with walnut whipped cream, top with second layer, spread with cream. Repeat with next two layers, leaving top of fifth layer plain for later icing. Save one-fourth of walnut whipped cream filling for decoration around sides of torte. Store torte, securely wrapped in foil, in refrigerator.

Several hours before serving, coat top of torte with lemon icing. When icing has set, apply remaining refrigerated whipped cream around sides of torte. Place quartered walnuts all around edge in 1½-inch intervals and place one walnut half in center of torte. Chill torte until serving.

Walnut Whipped Cream Filling: Place heavy cream into a cold bowl and beat. When cream begins to thicken, add sugar, then keep beating until stiff. Gently and gradually fold ground nuts into beaten whipped cream.

Note: If you do not have as many baking pans as required or the patience to bake each layer separately, I suggest you bake layers in flan rings, using cooky sheet as bottom. Divide dough into five parts. Roll each part between two sheets of wax paper to about the size of the flan ring. Refrigerate. When firm, remove top sheet of wax paper, invert dough into ring, gently remove second sheet of paper, and pat dough to fit ring. Bake, but watch carefully. With flan rings, less baking time is required. Let cool for several minutes. To avoid breakage, slide cardboard underneath before removing to wire rack.

LINZER TORTE

10–12 servings

1 cup flour (scant)
½ cup sugar (scant)
Rind of 1 lemon, grated
1 pinch cinnamon
1 pinch clove
1½ bars sweet butter, cold

2 egg yolks
3¼ cups finely ground unblanched almonds
¼ cup currant jelly or seedless raspberry jam

9 x 1½-inch baking pan with removable bottom

Blend flour, sugar, grated lemon rind, and spices together on pastry board. Make well in center, cut cold butter into it, add egg yolks. With knife, work ingredients quickly toward center and add ground almonds. Work dough with fingertips, then knead by hands into a smooth dough. Cover. Refrigerate for about 1 hour. Save one-third of dough for lattice. Keep refrigerated.

Place dough between two sheets of wax paper. Roll out to fit the bottom of a 9 × 1½-inch baking pan.

With refrigerated dough first make a long roll, about ¼ inch thick, and with it form a border all around torte. Thinly coat top of torte with currant jelly. Coating is best done with the back of a tablespoon. Return torte to refrigerator.

To form lattice, make 10 rolls, about ¼ inch thick, of different lengths to fit across top of torte. Brush border all around with lightly beaten egg white before placing first 5 rolls, about 1½ inches apart, across top of torte, pressing down firmly on border. Arrange remaining 5 rolls crosswise to form lattice. Brush lattice with lightly beaten egg white.

Bake in preheated oven (350° F) for 35–45 minutes until golden brown or torte shrinks from sides of pan.

Before serving, refill lattice spaces with currant jelly or raspberry jam. Dust top with confectioners' sugar.

Torte is best baked 3–4 days before serving.

LINZER TORTE (Stirred) LINZER TORTE (GERÜHRT)

12–14 servings

2¼ bars sweet butter, soft
¾ cup sugar
Rind of 1 lemon, grated
4 egg yolks
Juice of 1 lemon, medium size
4½ cups finely ground, toasted,
  blanched hazelnuts

¼ tsp. cinnamon
1¼ cups sifted flour
4 egg whites
2 bars or squares semisweet
  chocolate, grated

9 x 2½-inch springform pan

Cream together butter and sugar. Add lemon rind and egg yolks, beating until light and creamy. Gradually spoon lemon juice into batter and stir well. Add ground hazelnuts and cinnamon and blend. Delicately fold in flour and stiffly beaten (but not dry) egg whites. Combine until no lumps of egg whites show.

Pour half of batter into a buttered and floured 9 × 2½-inch springform pan. Sprinkle grated chocolate over surface, then pour remaining batter evenly over chocolate.

Bake in preheated oven (350° F.) for about 45 minutes, until golden brown and test done.

Dust with confectioners' sugar before serving.

Note: Blanched almonds, toasted and ground, may be substituted for hazelnuts.

LINZER TORTE (White)

LINZER TORTE (WEISS)

This torte is best when baked several days in advance. While some tortes get hard or brittle, others have a consistency that will improve with time just as certain cheeses or wines do.

8–10 servings

1¼ cups flour
2½ cups finely ground blanched
   almonds
⅓ cup sugar
1 bar sweet butter, cold

1 egg
Rind of 1 lemon, grated
1 egg white
¼ cup apricot jam

9 x 1½-inch baking pan with removable bottom

Mix flour, ground blanched almonds, and sugar on pastry board. Make a well in center and cut cold butter into it. Break whole egg into well and add grated lemon rind. With a table knife, work flour mixture toward well, and then, when ingredients are fairly well combined, knead with hands into a smooth paste. Form a ball, cover and chill for at least 1 hour. Save and refrigerate one-third of dough for lattice. Between two sheets of wax paper roll remaining dough to fit the bottom of a 9 × 1½-inch baking pan, or pat dough gently into pan.

Take dough for lattice from refrigerator and first make a long roll on pastry board, slightly more than ¼ inch thick, and place it around torte to form a border. Cover shell with apricot jam.

Next make lattice by forming 11 rolls about ¼ inch thick. Brush border with lightly beaten egg white. Place 5 rolls across torte, securing them by pressing ends down on border. Arrange remaining 6 rolls crosswise over first rolls to finish lattice. Brush with egg white.

If you prefer, instead of rolls you can make strips about ¼ inch wide to form your lattice. It is easier, but looks a little too commercial for my taste.

Return torte to refrigerator for a short time before placing in preheated oven (375° F.). After 15 minutes reduce heat to 350° F. and bake 25–35 minutes longer until torte is golden brown or shrinks from sides of pan.

Before serving, refill lattice spaces with apricot jam and dust with confectioners' sugar.

Keep torte in a cool place; it is not necessary to refrigerate.

MACAROON TORTE

8–10 servings

4 egg whites
¾ cup sugar (scant)
1 Tbs. sifted potato starch or
cornstarch
2½ cups finely ground blanched
almonds

2–3 Tbs. sifted bread crumbs
(plain)
¼ cup Apricot Glaze II
¾ cup heavy cream, whipped
(for filling)

Two 9 x 1½-inch baking pans with removable bottoms

Beat egg whites until firm. Gradually beat in sugar until very stiff. Combine sifted flour with ground almonds. Fold gently but thoroughly into beaten egg whites. Pour mixture into two generously buttered, lightly bread-crumb dusted 9 × 1½-inch baking pans.

Bake in preheated oven (325° F.) for 30–40 minutes until pale golden and test done.

When completely cool, same day or next, spread lightly sweetened whipped cream between layers. Sandwich together. (Double amount of heavy cream if used for decoration.)

Cover top of torte with apricot glaze. Through a pastry bag, filled with whipped cream and fitted with a plain tube with a small opening, draw rippled lines in half-inch intervals, starting from center (fanlike design). If you prefer, cover top with assorted chopped candied fruit instead.

MARASCHINO CHOCOLATE TORTE

MARASCHINO SCHOKOLADEN TORTE

12 servings

1 bar sweet butter, soft
½ cup sugar
7 egg yolks
5 bars or squares semisweet
  chocolate, grated
2 Tbs. maraschino liqueur
¾ cup thinly sliced, blanched
  almonds
6 egg whites
¼ cup sifted flour

½ cup (approx.) sour cherry
  preserve (Morellos)
Chocolate Icing

MARASCHINO ICING:

1½ cups confectioners' sugar
1 Tbs. lemon juice, strained
3 Tbs. maraschino liqueur
1 Tbs. boiling water

Two 9 x 1½-inch baking pans with removable bottoms

Cream together butter and sugar. Break in egg yolks two at a time, beating after each addition until light and creamy. Add grated chocolate to batter and stir until batter takes on a dark color and is very well mixed. Spoon in maraschino liqueur and blend. Take handfuls of sliced almonds, crushing them before stirring into batter. Beat egg whites until very stiff and fold with sifted flour gently but thoroughly into mixture. (Batter will be and should be on the soft side.) Pour batter, evenly divided, into two buttered and floured 9 × 1½-inch baking pans.

Place in preheated oven (350° F.) and bake for 30–40 minutes until test done, firm and springy to the touch. Do not open oven for first 15 minutes of baking. Allow cake to settle for 5 minutes before removing outer ring.

When completely cool, same day or next, spread sour cherry preserve generously between layers. Sandwich layers together. Keep refrigerated for 1–2 days before serving.

Since this torte requires two different icings that should not interfere with each other, I suggest you draw and cut out a 6-inch circle from heavy aluminum foil. Place circle in center of torte, then spread maraschino icing over outer, uncovered border. Refrigerate until firm. Gently remove aluminum foil. Coat inner circle and sides of torte with chocolate icing. Refrigerate.

Allow icing to set completely before placing whole cherries, from preserve, along seam between the two icings.

Maraschino Icing: Place sugar in porcelain or glass bowl. Add lemon juice, maraschino liqueur, and boiling water. With a wooden spoon, stir until smooth and shiny. When back of spoon is well covered with mixture, the icing has the right consistency.

If it should be too thick, add more lemon juice or liqueur; if too thin, add more sugar.

OLD VIENNA TORTE

About 12 servings

CHOCOLATE HAZELNUT LAYER

2 bars or squares semisweet chocolate, melted
½ bar sweet butter, soft
¼ cup sugar
3 egg yolks
1¼ cups finely ground, toasted, blanched hazelnuts
¼ cup sifted flour (scant)
3 egg whites

SPONGE LAYER

2 whole eggs
1 egg yolk

¼ cup sugar
½ cup sifted flour (scant)
¼ bar sweet butter, melted and clarified

CHESTNUT CREAM FILLING AND FROSTING

1 bar sweet butter, soft
¾ cup verifine sugar
1 egg yolk
2¾ cups cooked, peeled, and riced chestnuts (generous)
3 Tbs. cognac
Chocolate Icing

Two 9 x 1½-inch baking pans with removable bottoms

Chocolate Hazelnut Layer: Melt chocolate in top of double boiler. Cream together butter and sugar. Add egg yolks one at a time, beating after each addition until creamy. Stir in melted, cooled chocolate. Fold hazelnuts and flour, with stiffly beaten egg whites, into batter. Blend well. Pour into a buttered 9 × 1½-inch baking pan.

Bake in preheated oven (350° F.) for about 30 minutes or until cake shrinks from sides of pan. Remove outer ring. Let cool.

Sponge Layer: Place whole eggs, egg yolk, and sugar in a saucepan or bowl. Stir until smooth. Over low flame beat constantly until a bit warmer than lukewarm. Remove from heat. Keep beating until cool and batter becomes thick and foamy and volume has risen considerably. Fold in flour gently, but thoroughly, slowly adding slightly cooled melted butter.

Bake in preheated oven (350° F.) in a buttered, floured 9 × 1½-inch baking pan for about 30 minutes or until medium brown. Do not open oven for the first 15 minutes. Remove outer ring. Let cool.

When layers are completely cool, spread chocolate layer with one-third of chestnut cream. Place second layer on top. Refrigerate. Keep remaining filling also refrigerated.

Several hours before serving, spread chestnut cream over top and sides of torte. (If cream has thickened during refrigeration, allow it to reach a spreadable consistency.) Keep torte refrigerated until serving.

Fill a pastry bag, fitted with a plain pastry tube No. 2–4, with chocolate icing. Draw a circle all around border, and draw horizontal and vertical lines across top (lattice design).

Chestnut Cream Filling: Beat butter, sugar, and egg yolk until fluffy. Stir in riced chestnuts and gradually spoon in cognac. Mix until creamy.

ORANGE TORTE

14–16 servings

6 egg yolks, room temperature
1¾ cup confectioners' sugar
⅛ cup orange juice (generous)
Rind of 1 lemon, grated
6 egg whites
¼ cup sifted flour
½ cup potato starch or ⅔ cup
cornstarch

GLAZED ORANGE SECTIONS:
¾ cup water
1½ cups sugar

Drops of lemon juice, strained
3 oranges, small to medium size

ORANGE CREAM FILLING
AND FROSTING:
⅔ cup sugar
½ cup fresh orange juice, strained
⅛ cup lemon juice, strained
¼ cup white wine
3 egg yolks
1 Tbs. rice flour or cornstarch
1¼ bars sweet butter, soft
¼ cup heavy cream, whipped
Rind of 1½ oranges, grated

10 x 2½-inch springform pan

Sift flour and potato starch or cornstarch together.

Beat egg yolks and sugar together until light, creamy, and thick. Gradually add orange juice and lemon rind. Mix until fluffy. Fold stiffly beaten egg whites and sifted flour delicately into batter until well blended.

Pour into well-buttered and floured 10 × 2½-inch springform pan.

Bake in 350° F. oven for about 45 minutes until well browned and test done. Do not open oven for the first 15 minutes. After cake has settled for about 5 minutes, remove outer ring.

The following day cut torte in two layers. Spread about one-third of orange cream over one layer and top with second layer. Refrigerate for at least an hour. Keep remaining cream refrigerated.

Several hours before serving, spread chilled cream over top and sides of torte. Return to refrigerator.

Arrange glazed orange sections closely together in a circle around outer rim.

Orange Cream: In top of double boiler combine sugar, orange juice, lemon juice, wine, egg yolks, and flour. Stir until smooth. Place over medium heat and whisk until very thick. Remove from heat. Keep beating until cool. Beat creamed butter in small pieces into mixture. Fold in firmly beaten whipped cream and grated orange rind. Keep refrigerated.

Glazed Orange Sections: Cook water, sugar, and lemon juice over low flame, stirring continuously until sugar is completely dissolved. Let simmer. From time to time stir and skim foam from surface and sides of pan with spoon or moistened linen. As soon as syrup spins a fine thread when dropped from a spoon or the candy thermometer has reached 240–245° F., the syrup has reached the right stage.

Dip orange slices into slightly cooled syrup. Let soak for about 2 minutes, then remove slices with slotted spoon. Refrigerate.

When glaze has set, arrange slices on top of torte.

PEACH TORTE (Canned Fruit) (Hazelnut Short Dough)

PFIRSICH TORTE (EINGELEGTES OBST) (MÜRBER HASELNUSS TEIG)

10-12 servings

1⅓ cups flour
1 bar sweet butter, cold
⅛ tsp. salt
¼ cup sugar
1 pinch cinnamon
1 pinch clove
Rind of 1 lemon, grated
2 egg yolks
1¼ cups finely ground hazelnuts
½ cup Apricot Glaze II
10-12 halves of canned yellow cling peaches (depending upon size)

VANILLA CREAM TOPPING:

1 cup milk
3 egg yolks
¼ cup sugar
1½-2 Tbs. cornstarch
½ tsp. vanilla extract

PEACH JELLY GLAZE:

¾ cup juice from canned peaches, strained
1 envelope unflavored gelatin
2 Tbs. lemon juice
2 Tbs. cognac or rum

10-inch springform pan or pie shell

Place flour on pastry board, cut in butter, then crumble between your fingers into coarse pieces, and sprinkle with salt. Add sugar, combined with cinnamon and clove, and grated lemon rind. Mix. Make a well in center, break egg yolks in, and cover with ground hazelnuts.

Work ingredients quickly into a smooth dough until pastry board is clean. Form dough into a ball. Cover with wax paper and refrigerate for about 1 hour until firm but still spreadable.

Roll dough between two sheets of wax paper to fit a 10-inch springform pan or pie shell, overlapping 1½ inches all around to form a border. Refrigerate until almost firm. Gently remove top sheet of wax paper. Invert dough into pan. Remove second sheet of wax paper, pat dough against bottom and sides of pan. Cut to even height. If you prefer, pat dough by hand into baking pan to about ¼-inch thickness. Prick bottom and border of dough several times with a fork to prevent forming of air bubbles during baking.

Place in preheated oven (350° F.) for about 20-30 minutes or until crust shrinks from sides of pan. Allow to cool slightly before removing outer ring.

Four to six hours before serving, coat bottom thinly with apricot glaze. Refrigerate. When firm, cover glaze with cooled vanilla cream. Top vanilla cream with well-drained, paper-absorbed, canned peach halves and arrange closely together. Then pour a thin coat of peach glaze over cream and peaches. Chill for about 10 minutes. When firm, apply a second coating. Keep refrigerated until serving.

Vanilla Cream: Whisk ¼ cup cold milk, egg yolks, sugar, and flour together. Gradually add remaining milk (warmed) and stir until smooth. Heat in double boiler, beating until cream becomes thick. Remove from fire and combine with vanilla extract. Cool by placing pan in cold water, stirring from time to time to prevent forming of skin on top of cream.

Peach Glaze: Combine ½ cup peach juice with gelatin. Heat over low flame, stirring until completely dissolved. Remove from fire and add remaining peach juice, lemon, and liqueur.

When cool, cover torte with glaze.

Note: Canned apricots can be substituted for canned peaches.

PEACH TORTE (Fresh Peaches) (Short Dough)

PFIRSICH TORTE (FRISCHE PFIRSICHE) (MÜRBER TEIG)

Follow dough recipe for Apple Cake (Open Faced, Short Dough), p. 175, omitting egg for brushing.

The ingredients used for Apple Cake will give you dough for two Peach Tortes. If you plan on only one torte, divide dough into two equal parts and freeze or refrigerate one. The following ingredients for filling are for one torte only; double the amount for two.

6–9 servings

10–12 semi-ripe peaches, medium size   ½–¾ cup Apricot Glaze II

Two 9-inch baking pans with removable bottoms

Cut each peach into 4–6 sections.

On a lightly floured pastry board with a floured rolling pin, roll dough out to about ¼-inch thickness to fit bottom and sides of a 9-inch baking pan; add ¾ inch all around for border. Place into pan and pat to fit. Even out border. With a fork prick border only, several times all around.

In unbaked pastry shell arrange slices of peaches in a pinwheel pattern, overlapping slightly. Fill in small empty spaces with pieces cut in half.

Cover with slightly cooled, thick apricot glaze.

Bake in preheated oven (350° F.) for 20 minutes on lowest rack; place on center rack for 45–60 minutes more until edges of torte are slightly browned or until test done. Allow to settle for 5 minutes. Remove outer ring carefully, leaving torte on removable bottom.

Serve dusted with confectioners' sugar.

Note: To avoid excessive forming of liquid, do not sugar fruit before baking. If liquid should form during baking, carefully pour off and return to oven.

PISCHINGER TORTE

Pischinger Torte is made entirely the cold way. The only thing you have to do is buy a package of unfilled, plain wafers, about 9 inches round or square, which come ten to a package. They are imported and may be found in various specialty shops.

A delicious treat, quick and easy to make.

8–10 servings

5 wafers (Karlsbader Oblatten), plain
Chocolate Icing

HAZELNUT CHOCOLATE FILLING:
1 bar sweet butter, soft

⅔ cup confectioners' sugar
1½ bars or squares semisweet chocolate, grated
1 tsp. instant coffee (optional)
1 Tbs. hot water
2 cups finely ground hazelnuts

Spread the prepared filling thinly over wafers, one layer after the other, pressing them lightly together. Be careful with the first wafer since it breaks easily; after that the chances of breaking are slight. Keep top layer plain for the chocolate icing. Wrap in foil. Keep refrigerated for one or two days.

Several hours before serving pour chocolate icing over torte. Refrigerate.

Hazelnut Chocolate Filling: Dissolve 1 teaspoon instant coffee in 1 tablespoon hot water. Cream butter and sugar together. Add grated chocolate, beat until fluffy, then stir in coffee. Fold in ground hazelnuts and mix until well blended.

Note: Five layers are traditional, but make a rather thin torte. If you prefer, you may, of course, add more layers, but don't forget to prepare additional filling.

PLUM TORTE (Fresh Fruit) (Short Dough)

Follow dough recipe for Apple Cake (Open Faced, Short Dough) on p. 175, omitting egg for brushing.

The ingredients used for Apple Cake will give you dough for two Plum Tortes. If you plan on only one torte, divide dough into two equal parts and freeze or refrigerate one. The following ingredients for filling are for one torte only; double the amount for two.

6–8 servings

2–3 lbs. fresh plums   ½–¾ cup Apricot Glaze II

One or two 9-inch baking pans with removable bottoms

Quarter Plums.

On a lightly floured pastry board with a floured rolling pin, roll dough out to about ¼-inch thickness to fit a 9-inch baking pan; add ¾ inch all around for border. Place into pan and pat to fit. Even out border. With a fork, prick border only, several times all around.

In unbaked pastry shell arrange quartered plums in a pinwheel pattern, overlapping slightly. Fill in small empty spaces with pieces cut in half.

Cover with slightly cooled, thick apricot glaze.

Bake in preheated oven (350° F.) for 45–60 minutes until edges of torte are slightly browned or until test done. Allow to settle for 5–10 minutes. Remove outer ring carefully, leaving torte on removable bottom to cool.

Serve dusted with confectioners' sugar.

Note: To avoid excessive forming of liquid, do not sugar fruit before baking. If liquid should form during baking, carefully pour off and return to oven.

PUNCH TORTE (Sponge Butter Dough)

12 servings

3 whole eggs
¼ cup sugar
½ cup sifted flour (scant)
½ bar less 1 Tbs. sweet butter, clarified
Apricot Glaze I
Punch Icing
Chocolate sprinkles

RUM CREAM FILLING:
½ Tbs. flour
¼ cup heavy cream
2 egg yolks
¼ cup sugar (scant)
3 Tbs. rum
¼ cup heavy cream, whipped

9 x 2½-inch springform pan

Combine eggs and sugar in a saucepan or bowl until just blended. Heat mixture by beating constantly over low flame until a bit warmer than lukewarm.

Remove from flame. Beat until cool, light, and foamy like a mousse cream and volume increases considerably. Dust small amount of flour over mixture while alternately blending in cooled, clarified butter. When mixed, pour into a buttered, lightly floured 9 × 2½-inch springform pan.

In preheated oven (350° F.) bake for 30–35 minutes until springy to touch or golden brown. Do not open oven for the first 15–20 minutes.

When completely cool or, better still, the next day, cut torte into two layers. Spread bottom layer with rum cream and sandwich layers together. Refrigerate. A few hours before serving, spread top evenly with thin rum apricot glaze. Refrigerate. When glaze has set, pour punch icing over top and sides. When icing has set, apply chocolate sprinkles around sides of torte.

Rum Cream Filling: Blend flour and cream in a saucepan until smooth. Beat egg yolks and sugar together lightly with a fork and stir into flour mixture.

Place pan over low flame, stirring constantly. Do not allow mixture to come to a boil. Remove from heat occasionally to smooth out cream. When cream becomes very thick, remove from fire.

Keep stirring, gradually adding tablespoons of rum. Stir well after each addition. When completely cool, fold together with whipped cream. Refrigerate. When cream is firm, fill torte.

If you prefer, cook cream in double boiler.

SACHERTORTE

It is said that Sachertorte is the "King of Tortes." But whose Sachertorte is the real one? That is the question! Everybody claims to have
"*Die Echte*," meaning the right, the genuine recipe. Some are made
with ground nuts, some without. The torte must never be sliced
in half and filled with any kind of cream. It is only apricot glazed
and topped with a chocolate icing.

As far as I am concerned, the torte is a bit on the dry side. For
that reason I am adding one more egg white to *my* Sachertorte,
knowing very well that it is no longer the "genuine" one. Some
connoisseur may object, but with the help of the egg white I keep
my torte moist, and I prefer it that way.

Serve with lightly sweetened whipped cream and you will enjoy
it even more.

10–12 servings

3 bars or squares semisweet chocolate	4 egg yolks
1 Tbs. water	¾ cup sifted flour
½ bar sweet butter	5 egg whites
½ cup sugar (scant)	¼ cup Apricot Glaze II
	Chocolate Icing

9 x 1½-inch baking pan with removable bottom

Melt chocolate with 1 tablespoon water in top of double boiler.

Cream butter and sugar together. Add one egg yolk at a time,
beating well after each addition until very light and fluffy.

It is important to stir longer than usual since the success of the
torte depends on the length of time you work on it. Add melted
chocolate to batter and beat again for the same length of time as
previously. Gently fold in stiffly beaten (but not dry) egg whites
and sifted flour. Pour mixture into a buttered and floured 9 × 1½-
inch baking pan.

Preheat oven to 350° F. and bake for 45–55 minutes. Let set for five minutes before removing outer ring.

Next day spread top with apricot glaze and cover glazed top and sides with chocolate icing.

If you desire, you can write "SACHER" across top of torte with a pastry bag fitted with a small opening or, even better, since there is only a small amount of icing involved, with a paper cone (which you can make yourself) or with a pointed paper cup (make desired opening by cutting off tip).

Serve with whipped cream (optional).

SAND TORTE

8–10 servings

1¼ bars sweet butter, soft
1¼ cups confectioners' sugar
Rind of 1 lemon, grated
4 egg yolks (room temperature)
½ cup sifted flour

½ cup potato starch or ⅔ cup cornstarch
½ tsp. baking powder
4 egg whites
⅓ cup currant jelly
Lemon Icing

9 x 1½-inch baking pan with removable bottom

Cream together butter and sugar. Add grated lemon rind. Break in one egg yolk after another and stir after each addition until light and fluffy. Sift flour and baking powder together and fold gently with stiffly beaten (but not dry) egg whites and potato starch or cornstarch into mixture. Blend well until all white lumps have disappeared. Pour batter into a buttered 9 × 1½-inch baking pan.

Bake in preheated oven (350° F.) for 30–40 minutes or until test done and torte shrinks from sides of pan.

When completely cool, slice torte in two layers. Spread one layer wih currant jelly and sandwich together. Coat top of torte thinly with currant jelly before spreading top with lemon icing.

Refrigerate until icing has set. With knife or spatula remove dripped icing from sides of torte.

STRAWBERRY TORTE
(Fresh Strawberries)

One of those dream tortes . . .

There is hardly any torte more refreshing than a fruit torte, especially on a hot summer day, but among all of them, Strawberry Torte seems to be most people's favorite.

Nevertheless, it is, after all, a matter of taste, and therefore, if you decide on a fruit torte, I leave it up to you to use *your* favorite fruit.

10–12 servings

4 eggs
2 egg yolks
½ cup sugar
1 cup sifted flour
½ bar sweet butter, clarified

FILLING AND GARNISH:
2 cups heavy cream, whipped
4–6 Tbs. confectioners' sugar
2 pints fresh strawberries

10 x 2½-inch springform pan

Hull and wash strawberries. Dry thoroughly, placing them on absorbent paper to remove all moisture.

Divide strawberries about evenly. Select firm, ripe ones, if possible all the same size, for garnish. Slice remaining, less perfect berries for the filling. To avoid mushiness, do not sweeten strawberries.

Stir whole eggs, egg yolks, and sugar in a saucepan until just blended. Place over low flame and beat constantly until a bit warmer than lukewarm. If you prefer, you can use a double boiler. Remove from flame. Keep beating until mixture is cool and has become foamy and thick and volume has increased considerably. Dust flour over mixture and fold in gently. Add melted, lightly cooled butter. Blend carefully together. Pour batter into a buttered, floured, 10 × 2½-inch springform pan.

Place in preheated oven (350° F.) for about 30 minutes until golden brown and cake shrinks from sides of pan. Remove outer ring. When completely cool, return ring.

Next day slice torte in two layers. Spread one layer with strawberry whipped cream filling. Top with second layer. Refrigerate for 3-4 hours.

Shortly before serving, spread plain whipped cream over top and sides of torte. Arrange whole strawberries close together all around edge of torte. Select one large strawberry for center. Keep refrigerated.

Filling: Beat cream until it starts to thicken. Gradually add tablespoons of sugar. Keep beating until stiff. Reserve more than half to spread over top and sides of torte. Gently fold sliced strawberries into remaining whipped cream for filling.

TORTE WITH POT CHEESE FILLING

This is a cheese torte of great merit. The filling of ground almonds mixed with pot cheese is a very unusual combination—a torte that will melt in your mouth.

10 servings

1⅓–1⅔ cups flour
¼ cup sugar (scant)
Rind of 1 lemon, grated
1 bar sweet butter, cold
1 egg yolk
1 egg white

POT CHEESE FILLING:
½ lb. (8 ozs.) dry pot cheese
⅓ cup sugar
2 egg yolks
1 cup finely ground unblanched
   almonds
2 egg whites
1 Tbs. flour

9 x 1½-inch baking pan with removable bottom

Combine 1⅓ cups flour, sugar, and lemon rind on pastry board. Make a well in center, cut in butter, and add egg yolk. With a table knife blend ingredients together quickly. Work into a smooth, medium-firm dough. If necessary, add more tablespoons of flour until dough no longer sticks to hands and board. Form a ball. Cover with wax paper. Refrigerate for about 30 minutes.

Divide dough almost in half. Place larger part of dough on the removable bottom of a 9 × 1½-inch baking pan, cover with a sheet of wax paper, and roll out, adding 1–1½ inches all around to form rim. Remove wax paper.

Place bottom with dough in outer ring. Pat dough into pan to remove air pockets. Lightly press down rim to even out (will be thicker than bottom). With a fork or toothpick prick rim all around.

To form top layer of torte, roll second part of dough between two sheets of wax paper cut to the exact size of bottom of baking pan, using pan as guide. Refrigerate until almost firm.

Fill shell with cheese mixture. Remove top sheet of wax paper from refrigerated dough, fold dough gently over back of hand. After carefully removing second sheet of paper, place dough gently over top of cheese mixture, securing lightly against rim or place dough directly over cheese filling, and then remove wax paper gently. (If pieces of dough should break off, patch up.) With a pointed knife make four or five small incisions on top of torte. Brush torte with lightly beaten egg white.

Bake on lowest rack in preheated oven (350° F.) for 30 minutes. Remove to center rack for another 40 minutes or until golden brown and torte shrinks from sides of pan.

Before serving, sprinkle torte with confectioners' sugar. If you want your torte to look even more attractive, place a paper doily on top, then sprinkle with confectioners' sugar. Remove doily, being careful not to disturb the design.

Pot Cheese Filling: Strain pot cheese through a food mill. Add sugar and egg yolks and blend. Fold almonds into mixture. Add well-beaten egg whites and flour. Combine.

VIENNESE WALNUT STRAWBERRY TORTE
(Fresh Strawberries)

WIENER WALNUSS ERDBEERTORTE
(FRISCHE ERDBEEREN)

10–12 servings

2–3 pints fresh strawberries
1⅓ cups flour
¼ cup sugar
1 bar less 1 Tbs. sweet butter, cold

1 egg yolk
1½ cups finely ground walnuts
Currant Glaze

10 x 2½-inch springform pan

Hull and wash whole strawberries. Place on absorbent paper, changing paper several times to assure dryness. It is of greatest importance that the berries be free of excess moisture. Select firm strawberries for top of torte and use less perfect ones for slicing.

Mix flour and sugar on pastry board. Make a well in center and cut in butter. Add egg yolk. Cover with ground nuts. Combine with fingertips and work with hands quickly into a smooth dough until pastry board and hands are clean of all ingredients. Form a ball. Wrap in wax paper. Refrigerate for about 30 minutes.

Place ball between two sheets of wax paper. Flatten out slightly with hands. Roll ball out evenly to 1 inch larger than springform pan. Place on cardboard or a flat pot cover or any hard surface. Refrigerate.

When almost firm, remove top sheet of wax paper. Remove outer ring of springform. Place rolled-out dough on bottom of pan. Gently remove second sheet of wax paper. Attach outer ring. Fit dough firmly into pan to remove air pockets. Press sides down with a knife to form a straight border (so that border becomes slightly thicker than bottom). Prick sides and bottom several times with a fork.

If you prefer, pat dough evenly over springform pan to line bottom and form a border about 1 inch high.

Bake unfilled shell in preheated oven (350° F.) for 20–35 minutes, until golden.

Same day or next, when shell is completely cool, a few hours before serving, coat bottom with about half of currant glaze (p. 321). Refrigerate.

When firm, cover glaze with about 1½ cups sliced strawberries. Arrange whole strawberries on top of sliced berries, according to size, starting with largest one in center. Spoon or brush remaining currant glaze over berries. Refrigerate.

Before serving, sprinkle border lightly with confectioners' sugar. Best served with whipped cream.

WALNUT CHEESE LAYER TORTE

10–12 servings

1⅓ cups flour
¼ cup sugar
1 bar sweet butter, cold
1 egg yolk
1¾ cups finely ground walnuts

CHEESE FILLING:
1 lb. pot cheese
⅓ cup sugar
2 egg yolks
Rind of 1 lemon, grated
2 egg whites

*Three 9 x 1½-inch baking pans with removable bottoms or
9-inch round flan rings*

Mix flour and sugar on pastry board. Make a well in center, cut in butter. Add egg yolk and cover with ground nuts. With a table knife, mix ingredients together quickly. First with fingertips, then with hands, work into a smooth dough. At first, dough will crumble, but when all ingredients are kneaded in until pastry board is clean, dough will hold together nicely. Shape dough into a thick, short, oblong roll. Cover with wax paper. Refrigerate for 30 minutes.

Divide dough into three equal parts. Roll each part between two sheets of wax paper into a thin layer (if necessary, refrigerate) to fit baking pans approximately. If flan rings are used, use a cooky sheet as bottom. Instead of rolling out dough, you can gently pat dough into pan, starting from center, spreading toward edges.

Remove top sheets of wax paper from (refrigerated) layers of dough and invert each into a buttered and floured 9 × 1½-inch baking pan; carefully peel off second sheets of wax paper. Remove air pockets by patting dough into pans, fitting to pans at the same time. Prick bottoms several times with a fork.

In preheated oven (350° F.) bake two layers for 10–12 minutes until lightly colored. Keep third unbaked layer refrigerated. Do not overbake first two layers since they have to be baked once more with the filling. Bake third (top layer) about 20 minutes until lightly brown. Cool. Layers harden as they cool.

Same day or next, spread the two not fully baked layers with cheese filling, bake for 35 to 45 minutes until firm. Let cool. Before removing outer rings, loosen with a sharp knife all around edges. Sandwich cheese-filled layers together and slide third layer from bottom of pan into place on top. Top layer must be handled with greatest care since it breaks easily. Therefore remove it from baking pan only when completely cool or, even better, the following day by loosening edges, then sliding spatula gently under layer. If baked in flan ring, loosen, then slide cardboard under layer to remove.

Serve dusted with confectioners' sugar.

Cheese Filling: Strain pot cheese through a food mill. Combine with sugar, egg yolks, and grated lemon rind. Fold in well-beaten egg whites, and mix together gently.

4. Tortes Without Flour

Introduction

Tortes without flour are something super-special. They are exceptionally delicious, so much so that a dear Austrian friend for whom I baked a Mocha Almond Torte said to me: "If I could have this Torte once every month till the end of my life, I would be content." This is the greatest compliment one can get from an Austrian because, believe me, when it comes to food, the Austrians are hard to please. They are very generous with criticism, but very economical with praise.

ALMOND PEACH PLUM TORTE	*Mandel Pfirsich Zwetschgen Torte*
ALMOND TORTE WITHOUT FILLING	*Ungefüllte Mandeltorte*
CHEESE DOUGH TORTE	*Topfenteig Torte*
CHESTNUT ALMOND TORTE	*Kastanien Mandel Torte*
CHOCOLATE POPPYSEED TORTE	*Schokoladen Mohntorte*
CHOCOLATE SADDLE OF VENISON	*Rehrücken*
CHOCOLATE WALNUT TORTE	*Schokoladen Walnuss Torte*
DRY BEAN TORTE	*Bohnen Torte*
EGG WHITE ALMOND TORTE (ONE LAYER)	*Schnee Mandel Torte (Einblättrig)*

EGG WHITE ALMOND TORTE (THREE LAYERS)	Schnee Mandel Torte (Dreiblättrig)
EGG WHITE CHESTNUT TORTE	Eiweiss Kastanien Torte
EGG WHITE DATE TORTE	Schnee Dattel Torte
FARINA TORTE	Gries Torte
HAZELNUT TORTE	Haselnuss Torte
MERANER TORTE	Meraner Torte
MERINGUE TORTE	Schnee Torte
MOCHA ALMOND TORTE	Mocca Mandel Torte
ORANGE HAZELNUT TORTE	Orangen Haselnuss Torte
PLAIN POPPYSEED TORTE	Einfache Mohntorte
POPPYSEED ALMOND TORTE	Mohn Mandel Torte
POPPYSEED ALMOND TORTE WITH APPLES	Mohntorte mit Äpfeln
SIMPLE CHESTNUT TORTE	Einfache Kastanien Torte
SIMPLE HAZELNUT TORTE	Einfache Haselnuss Torte
THREE-LAYER HAZELNUT TORTE	Dreiblättrige Haselnuss Torte
WALNUT TORTE	Walnuss Torte

ALMOND PEACH PLUM TORTE

10–12 servings

1 bar sweet butter, soft
¾ cup sugar
6 egg yolks
2 cups finely ground, unblanched
   almonds
⅓ cup bread crumbs (scant)
6 egg whites

1 sheet of thin white wafer paper
   (Oblatten, available in specialty
   stores) (optional)

FILLING:
2–3 fresh peaches, medium size
12–14 fresh plums

9 x 2½-inch springform pan

Select semi-ripe fruit. Quarter plums and peaches, then cut quarters in half. Refrigerate.

Cream butter and sugar together well. Gradually add egg yolks. Beat until smooth, light, and fluffy. Combine ground almonds with bread crumbs and fold gently with stiffly beaten egg whites into batter. Blend well until no lumps of egg white show. Pour half of batter into a well-buttered, flour-dusted 9 × 2½-inch springform pan. Cover batter with wafer paper.

Alternately arrange rows of sliced peaches with rows of sliced plums. Cover with remaining batter, spreading it evenly with a spatula.

Bake in preheated oven (350° F.) for 50–60 minutes until medium brown and firm to touch. Do not open oven for the first 30 minutes. After 10 minutes cooling time, remove outer ring.

Before serving, sprinkle generously with confectioners' sugar.

Note: The largest wafer paper available is an oblong 8 × 11-inch size. Place bottom of your springform pan on top of wafer, draw a line around bottom, and cut along line. Save trimmings to fill in missing parts.

If wafers are unavailable, bake half of batter for 5–8 minutes until slightly firm. Arrange lightly floured fruit on top, trying to keep them as moisture free as possible. Cover with remaining batter, spreading evenly.

You may substitute pitted cherries for plums or you may use only one kind of fruit, either peaches or plums. Also, dried, barely stewed peaches or apricots, lightly sweetened, about 10–12 ozs., well drained, may be substituted for fresh fruit.

ALMOND TORTE WITHOUT FILLING

10–12 servings

1 whole egg
½ cup sugar
3 egg yolks
Rind of 1 lemon, grated
2 egg whites

2¼ cups finely ground, unblanched almonds
Apricot Glaze I
Chocolate Icing
2–3 Tbs. chopped blanched almonds, toasted

9 x 1½-inch baking pan with removable bottom

Beat whole egg with sugar. Add one egg yolk at a time, then grated lemon rind, beating until very light and foamy. Gently fold well-beaten egg whites and ground almonds into batter. Pour into a well-buttered 9 × 1½-inch baking pan with removable bottom.

Bake torte in preheated oven (325° F.) for about 45 minutes or until golden brown. Let cool.

Next day cover top with apricot glaze (optional), and pour chocolate icing over top and sides. Refrigerate.

When icing has set, sprinkle top lightly with toasted chopped almonds (see p. 19).

Note: This torte is very quick to make and does not call for a filling. If not overbaked, it will stay light and moist and will taste very, very good.

CHEESE DOUGH TORTE

A very fine, light, delectable cheese dough torte.

10–12 servings

¼ lb. (4 ozs.) pot cheese, strained (riced)
1 bar sweet butter
½ cup sugar
4 egg yolks

Rind of 1 lemon, grated
2½ cups finely ground blanched almonds
4 egg whites

9 x 1½-inch baking pan with removable bottom
or
9 x 9 x 1¾-inch square cake pan

Strain or rice pot cheese through a food mill.

Cream butter and sugar together. Add one egg yolk at a time, beating until light and fluffy. Add lemon rind and pot cheese. Combine. Fold ground almonds with stiffly beaten egg whites into batter. Mix gently together until well blended.

Pour into a buttered, floured 9 × 1½-inch baking pan or use a 9 × 9 × 1¾-inch square cake pan.

Bake in preheated oven (350° F.) for 40–45 minutes or until medium brown.

Before serving, dust torte with confectioners' sugar. For a more decorative effect, place a paper doily on top of torte before dusting with sugar. Remove doily, being careful not to disturb design.

Note: If pot cheese should contain too much moisture, press through a cheesecloth. If pot cheese is not available, farmer cheese may be substituted. If too dry, add spoonfuls of milk.

CHESTNUT ALMOND TORTE

12–14 servings

4 egg yolks
¾ cup sugar
2¼ heaping cups cooked, riced
  chestnuts
2 Tbs. dark rum
1 cup finely ground blanched
  almonds
5 egg whites

½ cup Apricot Glaze I or II
Chocolate Icing

CHOCOLATE WHIPPED CREAM FILLING:

3 bars or squares, semisweet
  chocolate
3–4 Tbs. water
1 cup heavy cream, whipped

10-inch springform pan

Boil fresh chestnuts (without incisions) for 15–20 minutes. Peel them, one by one, leaving remaining chestnuts in hot water. Rice chestnuts through a food mill or strainer.

Beat egg yolks and sugar until very light and fluffy. Gradually add riced chestnuts, sprinkled with rum. Mix well. Fold in ground almonds and stiffly beaten (but not dry) egg whites. Mix gently but thoroughly. Pour into a buttered, floured 10-inch springform pan.

Place in preheated oven (350° F.), reducing after 10 minutes to 325° F. Bake slowly for 45–60 minutes. Insert cake tester or toothpick; if it comes out dry, torte is done.

After removing outer ring of springform pan, let torte cool. Keep in dry place until you are ready to fill.

Slice into two layers. Spread chocolate filling over one layer, sandwich together. Refrigerate.

Several hours before serving spread apricot glaze on top of torte. Pour chocolate icing over top and sides. Refrigerate.

Allow icing to set. Place a sliced chestnut half in center of torte.

This is even more delicious when served with lightly sweetened whipped cream.

Chocolate Whipped Cream Filling: Place chocolate and water in a small pan. Let simmer over low flame. Keep stirring until chocolate sauce is smooth and all lumps have disappeared. If necessary, add more spoonfuls of water. Cool without refrigeration to keep sauce in liquid form. Combine with whipped cream when chocolate sauce is completely cool.

Note: If you prefer, you can replace the chocolate icing by preparing a double amount of chocolate whipped cream. Spread top and sides with it. Decorate either by piping some chocolate whipped cream through an open star tube around border or by simply sprinkling border with grated chocolate.

CHOCOLATE POPPYSEED TORTE

8–10 servings

1 bar less 1 Tbs. sweet butter
⅓ cup sugar
4 egg yolks
1¾ cups ground poppyseeds
2½ bars or squares semisweet
   chocolate, grated

4 egg whites
¼–⅓ cup apricot jam
Confectioners' sugar
1 cup heavy cream, whipped
   (optional)

9 x 1½-inch baking pan with removable bottom or
9 x 2½-inch springform pan

Cream together butter and sugar. Add egg yolks, beating until very light and fluffy. Mix poppyseeds with chocolate. Beat egg whites until stiff, but not dry. Gently fold poppyseed and chocolate mixture with egg whites into batter, blending until all lumps have been absorbed.

Pour batter into a buttered and lightly floured 9 × 1½-inch baking pan or a 9 × 2½-inch springform pan. Bake in preheated oven (350° F.) for about 30–40 minutes or until inserted cake tester comes out dry or cake shrinks from sides of pan.

When completely cool, preferably the next day, slice torte into two equal layers. Spread one with apricot jam, place the other on top. Refrigerate. Before serving, sprinkle with confectioners' sugar. For a more attractive looking effect, use a star design. Especially good when served with whipped cream.

CHOCOLATE SADDLE OF VENISON

I wonder who could have thought of such a strange name for such a delightful chocolate almond cake. Saddle of Venison is an unusual but very attractive cake.

It is baked in a long, tinned ring mold and, after chocolate glazed, is decorated with slivered almonds. Then it looks like a saddle of venison—if you use your imagination.

This is a well-loved cake in Austria, with a great tradition—a favorite of connoisseurs.

10–12 servings

6 egg yolks
½ cup sugar
Rind of 1 lemon, grated
3 bars or squares semisweet chocolate, grated
1 pinch clove
1 pinch cinnamon

1 pinch allspice
5 egg whites
2½ cups finely ground unblanched almonds
Chocolate Icing
½ cup blanched, slivered almonds (scant)

12-inch-long tinned ring mold

Beat egg yolks and sugar until light and creamy and add grated lemon rind. Mix chocolate with spices and stir well into mixture. Fold stiffly beaten (but not dry) egg whites with ground almonds into batter. Blend until no white lumps show. Pour into a well-buttered, *sugar*-dusted 12-inch-long tinned ring mold.

Bake in preheated oven (350° F.) for 45–55 minutes, until test done.

Allow cake to settle for about 5 minutes, then gently remove from pan. When completely cool, return to baking pan. Cover with foil. Refrigerate.

Next day, or two or three days later, cover whole cake with chocolate icing. Refrigerate.

When icing has set, garnish cake with 4-5 rows of slivered almonds along both sides of groove, sticking points of almonds straight into pastry. Refrigerate.

Serve with whipped cream.

Note: Don't be afraid to bake cake days in advance; refrigerated and wrapped, it will keep as fresh as if it were just baked.

CHOCOLATE WALNUT TORTE

12 servings

6 egg yolks
¾ cup sugar
3 bars or squares semisweet
chocolate, grated
3½ cups finely ground walnuts
3 Tbs. rum
6 egg whites
½ cup coarsely chopped walnuts
(generous)

FILLING and FROSTING:

1½–2 cups heavy cream (omit
¾–1 cup if cream is used only
for filling)
1–2 Tbs. liqueur of your choice
(optional)

9 x 2½-inch springform pan

Whisk egg yolks and sugar until very light and creamy. Add chocolate and stir well. Fold nuts, sprinkled with rum, and well-beaten egg whites into batter. Blend gently but thoroughly together. Pour batter into a well-greased 9 × 2½-inch springform pan.

Bake (350° F.) for about 45 minutes or until cake pulls away from sides of pan. Do not open oven for the first 20 minutes. Let cool slightly. Remove outer ring.

When completely cool—same day or next—slice torte into two layers. Spread bottom layer with lightly sweetened whipped cream, plain or liqueur-flavored to taste. Top with second layer.

Cover top and sides of torte with plain or liqueur-flavored whipped cream. Sprinkle coarsely chopped walnuts over top and sides.

Variation: If desired, you can decorate torte differently. Spread apricot glaze thinly over top, then cover top and sides with chocolate icing. Garnish by placing a walnut half in center of torte and making rows with quartered nuts (fanlike design) in 1½–2-inch intervals.

DRY BEAN TORTE

Although I am sure you do not need a conversation piece, nevertheless a Bean Torte will without doubt become an after-dinner topic of discussion.

Ask your guests to guess the ingredients of your torte. It will come as quite a surprise to them to learn that this delectable, light, pleasant, and very tasty torte contains white beans as main ingredient.

10–12 servings

3 egg yolks
¾ cup sugar (scant)
1 inch vanilla bean or ½ tsp.
  vanilla extract
1½ cups cooked dry, small white
  beans (generous)
2 Tbs. rum

3 egg whites
1¼ cups finely ground walnuts
  or hazelnuts
3–4 Tbs. apricot jam
Confectioners' sugar or Lemon
  Icing

9 x 2½-inch springform pan

Discard damaged or imperfect beans.

Soak dry beans in water overnight. Cook beans, well covered with water, over medium heat for about one hour or until tender. Drain off water. Steam over low flame to remove all excess dampness. *After measuring*, rice beans through a food mill.

Beat egg yolks with half amount of sugar until light and fluffy. Gradually add riced beans, vanilla, and rum. Mix until creamy and very well blended. Beat egg whites until soft peaks form. Spoon remaining sugar into egg whites, beating after each addition until very stiff. Fold gently into batter with ground nuts. Blend well. Pour batter into a well-buttered, floured 9 × 2½-inch springform pan.

Place in preheated oven (350° F.) for about 60 minutes or until firm and test done or torte shrinks from sides of pan.

Next day slice torte into two layers, spread apricot jam on one layer, and top with second layer. Dust with confectioners' sugar or apply lemon icing over top.

EGG WHITE ALMOND TORTE (One Layer)

SCHNEE MANDEL TORTE (EINBLÄTTRIG)

Follow same recipe as for Egg White Almond Torte (Three Layers), but bake as only one layer for about 45 minutes. Remove from pan and let cool.

Serve without filling, just glazed with an apricot glaze and covered with chocolate icing.

EGG WHITE ALMOND TORTE (Three Layers)

SCHNEE MANDEL TORTE (DREIBLÄTTRIG)

10–12 servings

2¾ cups finely ground blanched almonds
1½ cups confectioners' sugar, sifted
6 egg whites
Apricot Glaze II
Chocolate Icing
2 blanched almonds, split in half

COFFEE BUTTERCREAM FILLING:
2 tsps. instant coffee
3 Tbs. hot water
1 bar less 1 Tbs. sweet butter, soft
3 egg yolks
⅓ cup sugar

Three 9 x 1½-inch baking pans

Combine ground almonds with sifted sugar.

Beat egg whites until very stiff. Fold in almond mixture gently but thoroughly. Divide batter evenly and pour into three generously buttered 9 × 1½-inch baking pans. If only one or two baking pans are available, keep unused batter refrigerated during baking.

Bake at 325° F. for about 20 minutes until lightly golden and firm. Allow layers to settle for about 2 minutes before gently removing them to wire rack.

When cooled, spread two layers with coffee buttercream and sandwich together. Top with third, plain layer.

Refrigerate, securely wrapped (or stored in baking pan, well covered) two to three days before serving. Torte has to mellow before it is ready to be eaten.

Several hours before serving, spread top layer thinly with apricot glaze and pour chocolate icing over top and sides. With split almonds form a four-leaf clover in center.

Coffee Buttercream: **Dissolve** instant coffee in hot water. Stir butter until creamy.

In a double boiler, mix egg yolks, sugar, and coffee. Over low flame, beat mixture continuously until very thick. Remove from flame. Set pan in ice water and keep beating until cool. Spoon mixture gradually into creamed butter, beating well after each addition.

EGG WHITE CHESTNUT TORTE

10–12 servings

3 cups boiled, riced chestnuts
6 egg whites
¾ cup sugar
2 Tbs. vanilla sugar or ½-inch
vanilla bean

3–4 Tbs. apricot jam
1½ cups heavy cream, whipped
Grated chocolate curls

9 x 1½-inch baking pan with removable bottom

Cook, peel, and rice chestnuts through a food mill. (See p. 20.)

Beat egg whites until very stiff. Gradually spoon in half of sugar, beating after each addition. Fold chestnuts, remaining sugar, and vanilla into egg whites. Pour mixture into a well-buttered, flour-dusted, 9 × 1½-inch baking pan. Spread evenly.

Bake in moderate oven (325° F.) for about 1 hour until golden and torte shrinks from sides of pan.

The following day slice torte into two layers. Spread one layer with apricot jam. Top jam with lightly sweetened whipped cream. Cover with second layer.

Spread remaining whipped cream over top and sides. Dust with grated chocolate curls. Refrigerate.

EGG WHITE DATE TORTE

8–10 servings

1½ cups sliced pitted dates

⅔ cup sugar

3½ cups finely ground, blanched almonds

5 egg whites

Heavy cream, whipped

9 x 1½-inch baking pan with removable bottom

Cut dates lengthwise in half and then into thin strips. Add ground almonds, sugar, and stiffly beaten egg whites. Blend ingredients well. Pour mixture into a buttered, floured, 9 × 1½-inch baking pan with removable bottom. Bake in preheated oven (350° F.) for about 45–60 minutes or until golden.

Serve with whipped cream. (Optional.)

Note: If unpitted dates are used, roll dates very lightly in flour to prevent them from sticking to fingers while pits are being removed.

FARINA TORTE

8 servings

4 egg yolks
¾ cup sugar
Rind of 1 lemon, grated
Juice of 1 medium-sized lemon,
   strained

1½ cups finely ground blanched
   almonds
4 egg whites
½ cup farina
¼ cup apricot jam

9 x 2½-inch springform pan

Beat egg yolks, sugar, and lemon rind until pale and creamy. Gradually add strained lemon juice and ground almonds. Fold stiffly beaten egg whites and farina alternately into mixture Blend thoroughly. Pour into buttered, flour-dusted 9 × 2½-inch springform pan.

Bake in preheated oven (325° F.) for about 1 hour or until golden brown and cake shrinks from sides of pan.

Next day slice into two layers. Spread with apricot jam and sandwich layers together. Keep refrigerated.

Before serving, dust torte generously with confectioners' sugar.

Note: For a more decorative effect, place a laced paper doily on top of torte before dusting with confectioners' sugar. Then remove doily, being careful not to disturb design.

HAZELNUT TORTE

8–10 servings

4 egg yolks
⅓ cup sugar (generous)
Rind of 1 lemon, grated
1 Tbs. lemon juice
1 Tbs. rum
2 cups finely ground hazelnuts
⅛ tsp. allspice
⅛ tsp. clove

4 egg whites
3–4 Tbs. apricot jam

HAZELNUT WHIPPED CREAM:

1 cup heavy cream, whipped
1–2 Tbs. confectioners' sugar
¾ cup finely ground hazelnuts

9 x 1½-inch springform pan

Beat egg yolks and sugar until pale and creamy. Add grated lemon rind and, gradually, lemon juice and rum. Stir. Combine ground hazelnuts with spices. Fold into batter with stiffly beaten egg whites. Blend well until no lumps of egg white show. Pour into a buttered, floured 9 × 1½-inch springform pan.

Bake in preheated oven (350° F.) for 30–35 minutes or until test done.

When completely cool, slice torte into two layers. Spread with apricot jam. Sandwich together. Cover top and sides with hazelnut whipped cream or, if you prefer, with slightly sweetened, plain whipped cream, sprinkled with sliced hazelnuts.

Hazelnut Whipped Cream: Beat heavy cream until it starts to thicken. Gradually add sugar. Beat until stiff. Gently fold hazelnuts into cream.

MERANER TORTE

A plain and simple, good chocolate torte.

8–10 servings

1 bar sweet butter, soft
⅔ cup sugar (scant)
3 egg yolks
2 bars or squares semisweet
   chocolate, grated

2 cups finely ground unblanched
   almonds
⅛ tsp. cinnamon
⅛ tsp. clove
3 egg whites

9 x 1½-inch baking pan with removable bottom

Cream together butter and sugar. Add egg yolks and beat until very light and fluffy. Stir in grated chocolate until well blended. Combine ground almonds with spices and add one-fourth of it to batter. Stir lightly. Gently fold well-beaten egg whites and remaining ground almonds into batter. Pour into a lightly buttered and floured 9 × 1½-inch baking pan with removable bottom.

Bake in preheated oven (350° F.) for 35–45 minutes until test done or torte shrinks from sides of pan.

Let cool in pan for about 15 minutes before removing outer ring. Serve dusted with confectioners' sugar.

MERINGUE TORTE

You can bake meringue layers in advance; keep in a dry place and use at your convenience.

8–10 servings

5 *egg whites*
1 *inch vanilla bean or 1 Tbs. vanilla*
sugar
1 *cup sugar (scant)*

COCOA WHIPPED CREAM:
2 *cups heavy cream, whipped*
5–6 *Tbs. confectioners' sugar*
3–4 *tsps. sifted, dark unsweetened cocoa*

One or two baking pans

Beat egg whites until almost firm. Add vanilla. Gradually add sugar, ¼ cup at a time, beating after each addition at length until very thick and glossy.

Line baking pans with wax paper.

Use rim or bottom of a cake pan as guide to draw three circles 9 inches in diameter on wax paper. Grease paper. Starting from center of each circle, draw batter spirals, close together, on the paper, using a pastry bag fitted with a No. 4 pastry tube. Or spread mixture evenly over drawn circles.

Bake meringue layers in very low oven (200° F.) to dry them rather than to bake them, for 40–50 minutes or longer, until very dry and wax paper pulls off easily when tested.

Gently turn layers over on pastry rack and remove paper with great care.

When completely cool, spread bottom layer with cocoa whipped cream, top with second layer, again spread with cocoa whipped cream, top with third layer. Cover top and sides of torte with cocoa whipped cream.

Through a pastry bag fitted with a star tube and filled with plain whipped cream, press small rosettes around outer border.

Cocoa Whipped Cream: Beat cream until it starts to thicken, gradually beating sugar into it until thick. Remove one-third of beaten cream for garnish. Fold sifted cocoa into remaining cream.

Variations: Instead of cocoa whipped cream, you can use different fillings—plain whipped cream, rum- or liqueur-flavored whipped cream, or coffee whipped cream. And don't forget the varieties of fruits such as strawberries or raspberries combined with whipped cream.

Note: Instead of using wax paper, you can generously butter and lightly flour the pan.

MOCHA ALMOND TORTE

12–14 servings

6 egg yolks
¾ cup sugar
3½ cups finely ground blanched
   almonds
7 egg whites
16 blanched almonds, split in half
Chocolate Icing

COFFEE CREAM FILLING:
2 tsps. instant coffee
1 Tbs. hot water
1 bar sweet butter, soft
⅓–½ cup verifine sugar
1 egg yolk
1 inch vanilla bean or 1 tsp. extract

Two 10 x 2½-inch springform pans

Beat egg yolks and sugar until very light and fluffy. Carefully fold in ground almonds with stiffly beaten (but not dry) egg whites. Pour equally divided batter into two buttered and floured 10 × 2¼-inch springform pans.

Bake in preheated oven (350° F.) for 15–20 minutes until lightly browned or cake tester inserted in center comes out dry. Remove outer rings immediately, carefully loosening layers of cake from bottoms of pans. Let cool.

Next day spread coffee cream filling between the two layers. Refrigerate.

A few hours before serving, pour icing over top and sides. When icing has almost set, place split blanched almonds around the top of the torte, close to edge, at 1-inch intervals. In the center of the torte arrange four split almonds to form a four-leaf clover. Refrigerate.

Coffee Cream Filling: Dissolve instant coffee in one tablespoon of hot water. Cream butter and sugar together in a small bowl. Add egg yolk and cooled coffee extract, stirring until light and fluffy and sugar is completely dissolved.

Note: If only one springform is available, keep other half of batter refrigerated. Remove baked layer from bottom of pan carefully to wire rack. Before regreasing and reflouring bottom of springform pan, clean with paper towel to remove crumbs. Pour rest of batter into form and bake as directed.

ORANGE HAZELNUT TORTE

ORANGEN HASELNUSS TORTE

10–12 servings

6 egg yolks
¾ cup sugar (generous)
Rind of 1 orange, grated
2–3 Tbs. fresh orange juice (or frozen concentrate, diluted with ½ the usual amount of water)
4 cups finely ground hazelnuts
6 egg whites
Chocolate Icing

2 Tbs. chopped, toasted, blanched hazelnuts

ORANGE BUTTERCREAM FILLING:

1½ bars sweet butter, soft
⅓–½ cup verifine sugar
Rind of 1½ oranges, grated
Juice of 1 orange, strained

9 x 2½-inch springform pan

Beat egg yolks and sugar until pale and creamy. Add grated orange rind and orange juice by the tablespoonful, mixing after each addition. Gently fold ground hazelnuts with stiffly beaten egg whites into batter until all ingredients are well blended. Pour into a buttered, flour-dusted 9 × 2½-inch springform pan.

Bake in preheated oven (350° F.) for 60–70 minutes or until tester inserted comes out dry. Remove outer ring.

Next day or the day after, slice torte into three layers. Spread orange buttercream between two layers, leaving top layer plain. Sandwich together. Refrigerate.

Several hours before serving, glaze top with chocolate icing. Refrigerate.

When icing has set, scatter chopped, toasted, blanched hazelnuts over top of torte.

Orange Buttercream: Cream butter and sugar. Add grated orange rind and, gradually, orange juice. Beat until fluffy.

PLAIN POPPYSEED TORTE

Everybody likes to try something new—a poppyseed torte perhaps?

Poppyseeds are known in this country, but they are mostly used for filling or as garnish for bread and rolls or a variety of warm desserts. But rarely are they used for tortes.

You can combine the poppyseeds with chocolate or apples or almonds without adding a bit of flour, since the poppyseeds act as a binding. (For Chocolate Poppyseed Torte, see p. 143.)

All recipes for poppyseed tortes included here are easy to make and take very little time.

Note: It is advisable to buy poppyseeds only in reliable stores. They have to be fresh and also clean of all shells (the shells will give a bitter taste to ground poppyseeds). Keep ground poppyseeds refrigerated, but no longer than about six weeks. There is no time limit for ground or unground poppyseeds if frozen.

8 servings

4 egg yolks
½ cup sugar
2 cups ground poppyseeds
Rind of 1 lemon, grated
⅛ tsp. cinnamon

⅛ tsp. clove
4 egg whites
4–5 Tbs. apricot jam
Chocolate Icing

9 x 1½-inch round baking pan with removable bottom

Beat egg yolks with sugar until very pale and creamy. Combine with grated lemon rind, cinnamon, and clove. Beat egg whites until stiff, but not dry. Add beaten egg whites and poppyseeds to batter, gently folding mixture together.

Pour into a well-buttered, lightly flour-dusted 9 × 1½-inch round baking pan with removable bottom.

Bake in preheated oven (350° F.) for about 30–40 minutes. Torte is done when springy to touch or when it shrinks from sides of pan. When completely cool, slice torte into two layers. Spread apricot jam betweeen layers and sandwich together. Refrigerate.

Several hours before serving, cover top and sides with chocolate icing. When icing has set, sprinkle a small amount of whole poppy-seeds in center and around border on top of torte. This decoration is not absolutely necessary, but it looks nice and will show your guests what kind of torte you are serving. Torte can also be served plain, dusted with confectioners' sugar.

POPPYSEED ALMOND TORTE

12 servings

1¼ bars sweet butter, soft
¾ cup sugar
5 egg yolks
Rind of 1 lemon, grated
½ inch vanilla bean or ½ tsp.
  extract
⅛ tsp. clove
Juice of 1 lemon (medium size)

2 cups finely ground unblanched
  almonds (scant)
2½ cups ground poppyseeds
5 egg whites
3–4 Tbs. apricot jam
¼ cup Apricot Glaze II
Chocolate Icing
Poppyseeds (for garnish)
Heavy cream, whipped (optional)

9 x 2½-inch springform pan

Cream butter and sugar. Beat in one egg yolk at a time. Add grated lemon rind, vanilla bean or extract, and clove. Blend. Sprinkle lemon juice over almonds and stir into batter. Gently fold in ground poppyseeds and well-beaten egg whites and combine thoroughly.

Pour batter into a well-buttered and floured 9 × 2½-inch springform pan.

Bake in preheated oven (350° F.) for 45–55 minutes or until test done and cake tester or toothpick inserted in center comes out dry.

When completely cool, split torte into two layers. Spread one layer with apricot jam and top with second. Brush top with Apricot Glaze. Pour chocolate icing over top and sides. Refrigerate.

When chocolate icing has set, form a small circle with whole poppyseeds in center.

Serve with whipped cream (optional).

POPPYSEED TORTE WITH APPLES

MOHNTORTE MIT ÄPFELN

8–10 servings

4 egg yolks
¾ cup verifine sugar
1½ cups ground poppyseeds

1¾ cups finely ground walnuts
2 medium-sized tart apples
4 egg whites

9 x 2½-inch springform pan

Peel, core, and quarter apples and cut into thin slices.

Beat egg yolks and sugar until creamy and light. Separately mix ground poppyseeds, nuts, and finely sliced apples. Fold into batter with stiffly beaten egg whites. Blend thoroughly. Pour batter into a buttered, lightly floured 9 × 2½-inch springform pan.

Bake in preheated oven (350° F.) for about 1 hour or longer until test done and top becomes medium brown and firm. Let cool for 10 minutes. Remove outer ring.

Before serving, dust top with confectioners' sugar. For a more attractive looking effect, use a star design.

SIMPLE CHESTNUT TORTE   EINFACHE KASTANIEN TORTE

8–10 servings

4 egg yolks
½ cup sugar
2¼ cups cooked, riced chestnuts
1 Tbs. lemon juice
1 Tbs. rum
Rind of 1 lemon, grated
½ inch vanilla bean

4 egg whites
¼ cup apricot jam
¼ cup Apricot Glaze II
Chocolate Icing
2 Tbs. finely ground pistachio nuts
  (approx.)
Heavy cream, whipped (optional)

9 × 2½-inch springform pan

Boil fresh chestnuts for 15–20 minutes, peel and rice through a food mill. (See p. 20 for further instructions.)

Whisk egg yolks and sugar until very pale and creamy. Gradually add three-fourths of riced chestnuts, moistened with lemon juice and rum. Add lemon rind and vanilla and mix well. Fold in stiffly beaten egg whites with remaining riced chestnuts and blend thoroughly. Pour batter into a generously buttered and floured 9 × 2½-inch springform pan. Spread evenly over surface.

Place in preheated oven (350° F.) and bake for about 1 hour or until test done. When slightly cool, loosen torte from ring with a sharp knife. Remove and let cool.

Next day, split torte in half. Spread apricot jam between layers. Sandwich together. Refrigerate.

Several hours before serving, spread top with plain apricot glaze and pour chocolate icing over top and sides. Refrigerate.

Before serving, sprinkle chocolate icing with ground pistachio nuts. Serve plain or with lightly sweetened whipped cream on the side.

SIMPLE HAZELNUT TORTE EINFACHE HASELNUSS TORTE

Some day when you are in a real rush, but still want to produce a delicious torte, try this one. It is one of the easiest tortes to make. You don't even have to separate the eggs. Just mix all ingredients together well, pour the mixture into the prepared pan, and bake it.

Do you know a quicker and easier way to make a torte?

12–14 servings

2 tsp. sifted baking powder
5 cups finely ground hazelnuts
6 whole eggs, room temperature
1 egg white
1¼ cups sugar (scant)
Rind of 1 lemon, grated

¼ cup sifted bread crumbs
½–1 pint heavy cream, whipped
  (optional)
4–5 Tbs. apricot jam
⅓ cup Apricot Glaze
Chocolate Icing

10 x 2½-inch springform pan

Sift baking powder into ground hazelnuts. Mix thoroughly. Break 6 whole eggs and 1 egg white into a large bowl. Add sugar, grated lemon rind, and ground hazelnuts. Fold mixture together thoroughly. Pour batter, evenly spread, into a well-buttered, breadcrumb-dusted 10 × 2½-inch springform pan.

Bake in preheated oven (375° F.) for 20 minutes. Reduce heat to 350° F. and bake 20–30 minutes longer until test done or golden brown. Don't open oven for the first 15 minutes. Let cool.

Same or next day, slice torte into two layers. Spread apricot jam between layers and sandwich together.

Serve dusted with confectioners' sugar.

Variations: If you want the torte to look more festive, cover top with apricot glaze. Pour a chocolate icing over top and sides. Decorate with hazelnuts, sliced in half, all around edge.

Torte can also be served without the apricot filling, just sprinkled with confectioners' sugar, with whipped cream on the side.

You can also fill and top your Hazelnut Torte with a chocolate buttercream, served with or without whipped cream. It depends on your own mood and the occasion.

THREE-LAYER HAZELNUT TORTE

DREIBLÄTTRIGE HASELNUSS TORTE

12 servings

5 egg whites
½ cup sugar
2 egg yolks
3½ cups finely ground hazelnuts

4–5 Tbs. apricot jam
4–5 Tbs. raspberry jam
Lemon Icing
Hazelnuts, split in half

Three 9 x 1½-inch baking pans with removable bottoms

Beat egg whites to almost firm consistency. Gradually add sugar by tablespoons, beating after each addition, until egg whites become very stiff. Break egg yolks one at a time into egg whites, alternately sprinkling in hazelnuts. Fold mixture delicately but thoroughly together.

Pour batter, evenly divided, into three well-buttered, floured, 9 × 1½-inch baking pans.

Bake in preheated oven (350° F.) for 15–20 minutes or until very lightly colored and springy to touch. Remove layers carefully to wire rack. When completely cool, spread first layer with apricot jam, top with second layer, and spread second layer with raspberry jam. Place third plain layer on top.

Several hours before serving, pour a lemon icing over top. Refrigerate.

When icing has set slightly, place hazelnuts, split in half, all around border. Arrange four halves in center to form a four-leaf clover.

Keep refrigerated until serving.

Note: If you do not have three baking pans available, bake one layer at a time and keep remaining batter refrigerated.

WALNUT TORTE

There are quite a variety of ways, simple or elaborate, to fill and garnish this torte. For a filling and topping I suggest whipped cream, plain or flavored, or Parisian Cream, and there is nothing wrong with using any good chocolate cream.

14–16 servings

6 egg yolks
½ cup sugar
Rind of 1 lemon, grated
¼ cup breadcrumbs (scant)
Juice of ½ lemon
2½ cups finely ground walnuts
6 egg whites
Walnut halves or quarters

CHOCOLATE CREAM FILLING and GARNISH:

2 bars or squares semisweet
 chocolate, melted
1 bar sweet butter, soft
2–4 Tbs. sugar
1 whole egg
1 tsp. instant coffee
½ inch vanilla bean or ½ tsp.
 vanilla extract

10 x 2½-inch springform pan

Beat egg yolks and sugar until very light and foamy. Add grated lemon rind and breadcrumbs, sprinkled with lemon juice. Stir. Gently fold in ground walnuts with stiffly beaten (but not dry) egg whites. Blend until no white shows. Pour batter into a well-buttered 10 × 2½-inch springform pan.

Bake in preheated oven (350° F.) for 30–40 minutes until test done or springy to touch. Remove outer ring. Let cool.

Slice torte into two layers. Spread filling between layers and sandwich together.

If you choose chocolate cream for your filling, omit the cream topping. Sprinkle top of torte with confectioners' sugar. Use remaining cream to form truffles. Before forming truffles, refrigerate chocolate cream.

Chocolate Cream Filling and Garnish: Melt chocolate in double boiler. Cream butter and sugar. Add lightly beaten egg and stir. Add cool melted chocolate, coffee, and vanilla. Blend well. If cream is too soft, chill to spreading consistency.

Truffles: Between the palms of your hands, roll small balls of chocolate cream, about the size of a small walnut; then roll in cocoa. Flatten them out slightly. Place truffles around edge of torte in 1½-inch intervals. Place one in center, and top each truffle with walnut half or quarter.

5. Various Pastries

Introduction

These pastries include known and unknown pastries, from Apple Cake to Sponge Rolls, from Linzer Tartlets to Indian Puffs, and some of them you will find most unusual; for example, Almond Squares or Cognac Slices. Bishop's Bread, made with pignolia and pistachios might be new to you, and let's not forget various cheese pastries with cheese used either in the dough or as a filling.

Try them all, and with these various pastries a fascinating new chapter of baking will open for you.

ALMOND SQUARES	*Mandel Würfel*
APPLE CAKE (OPEN FACED, SHORT DOUGH)	*Apfelkuchen (Mürber Teig)*
APPLE TURNOVERS (PUFF PASTE)	*Polsterzipf (Blätterteig)*
BISHOP'S BREAD WITH PINE NUTS (PIGNOLIA NUTS) AND PISTACHIOS	*Bischofsbrot mit Pignolia Nüssen und Pistachios*
BLUEBERRY CAKE OR BLUEBERRY TORTE (FRESH BLUEBERRIES)	*Heidelbeer Kuchen or Heidelbeer Torte (Frische Heidelbeeren)*
CHEESE ROLL (SHORT DOUGH)	*Topfen Rolle (Mürber Teig)*

CHERRY CAKE OR CHERRY TORTE	Kirschen Kuchen or Kirschen Torte
CHOCOLATE ALMOND SLICES	Schokoladen Mandel Schnitten
CHOCOLATE BUTTER ROLL	Schokoladen Butter Roulade
COGNAC SLICES	Kognakscheiben
CONTINENTAL CHEESE SLICES	Topfen Schnitten
CREAM PUFFS (PÂTE À CHOUX)	Brandteig Krapferl
EMPEROR CAKE	Kaiserkuchen
FRUIT TARTLETS	Obst Körbchen
INDIAN PUFFS	Indianer Krapfen
LINZER SLICES	Linzer Schnitten
LINZER TARTLETS	Linzer Törtchen
MARBLE CAKE	Marmorierter Gugelhupf
OLD VIENNA GUGELHUPF (WITH BAKING POWDER)	Alt Wiener Gugelhupf mit Backpulver
PALM LEAVES (PUFF PASTE)	Palmenblätter (Blätterteig)
PRUNE BUTTER (LEKVAR) ROLL (SHORT DOUGH)	Powidl Rolle (Mürber Teig)
PUFF PASTE	Blätterteig
RAISIN CAKE OR BALANCED CAKE	Gleichgewichtskuchen
SPONGE ROLL WITH APRICOT JAM	Biskuit Roulade mit Marillen Marmelade
SPONGE ROLL WITH COFFEE CREAM	Biskuit Roulade mit Kaffee Creme
SPONGE ROLL WITH WHIPPED CREAM	Biskuit Roulade mit Schlagobers
STRAWBERRY STRIPS (PUFF PASTE)	Erdbeerschnitten (Blätterteig)

ALMOND SQUARES

About 24 servings

2¼–2½ cups flour
¾ cup verifine sugar
Rind of 1 lemon, grated
⅓ cup finely chopped, candied
  lemon peel or citron (generous)
¼ tsp. allspice
1¾ bars sweet butter, cold
3 hard-boiled egg yolks, mashed
1 whole egg

1½ cups sliced blanched almonds
1–1½ cups currant or sour cherry
  jam (or any other tart jam)

MERINGUE:
½–¾ cup confectioners' sugar,
  sifted
2 egg whites

10 x 16-inch baking pan

Since hard-boiled egg yolks are used in Almond Squares, it would be a shame to waste the egg whites. They can be saved for the meringue.

Separate the yolks from the whites. Place yolks into a greased oven-proof dish or in separate cups and place in a saucepan with water half covering dish or cups. Cover saucepan and let simmer over low flame until egg yolks are firm. Strain egg yolks through a food mill.

Combine flour, sugar, lemon rind, candied lemon peel, and allspice on pastry board. Make a well in center, cut in butter, and add strained egg yolks and the whole egg. With a table knife cover well with flour mixture. Add crushed sliced almonds. Work ingredients by hand into a smooth, workable dough until it no longer sticks to board or hands. If necessary, add more flour. Form a ball. Cover with wax paper. Refrigerate for about 1 hour.

Roll dough between two sheets of wax paper to about ¼-inch thickness to fit approximately a 10 × 16-inch baking pan. Remove top sheet of wax paper from dough. Invert dough into pan. Remove second sheet carefully and pat out dough gently and evenly to fit the pan.

Bake unfilled shell in preheated oven (350° F.) for 12–15 minutes until lightly colored. When cool, spread top of cake with jam. Cover jam entirely with meringue or fill a pastry bag, fitted with a plain No. 3 pastry tube, with mixture and draw a lattice across top in about 2-inch intervals. This involves a little more work, but will make your squares look very colorful.

Return pastry to oven (300° F.) until meringue gets browned and crisp.

Before serving, cut pastry into about 2½ × 2½-inch squares with a knife dipped in hot water. Be sure to wipe knife after slicing each row or you won't get a clean cut. Apply a new thin coating of jam if dried out during baking.

Meringue: Beat egg whites to soft peaks. Gradually spoon in sugar, beating 2–3 minutes after each addition, until egg whites are very stiff and shiny.

APPLE CAKE (Open Faced, Short Dough)

12–14 servings

2 cups flour
⅓ cup sugar
Rind of 1 lemon, grated
1¼ bars sweet butter, cold
1 whole egg
1 egg yolk
⅛ tsp. salt
¾ Tbs. white vinegar, mixed with
 ¾ Tbs. cold water

1 whole egg (for brushing)
4 large apples, sliced (approx.)
½ cup blond raisins (approx.)
⅓–½ cup finely chopped almonds
 or walnuts
½ cup sugar (approx.)
2 tsp. cinnamon
3–4 Tbs. sweet butter, melted

11 x 17-inch baking pan or jelly-roll pan

Mix flour and sugar on pastry board. Add grated lemon rind. Make well in center, cut in butter, and add whole egg, egg yolk, and salt. Fold together with table knife and gradually add watered vinegar. Work first with fingertips, then knead by hand quickly into a medium-firm dough. From time to time scrape sticky dough off pastry board until it is clean of all ingredients. If necessary, add a little more flour. Form into a ball. Cover and refrigerate for 20–30 minutes.

While dough is chilling, peel apples and cut into ⅛-inch (or a bit thicker) slices. To prevent apples from discoloring, cover and refrigerate.

With a floured rolling pin, roll dough out on a floured pastry board into an 18–19-inch-long and 10–12-inch-wide piece. To prevent dough from sticking to pastry board, turn it over from time to time on flour-sprinkled board until it is stretched to the desired size. Fold dough over back of hand and transfer to baking pan.

Cover sheet of dough with one layer of slightly overlapping slices of apples, leaving a 1½–2-inch margin all around. Scatter two-thirds of chopped almonds or walnuts and half of raisins over apples.

Combine sugar and cinnamon and dust apples with one-half to two-thirds of it. Cover with a second layer of sliced apples and scatter with remaining nuts and raisins. Dust to taste with cinnamon sugar.

Fold margin over, first short sides, then long sides. Spoon 3-4 tablespoons of melted butter over filling and brush border of dough with lightly beaten egg.

Bake in preheated oven (350°F.) for 35-45 minutes until golden or test done.

Before serving, cut cake into about 1-inch slices and sprinkle with confectioners' sugar.

APPLE TURNOVERS (Puff Paste)

POLSTERZIPF (BLÄTTERTEIG)

This recipe uses puff paste (p. 198) and the apple filling for Apple Torte (Butter Dough) on p. 84.

Roll dough out to less than ¼-inch thickness. Trim edges straight. Cut into 4-inch-wide strips and cut the strips into squares. Brush squares thinly with apricot jam and place a teaspoon of apple filling in each center. Spread out filling slightly. Brush each square close to edges with lightly beaten egg white. Fold corners over to form a triangle. Press lightly together without pressing edges. Brush top of pastry with remaining egg white. Refrigerate.

Bake in preheated oven (425° F.) for about 10 minutes. Reduce to 350° F. and bake 15–20 minutes longer, until golden brown.

Note: Apple filling can be replaced with apricot jam only.

BISHOP'S BREAD WITH PINE NUTS (Pignolia Nuts) AND PISTACHIOS

36 servings (approx.)

6 egg yolks
1 cup sugar (scant)
⅓ cup finely chopped pine nuts (pignolia nuts)
⅓ cup sliced blanched almonds, slightly crushed
½ cup finely chopped pistachio nuts

1 bar or square semisweet chocolate, finely chopped
¼ cup golden raisins (generous)
¼ cup currants (generous)
¼ cup finely chopped, candied lemon peel
1 cup sifted flour
6 egg whites

14-inch tinned ring mold

Beat egg yolks and sugar until very pale and fluffy. Fold in nuts (almonds, pine nuts, and pistachio nuts) and chocolate. Add raisins and candied lemon peel, lightly sprinkled with flour (which will prevent them from sinking to the bottom of the mold). Blend. To batter, add stiffly beaten egg whites and flour, folding until all white lumps have disappeared. Pour into a well-buttered, floured, 14-inch tinned ring mold.

Bake in preheated oven (400° F.) for 20 minutes. Reduce heat to 350° F. and bake about 30 minutes more or until test done.

Bishop's Bread should be baked 2–3 days in advance.

Before serving, cut into slices ⅓-inch thick. Sprinkle lightly with confectioners' sugar.

Note: If no ring mold is available, a bread or loaf pan can be substituted.

BLUEBERRY CAKE OR BLUEBERRY TORTE
(Fresh Blueberries)

HEIDELBEER KUCHEN OR HEIDELBEER TORTE (FRISCHE HEIDELBEEREN)

10 servings

Follow recipe for Cherry Cake (p. 180), substituting 2 cups (approx.) fresh blueberries for cherries.

Keep blueberries moisture free when dropping into batter.

CHEESE ROLL *(Short Dough)*

TOPFEN ROLLE (MÜRBER TEIG)

Follow recipe for Prune Butter Roll (p. 196), replacing prune butter with cheese filling.

About 18 pieces

POT CHEESE FILLING:
2 Tbs. sweet butter, melted
¾ lb. pot cheese
⅓ cup sugar
2 egg yolks

½ cup blond raisins or currants (generous)
Rind of 1 lemon, grated or ½ tsp. vanilla extract
1–2 egg whites

Stir melted butter into strained pot cheese. Add sugar, egg yolks, raisins or currants, and grated lemon rind or vanilla extract. Fold in beaten egg whites. Use only 1 egg white if cheese is moist; use 2 if dry. Bake for 35–45 minutes in preheated oven (350° F.) or until golden brown.

CHERRY CAKE OR CHERRY TORTE

KIRSCHEN KUCHEN OR KIRSCHEN TORTE

10 servings

½ bar sweet butter, soft
⅔–¾ cup sugar
5 egg yolks
1 cup sifted flour
5 egg whites

1 lb. fresh Bing cherries, pitted, or
   a 16-oz. can black Bing cherries
2–3 Tbs. sliced blanched almonds
1 whole egg

*9 x 1½-inch round baking pan with removable bottom or
a 9-inch square pastry pan*

Cream butter and sugar. Add egg yolks and beat until light and fluffy. Alternately fold flour with well-beaten egg whites into mixture. Pour batter into a buttered, lightly floured, 9 × 1½-inch round baking pan or 9-inch square pastry pan. Drop paper-absorbed, moisture-free cherries, rolled lightly in flour, into batter. Brush top with beaten egg and scatter top of cake with sliced almonds.

Bake in preheated oven (400° F.) for 10 minutes, then reduce to 350° F. and bake for about 25 minutes longer until top is deep golden and springy to touch.

If fresh cherries are used, pit them with a cherry pitter.

CHOCOLATE ALMOND SLICES

20 servings

1¼ bars sweet butter, clarified
¾ cup sugar (generous)
3½ bars or squares semisweet
chocolate
2 cups finely ground unblanched
almonds
4 egg yolks

⅔ cup sifted flour
4 egg whites
1 whole egg
½ cup thinly sliced blanched
almonds
2–3 Tbs. white crystal sugar (also
called harlequin sugar)

10 x 16 x 2-inch baking pan

Heat butter over low flame. Add sugar and chocolate. Keep stirring until ingredients are completely dissolved to an even consistency. Remove from flame. When cool, add ground almonds and keep stirring until completely cool. Break one yolk at a time into batter, blending well after each addition. Lightly stir in half amount of flour. Fold stiffly beaten egg whites sprinkled with remaining flour into batter.

Pour batter into a lightly buttered 10 × 16 × 2-inch baking pan, spreading evenly. Glaze with well-beaten egg, and scatter sliced almonds and crystal sugar over top.

Bake in preheated oven (350° F.) for 25–30 minutes or until cake shrinks from sides of pan.

Next day cut into 1½ × 4-inch slices.

CHOCOLATE BUTTER ROLL   SCHOKOLADEN BUTTER ROULADE

8–10 servings

1½ bars sweet butter, soft
¾ cup sugar
5 egg yolks
5 bars or squares semisweet chocolate, melted
¾ cup sifted flour

¾ tsp. baking powder
5 egg whites
Cocoa, unsweetened, sifted
2 cups heavy cream, whipped, plain or combined with liqueur or fresh fruit of your choice

10 x 16-inch baking pan or jelly-roll pan

Cream butter and sugar. Add one egg yolk at a time beating well after each addition. When pale and creamy, stir in cooled chocolate thoroughly. Sift flour with baking powder, fold gently into batter with stiffly beaten egg whites until all white lumps have disappeared.

Pour batter into a buttered, flour-dusted 10 × 16-inch baking pan, spreading evenly.

Place in preheated oven (375° F.). Reduce temperature to 350° F. and bake for about 20 minutes until springy to touch. Turn over immediately on a sheet of wax paper generously sprinkled with sifted cocoa. Roll up jelly-roll style, including paper. When cool, unroll, removing wax paper. Spread surface with lightly sweetened, plain, whipped cream. Roll up loosely once more. For a pleasant change use whipped cream flavored with liqueur or combined with fresh blueberries, strawberries, or raspberries. Keep refrigerated.

Before serving, sprinkle with confectioners' sugar. Serve whipped cream on the side (optional).

COGNAC SLICES

16–18 servings

2¼–2½ cups flour
½ cup sugar
Rind of 1 lemon, grated
1¾ bars sweet butter, cold
2 egg yolks
2 cups finely ground unblanched
 almonds
1 whole egg for brushing
8–9 blanched almonds, split in half

COGNAC-ALMOND FILLING:

1¾ cups ground unblanched
 almonds
1–1¼ cups confectioners' sugar,
 sifted
2 Tbs. milk to 3 Tbs. cognac or
3 Tbs. milk to 2 Tbs. cognac

11 x 17-inch baking pan

Combine flour and sugar on pastry board. Add lemon rind. Make well in center. Cut butter and break egg yolks into well. Add ground almonds. Fold ingredients together with a table knife. First with fingertips, then with hands, work quickly into a smooth dough. If necessary, add more flour. Form a ball and wrap in wax paper. Refrigerate for 1–2 hours.

Divide dough into two parts. Keep one part refrigerated.

Place dough between two sheets of wax paper, flatten out slightly by hand, then roll out to about ⅛-inch thickness. With a rectangular cooky cutter, also called gingerbread cooky cutter, cut dough into 2–3½-inch slices, one next to the other. Save trimmings to be re-used.

Transfer slices gently to baking pan. Brush half the slices with lightly beaten egg and garnish center of each brushed slice with a blanched almond half. Leave other slices plain.

Bake in preheated oven (350° F.) for about 10–15 minutes or until golden. Let cool on baking pan.

Spread prepared filling over plain slices, placing them flat on a table to avoid breakage. Sandwich together with the almond-decorated slices.

Cognac-Almond Filling: Mix almonds and sugar; combine with milk and cognac. Stir until you obtain a smooth medium-dry paste. If necessary, spoon in more milk or cognac.

CONTINENTAL CHEESE SLICES

12 servings

2⅓–2¾ cups flour
⅓ cup sugar
Rind of 1 lemon, grated
1¾ bars sweet butter, cold
2 egg yolks
1 egg white

CHEESE FILLING:

1 lb. dry pot cheese
⅓ cup sugar
2 egg yolks
1 tsp. vanilla extract or 1 Tbs. vanilla sugar
½ cup blond raisins (generous)
2 egg whites, beaten

9 x 13-inch baking pan

Blend flour with sugar on pastry board. Add lemon rind. Make a well in center and cut in butter. Add egg yolks. With a table knife spread flour over butter and egg yolks, working ingredients together quickly. Knead into a smooth, firm, workable dough. If necessary, add more flour. Form a ball. Cover and refrigerate for about 1 hour.

Between two sheets of wax paper, roll about two-thirds of dough into ⅛-inch thickness to fit a 9 × 13-inch baking pan, adding 1 inch all around to form border. Remove top wax paper. Invert dough into baking pan and gently peel off remaining wax paper. Pat dough well into form and cut border straight. Prick border several times with toothpick or fork. Spread filling evenly over bottom.

With remaining dough, make rolls about ⅛-inch thick to form lattice. Brush border with beaten egg white, then place rolls crosswise and lengthwise, pressing ends down lightly on border. Brush rolls with lightly beaten egg white before placing cake in preheated oven (350° F.). Bake for 30 minutes on lowest rack, then transfer to center rack for another 30–45 minutes until browned and filling has become firm.

Before serving, cut into about 3 × 3-inch slices. Dust with confectioners' sugar.

If so desired, slices can be served slightly warm.

Cheese Filling: Strain pot cheese through a food mill. Add sugar, egg yolks, and vanilla and blend. Stir in raisins, then fold in well-beaten egg whites.

Note: Since a lattice top is widely used on a variety of cakes, you may want to use a different decorative cut-out top.

This is one of my favorites. Roll remaining dough between two sheets of wax paper to match size of bottom. Remove top sheet of wax paper. Using a big scalloped round cutter, about 1–1½ inches in diameter, cut out dough, leaving a 1-inch margin all around edge. Refrigerate. When just firm enough to be handled, invert dough over top of cheese filling. Remove paper very carefully. Press dough gently down on border, patching up broken parts.

Bake and proceed as indicated above.

CREAM PUFFS (Pâte à Choux)

When cream puffs are filled with whipped cream and dusted with confectioners' sugar, they look like clouds, big and small, and taste heavenly good.

They will add a festive appearance to your table whenever served, with a hot chocolate sauce at an elegant luncheon or with chocolate or coffee icing in the afternoon and after dinner.

They require only a little work and can be done in a very short time. Before baking, the mounds are small, then they puff up—the inside moisture does it—expanding into a delicate and delightful dessert.

About 15 pieces
(medium size)

½ cup water

1½ Tbs. sugar

½ bar sweet butter

½ cup sifted flour (generous)

⅛ tsp. salt.

2–3 whole eggs, room temperature

1 egg white

Heavy cream, whipped

11 x 17 x 2-inch baking pan

Place water, sugar, and cut-up butter in saucepan. Bring to a boil, and when butter is melted, reduce to a very low flame. Add sifted flour, combined with salt, all at once, stirring vigorously until smooth, and mixture no longer clings to sides of pan and spoon. Remove from flame.

Change to a wooden spoon. While batter is still hot, add one egg at a time, beating very well after each addition. Keep beating for about 10 minutes until dough becomes smooth and glossy and medium firm, just enough to hold its shape.

Drop teaspoonfuls of paste, about 1½ inches in diameter, 2½ inches apart on a lightly buttered 11 × 17 × 2-inch baking pan. With the help of a second spoon, mold into mounds as high as possible.

Brush puffs with beaten egg white. Place in preheated oven (400° F.), bake for 10 minutes, reduce to 350° F., and bake 20–30 minutes longer until golden brown. Do not open oven for the first 15 minutes. When baked, pierce puffs 2–3 times with a cake tester or with the point of a knife to let steam escape. Return to turned-off oven to let dry for 10–15 minutes to prevent inside moisture.

After removing puffs from oven, leave them in the warm kitchen (protect them from sharp temperature changes).

Before serving, slice puffs in half horizontally with a sharp knife and fill with slightly sweetened whipped cream. (To prevent sogginess, fill only shortly before serving.)

Sprinkle with confectioners' sugar.

Note: There are three possible ways to serve filled Cream Puffs: (1) sprinkled with confectioners' sugar, (2) topped with a hot chocolate sauce, especially recommended after lunch or dinner, and (3) glazed on top with chocolate or coffee icing, to be served in the afternoon. (Omit brushing puffs with beaten egg white, if glazed.)

EMPEROR CAKE

16–18 pieces

3 whole eggs, room temperature
½ cup sugar
Rind of 1 lemon, grated
¾ cup sifted flour

¼ cup chopped blanched almonds
⅓ cup blond raisins
⅓–½ cup currants

10-inch-long tinned ring mold or loaf pan

Beat eggs with sugar until very pale, foamy, and thick. Add grated lemon rind. Gently but thoroughly fold sifted flour gradually into batter, saving a tablespoon of flour. Stir in almonds. Mix raisins and currants with remaining tablespoon of flour and fold into batter.

Pour batter into a generously buttered, lightly floured, 10-inch-long tinned ring mold. (A loaf pan can replace the ring mold, but the finished cake will not look quite as attractive.)

Bake in preheated oven (400° F.) for 10 minutes. Reduce to 350° F. and bake about 40–50 minutes longer or until brown and test done. Let settle for 10 minutes, then invert on pastry rack. When cool, return to ring mold.

Next day or the day after, cut into thin slices.

Serve lightly sprinkled with confectioners' sugar.

Note: Emperor Cake can also be served toasted; then it is called Zwieback.

Cut into medium-thin slices and place on an ungreased baking pan. Toast in preheated oven (350° F.) on lowest rack for about 15 minutes or until golden brown. Remove. While still hot, dust slices generously with vanilla sugar on both sides.

FRUIT TARTLETS

Any short dough, plain or with hazelnuts or walnuts, will lend itself very well to baking tartlet crusts. Follow any recipe of your
choice. The crusts can be baked many days in advance and will keep
well in a dry, cool place.

The small tartlet not only looks decorative but tastes divine. It is
an all-season pastry, very tempting, and will please the fanciest and
the simplest tastes. The crust can be filled with a variety of fresh
or canned fruits, for example, with strawberries and a currant glaze
(see Viennese Walnut Strawberry Torte) or with fruit embedded in
a base of vanilla cream (see Peach Torte, Canned Fruit). Or brush
the crust first with currant or strawberry glaze and then fill it
with sliced strawberries, combined with lightly sweetened whipped
cream. Decorate with a single strawberry.

The crust can be baked in an assortment of small, differently
shaped forms. In Vienna, a boat-shaped tartlet (*Schifferl*) is the most
preferred.

Before you start, butter tartlet molds lightly.

Roll dough out, between two sheets of wax paper, to less than
¼-inch thick. Remove top sheet of wax paper. Cut dough, including bottom paper, in strips wider than the mold. Cut strips in pieces
large enough to cover two molds placed close together. Invert dough
with paper over molds, and with the palm of your hand cut dough
out against edge of molds. Gently remove wax paper. Let dough
settle in molds. Re-use scraps and roll out. When all molds are covered with dough, line inside of each by pressing dough firmly and
evenly to fit fluted sides and bottom.

Arrange molds on cooky sheet and bake in preheated oven
350° F.) for about 15 minutes or until lightly browned. When
slightly cooled, remove crust by turning mold over and tapping
bottom gently with a knife. Lift mold off carefully. Handle crust
only when completely cool.

Note: Be especially careful of nut short dough, for it breaks easily.

INDIAN PUFFS

An Indian Puff is an all-time favorite.

If you want to be successful with your finished creation, do not lose time and energy in baking puffs without any forms or molds as is often suggested. The result will be that the dough will spread quicker than you can bake it and you will get flat cookies instead of well-formed balls.

If you have no biscuit forms with round bottoms or if none are available, popover or cupcake molds can be substituted.

12–14 servings

6 egg yolks
⅓ cup sugar
1 inch vanilla bean
6 egg whites
¼ sifted flour

½ cup potato flour or ⅔ cup cornstarch
Apricot Glaze II
Chocolate Icing
2 cups heavy cream, whipped
2–3 tsps. confectioners' sugar

2–4 biscuit forms with 6 cups or 12-cup popover or cupcake pan

Beat egg yolks and sugar until light, creamy, and thick. Add vanilla. Gently fold in stiffly beaten (but not dry) egg whites with sifted flour and potato flour or cornstarch. Blend until no lumps of egg whites show.

Butter generously and lightly flour cups of biscuit forms (or popover or cupcake pan). Fill each cup ¾-full of batter.

Bake in preheated oven (325° F.) for about 20 minutes until golden brown. Remove puffs to pastry rack.

When completely cool, same day or next, first scoop out each puff from flat side with a spoon. Divide puffs in two equal parts. Place one part on a pastry rack, brush with apricot glaze, and coat with chocolate icing. Refrigerate. Leave other part plain.

If baked in biscuit forms, cut off tips of plain puffs shortly before serving to prevent them from toppling over.

Fill plain puffs with lightly sweetened whipped cream and top with chocolate-covered puffs.

Keep refrigerated until serving.

LINZER SLICES

20 servings (approx.)

1⅔ cups flour
1 pinch cinnamon
1 pinch clove
⅓ cup sugar
1 bar plus 1 Tbs. sweet butter, cold
1 egg yolk

Rind of 1 lemon, grated
1¼ cups finely ground blanched
    almonds
Currant or raspberry-currant jam
1 egg white

10 x 16-inch baking pan

Place flour, combined with spices and sugar, on pastry board. Make a well in center and cut in small pieces of butter. Add egg yolk and lemon rind; cover with almonds. With a table knife, combine until mixture holds together. Knead by hand quickly into a workable dough. Form a ball, wrap in wax paper, and refrigerate for about 1 hour.

Divide dough into two parts, and return one part to refrigerator. Place the other between two sheets of wax paper and flatten out lightly by hand. Roll to about ¼-inch thickness. Proceed same way with remaining part. Refrigerate. When dough is firm enough, remove top sheet of wax paper and cut with pastry cutter into 2 × 3½-inch slices.

With a spatula, transfer slices to an ungreased 10 × 16-inch baking pan.

Combine scraps of dough and roll out. Cut into ¼-inch-wide strips, then cut strips into 2-inch lengths. Place strips on top of linzer slices, one at each end. Spread jam thinly over slices. Brush strips with lightly beaten egg white.

Bake in preheated oven (350° F.) for 15–18 minutes until golden brown. Let cool in pan.

Since jam will have dried out during baking, recolor and refresh slices by spreading with jam before serving.

Dust lightly with confectioners' sugar.

LINZER TARTLETS

18–20 pieces

1¼ cups flour (scant)
½ cup sugar (scant)
1 pinch cinnamon
1 pinch clove
1 bar sweet butter, cold

Rind of 1 lemon, grated
2½ cups finely ground unblanched
almonds
½ cup apricot, currant, or
strawberry jam

11 x 17-inch baking pan or cooky sheet

Combine flour, sugar, and spices on pastry board. Cut in cold butter. Add grated lemon rind and almonds. Work by hand into a smooth dough until all ingredients from pastry board are picked up. Form into a ball and wrap in wax paper. Refrigerate for 30 minutes. Divide dough in half. Return one half to refrigerator.

Between two sheets of wax paper, roll dough to about ⅛-inch thickness. Use one 2¾-inch biscuit cutter and one doughnut cutter (plain or crinkled). With both cutters, cut out equal numbers of rounds. Transfer carefully to baking pan. Re-use scraps of dough.

Proceed same way with second half of dough.

Bake 12–15 minutes in preheated oven (325° F.) until lightly pale.

When completely cool, remove from pan. Spread plain rounds with jam of your choice and sandwich together with rounds cut out with doughnut cutter.

Serve lightly dusted with confectioners' sugar.

Note: If a doughnut cutter is not available, you can use a ¾-inch cutter or a thimble for cutting out centers.

Note: If dough is very crumbly, a very small amount of butter should be added.

MARBLE CAKE

10–12 servings

1¼ bars sweet butter, soft
1 cup sugar
½ tsp. vanilla sugar or ½ inch
  vanilla bean
3 egg yolks
½ cup milk

Rind of 1 lemon, grated
1¾ cups sifted flour
2 tsps. baking powder
3 egg whites
5 tsps. unsweetened dark cocoa
2 Tbs. cold water

8- or 9-inch Turk's head (Gugelhupf form) or ring mold

Mix cocoa with cold water to make a smooth paste.

Cream butter, sugar, and vanilla until smooth. Add egg yolks and grated lemon rind and beat until very pale and fluffy. Sift flour with baking powder and stir about half of it alternately with milk into batter. Fold in beaten (but not dry) egg whites with remaining flour and blend well. Pour two-thirds of the batter into a well-buttered, floured, 8- or 9-inch Turk's head or ring mold. Blend cocoa paste thoroughly with remaining batter. Pour over top of white batter or alternately pour both batters into form.

Bake in preheated oven (350° F.) for about 1 hour or until test done. Cool.

Serve lightly dusted with confectioners' sugar.

OLD VIENNA GUGELHUPF
(With Baking Powder)

ALT WIENER GUGELHUPF MIT
BACKPULVER

10–12 servings

1 bar less 1 Tbs. sweet butter, soft
½ cup sugar (generous)
½ tsp. vanilla sugar or ½ tsp.
vanilla extract
4 egg yolks

⅓ cup milk
2¼ cups sifted flour
1½ tsps. baking powder
4 egg whites

8- or 9-inch Turk's head (Gugelhupf form)

Cream butter and sugar. Add vanilla sugar or extract. Add egg yolks one at a time, beating until light and fluffy. Add half of sifted flour alternately with milk into batter. Stir well. Fold in stiffly beaten egg whites and remaining flour sifted with baking powder. Blend ingredients together gently. Pour into a well-greased, floured, 8- or 9-inch Turk's head. Spread batter evenly with a spatula.

Bake in preheated oven (375° F.) for 50–60 minutes or until cake tester or toothpick inserted into cake comes out dry.

Let cool for 10–15 minutes before gently removing from form. Dust with vanilla confectioners' sugar before serving.

PALM LEAVES (Puff Paste) PALMENBLÄTTER (BLÄTTERTEIG)

Follow directions for puff paste on p. 198.

On a generously sugared pastry board, roll out dough evenly into a rectangle about ¼ inch thick. Cut edges straight, sprinkle surface with sugar, and roll dough firmly, jelly-roll style, from both long sides toward center until both rolls meet. Cover lightly with wax paper. Refrigerate.

When firm, cut roll into ¼-inch slices. Place each slice on baking pan, keep halves slightly separated.

Bake in preheated oven (425° F.) for about 10 minutes. Reduce heat to 350° F. and bake until crisp and golden brown. Turn pastry over with a spatula and bake 15–20 minutes longer, until crisp and golden brown.

PRUNE BUTTER (Lekvar) ROLL (Short Dough)

POWIDL ROLLE (MÜRBER TEIG)

About 18 pieces

2 cups flour (approx.)
¼ cup sugar
1¼ bars sweet butter, cold

2 egg yolks
1 egg white
Prune butter (lekvar), thick

10 x 16 x 2-inch baking pan

Combine flour and sugar on pastry board. Make well in center, cut in butter, break egg yolks into it, and cover with flour mixture. With a table knife, quickly combine ingredients. Work first with fingertips, then knead by hand into a smooth dough until it no longer sticks to hands or board and all ingredients are worked in. If necessary, gradually add more flour. Form dough into a ball. Cover. Refrigerate.

Divide dough, keeping unused part refrigerated. Roll dough between two sheets of wax paper to about a 12-inch-long, 10-inch-wide piece ⅛ inch thick. Dough will spread easier during rolling if, from time to time, you turn it over and then lift the top sheet of wax paper. Refrigerate between wax paper. Proceed same way with second half of dough.

Remove top sheet of wax paper from first half of dough and cut edges straight. Place dough with long side toward you and spread with thick prune butter, leaving ¼ inch at top edge and about ⅛ inch on both short sides free of filling. With the help of wax paper fold dough into one large roll about 4 inches wide, starting with long side closest to you, then folding opposite side over. Press seam down lightly and pinch sides securely together. Refrigerate.

When firm, invert first roll, seam down, into a 10 × 16 × 2½-inch baking pan. Remove wax paper. Place second roll next to first in pan. Brush top of rolls with egg white lightly beaten with 1 or 2 tablespoons of water.

With a sharp knife, cut several small incisions diagonally into top to let steam escape and to avoid bursting of rolls.

Bake in preheated oven (375° F.) for 30–35 minutes or until golden brown. Remove from pan when completely cool.

Before serving cut into 1–1½-inch slices. Sprinkle with confectioners' sugar.

PUFF PASTE

BLÄTTERTEIG

Puff paste is used in the recipes for Apple Turnovers, Palm Leaves, and Strawberry Strips.

2 cups sifted flour
¼ tsp. salt
1 egg yolk
2 Tbs. white wine

9 Tbs. cold water
1 Tbs. lemon juice
2 bars sweet butter

Sift flour and salt into a bowl or on a pastry board. Make a well, add egg yolk, and combine with a knife. Whisk wine, water, and lemon juice together and gradually pour into well, mixing continuously until liquid is absorbed. Then combine with fingertips until paste holds together. Knead on pastry board and keep kneading and pounding dough for about 20 minutes until you obtain a smooth, elastic dough. Dough and butter should have about the same consistency, firm but not hard. From time to time, dip fingers into cold water to keep dough elastic, as you will be more successful if dough is kept a bit on the moist rather than dry side. Work into a ball. Wrap ball in a barely damp cloth and refrigerate for about 30 minutes.

While dough is chilling, combine 2 bars of butter by pressing them together until you obtain one smooth brick. Sprinkle lightly with flour all around and roll out to flatten brick slightly. Wrap in foil. Refrigerate.

On a lightly floured pastry board roll dough out into an approximate 9-inch square, leaving center slightly thicker than edges. Place the lightly floured butter brick in center of square. Fold the four corners of dough over butter brick, overlapping slightly so that butter brick is completely sealed in.

On a lightly floured board, gently and evenly roll out package of dough containing butter brick, always rolling away from you, into a rectangle about 8 inches wide and 16 inches long, with short end facing you. Avoid breakthrough of butter brick. Flatten out short end close to you to same thickness as rest of dough. Now, fold both ends of rectangle toward center until they meet. Brush away excess flour. Then fold dough in half along center line as though closing an open book. Brush away excess flour. Cover dough with a barely damp cloth and refrigerate for about 30 minutes.

Place chilled dough on a lightly floured pastry board with short (open) end toward you.

Repeat all steps—rolling, brushing, folding, and chilling—for a total of four to five times.

After the final rolling, keep dough, covered with a barely damp cloth, refrigerated for at least 2 hours or even overnight.

RAISIN CAKE OR BALANCED CAKE

Here is another one of those simple cakes that are extremely good and very easy to make. You will enjoy this cake any time of the day —for breakfast, as a snack, with coffee, tea, or cold drinks or with stewed fruit or fruit salad.

20–24 servings

2 bars sweet butter, soft
1 cup sugar (approx.)
4 egg yolks
1 cup blond raisins or currants
   (approx.)

Rind of 1 lemon, grated
2 cups sifted flour
¾ tsp. baking powder
4 egg whites

10-inch loaf pan

Cream butter and sugar well. Add egg yolks and beat until pale and fluffy. Add grated lemon rind. Blend flour-dusted raisins or currants (or mixture of both) into batter. Sift flour and baking powder together and fold into batter with stiffly beaten (but not dry) egg whites. Mix thoroughly. Pour into a well-buttered, lightly floured 10-inch loaf pan.

Bake in preheated oven (375° F.) for 10 minutes. Reduce heat to 350° F. and bake for 50–60 minutes longer or until toothpick or cake tester inserted comes out dry. Remove from pan when slightly cool.

Before serving, sprinkle with confectioners' sugar.

SPONGE ROLL WITH APRICOT JAM

BISKUIT ROULADE MIT MARILLEN MARMELADE

Best eaten the same day.

8–10 servings

4 egg yolks, room temperature
⅓ cup sugar
Rind of 1 lemon, grated
4 egg whites

⅔ cup sifted flour
1 cup apricot jam, room
  temperature or slightly heated

10 x 16-inch jelly-roll pan or baking pan

Beat egg yolks and sugar well until light, thick, and creamy. Stir in grated lemon rind. Gently fold stiffly beaten egg whites, dusted with flour, into batter. Blend thoroughly.

Pour batter into a generously buttered, lightly floured 10 × 16-inch jelly-roll pan and spread evenly over surface of pan.

Bake in preheated oven (400° F.) for 10 minutes, then reduce to 350° F. and bake for about 5 minutes more, until golden brown and test done. Do not overbake or it will dry out.

Turn sponge cake immediately over on wax paper dusted with confectioners' sugar. Spread with apricot jam while still hot. Roll up sponge cake jelly-roll style, beginning with long side. Let cool on pastry rack. Cut into about 2-inch diagonal slices.

Serve sprinkled generously with confectioners' sugar.

SPONGE ROLL WITH COFFEE CREAM FILLING

Follow recipe for Sponge Roll with Apricot Jam (p. 200), substituting filling.

8–10 servings

COFFEE CREAM FILLING:
2 tsps. instant coffee
1 Tbs. hot water
1 bar sweet butter, room temperature

⅓–½ cup verifine sugar
1 egg yolk
½ inch vanilla bean or ½ tsp. vanilla extract

10 x 16-inch baking pan or jelly-roll pan

Grease a 10 × 16-inch baking pan or jelly-roll pan. Line pan with wax paper and brush paper with melted butter. Pour batter into pan and spread out evenly.

Bake in preheated oven (400° F.) for 12–15 minutes or until test done. Do not overbake.

Remove cake with wax paper quickly from pan (but do not invert). Roll lengthwise, jelly-roll stye, including wax paper. Let cool on pastry rack.

When completely cool, unroll carefully. Spread coffee cream evenly over surface. Roll up sponge cake once more, removing wax paper as you proceed. Refrigerate.

Serve dusted with confectioners' sugar.

Coffee Cream Filling: Dissolve instant coffee in hot water. Cream butter and sugar. Break egg yolk into mixture. Blend. Add vanilla and coffee solution. Beat until very fluffy.

SPONGE ROLL WITH WHIPPED CREAM

BISKUIT ROULADE MIT SCHLAGOBERS

Follow recipe for Sponge Roll with Apricot Jam (p. 200), substituting filling.

8–10 servings

WHIPPED CREAM FILLING:
1½–2 cups heavy cream, whipped
1–2 Tbs. confectioner's sugar
½ inch vanilla bean

3–4 Tbs. liqueur of your choice (optional)
Chocolate Icing
1 Tbs. finely ground, unsalted pistachio nuts

10 x 16-inch jelly-roll pan or baking pan

Grease a 10 × 16-inch jelly-roll pan. Line pan with wax paper and brush paper with melted butter. Pour batter into pan, spreading out evenly.

Bake in preheated oven (400° F.) for 12–15 minutes or until test done. Do not overbake.

Remove cake with wax paper quickly from pan (but do not invert). Roll lengthwise, jelly-roll style, including wax paper. Let cool on pastry rack.

When completely cool, unroll carefully. Spread whipped cream, flavored to taste, evenly over surface. Roll up sponge cake once more, removing wax paper as you proceed. Refrigerate.

Shortly before serving, spread top with chocolate icing. Chill. When icing has set, sprinkle top of roll with ground pistachio nuts. Refrigerate again.

Whipped Cream Filling: Whip heavy cream until it starts to thicken. Gradually add sugar and vanilla. Keep beating until stiff, then add flavoring of your choice. Keep refrigerated.

202   THE VIENNESE PASTRY COOKBOOK

STRAWBERRY STRIPS
(Puff Paste)
1 pint fresh strawberries

ERDBEERSCHNITTEN (BLÄTTERTEIG)

¾ cup Currant or Raspberry
Currant Glaze

14 x 4½ x 1-inch flan ring

Follow directions for puff paste on p. 197.

On a lightly floured pastry board roll dough out into a long strip of about ⅛ inch thick, 14 inches long, and 4½ inches wide, adding 1 inch of dough all around. Place flan ring on baking pan. Invert rolled-out dough into flan ring and pat very lightly to fit. Cut edges straight. Refrigerate for about 10 minutes.

Prick strip all over with a fork before placing in preheated oven (425° F.) for 10 minutes. Reduce heat to 350° F. and bake 15–20 minutes longer until golden and puffy.

Several hours before serving, brush pastry with currant or currant-raspberry glaze. Refrigerate. When firm, top glaze with moist-free strawberries, neatly arranged. Top strawberries with remaining glaze. Refrigerate. Before serving, cut into about 2-inch strips.

Can also be served with whipped cream on the side.

Note: You can also spread whipped cream over top of currant glaze. Cover whipped cream with closely arranged strawberries. Before serving, sprinkle berries with sugar.

6. Various Pastries Without Flour

Introduction

Here we have once more pastries without flour, and some of the finest. Bake and eat your way through these recipes and choose your favorites. Chocolate Rolls or Almond Rolls may well be the most outstanding ones among these pastries; they are easy to make, and their fine taste should please even the most severe critic.

ALMOND ROLL

CHESTNUT PASTRY

CHOCOLATE ALMOND ROLL

CHOCOLATE ROLL

HAZELNUT CHESTNUT SQUARES

HAZELNUT CHOCOLATE STRIPS

WALNUT SQUARES

Mandel Roulade

Kastanien Bäckerei

Schokoladen Mandel Roulade

Schokoladen Roulade

Haselnuss Kastanien Würfel

Haselnuss Schokoladen Schnitten

Walnuss Würfel

ALMOND ROLL

One of the finest and daintiest rolls among the many you will find in this book, and very easy to make.

8–10 servings

5 egg yolks
1 cup confectioners' sugar
  (generous)
5 egg whites

2¼ cups finely ground, blanched almonds
1½–2 cups heavy cream, whipped
Chocolate Icing

10 x 16-inch baking pan or jelly-roll pan

Beat egg yolks and sugar until pale, creamy, and thick. Beat egg whites until very stiff and fold into mixture with ground almonds. Blend gently but thoroughly.

Butter a 10 × 16-inch baking or jelly-roll pan. Line with wax paper (cut wax paper at corners to make it fit smoothly). Butter wax paper and pour batter, spreading evenly, into pan.

Place pan in preheated oven (400° F.). Reduce immediately to 350° F. and bake 15–20 minutes until lightly browned and springy to touch. Remove cake with wax paper from pan. Roll lengthwise, jelly-roll style, including wax paper. Place on wire rack. When cool, gently unroll, spread whipped cream evenly over surface. Reroll, removing wax paper as you proceed. Refrigerate.

Several hours before serving, spread chocolate icing over top. Refrigerate again.

Serve with whipped cream on the side. (Optional)

CHESTNUT PASTRY

24–30 servings

4 egg whites
1¾ cups finely ground hazelnuts
¾ cup sugar

CHESTNUT FILLING:
⅓ cup milk
1½ lb. unpeeled chestnuts
⅓ cup sugar
2 Tbs. rum or maraschino liqueur
½ tsp. vanilla extract
¾ cup heavy cream, whipped
Chocolate Icing

10 x 16-inch cooky sheet or baking pan

Boil chestnuts without incision for 15–20 minutes. Peel. Rice through a food mill.

Combine stiffly beaten egg whites with sugar and ground hazelnuts. Fold all ingredients together gently. Drop full teaspoons of mixture on a buttered, floured 10 × 16-inch cooky sheet or baking pan, spreading to about 2-inch flat rounds with the back of a spoon, or use a pastry bag fitted with a No. 5 or 7 plain pastry tube.

Bake in preheated oven (350° F.) for 10–15 minutes or until lightly browned. While still warm, remove to wire rack.

Let cool. Top each round with chestnut paste, covering the whole surface and molding the paste into 1-inch high mounds. Refrigerate.

Cover pastry entirely with chocolate icing.

Chestnut Filling: Bring milk to boiling point and pour over riced chestnuts combined with sugar. Mix. Stir in rum and vanilla extract. Add whipped cream and fold into mixture. Combine well.

CHOCOLATE ALMOND ROLL

SCHOKOLADEN MANDEL ROULADE

8–10 servings

5 egg yolks	5 egg whites
⅔ cup sugar	1¾ cups finely ground unblanched
2½ bars or squares semisweet	almonds
chocolate, grated	1½–2 cups heavy cream, whipped

10 x 16-inch baking pan or jelly-roll pan

Beat egg yolks and sugar until pale and creamy. Add grated chocolate, stirring until chocolate is well blended. Fold stiffly beaten egg whites and ground almonds into mixture. Combine gently but thoroughly.

Butter a 10 × 16-inch baking or jelly-roll pan. Line with wax paper (cut into each corner of paper to make it fit pan smoothly). Butter wax paper. Pour batter into pan, spreading evenly.

Place pan in preheated oven (400° F.). Immediately reduce temperature to 350° F. and bake for about 20 minutes until firm but springy to touch.

Remove cake from pan. When still hot, roll cake lengthwise, jelly-roll style, without removing wax paper. Place on wire rack.

When completely cool, unroll, spread whipped cream over whole surface, and reroll, removing wax paper gently as you proceed. Refrigerate.

Before serving, dust with confectioners' sugar.

Serve with whipped cream on the side. (Optional)

CHOCOLATE ROLL

A delicious and exceptionally delicate treat. Easy to make, if you follow recipe exactly.

9–10 servings

5 bars or squares semisweet chocolate, melted
4 Tbs. water
5 egg yolks
¾ cup sugar
5 egg whites
2–3 Tbs. sifted unsweetened cocoa

1½ cups heavy cream, whipped
½ tsp. vanilla sugar or ½ inch vanilla bean
Chocolate Icing
2–3 Tbs. finely ground pistachio nuts

10 x 16 x 2-inch baking pan

Dissolve chocolate in water in a double boiler over medium heat, stirring occasionally until smooth.

Beat egg yolks and sugar until light and fluffy. Gradually add cooled, melted chocolate and blend well. Fold in stiffly beaten egg whites, combining gently but thoroughly.

Butter or oil a 10 × 16 × 2-inch baking pan, cover with wax paper, then butter or oil wax paper. Pour in batter and spread evenly over wax paper.

Place in preheated oven (400° F.), immediately reducing heat to 350° F. Bake for 15–20 minutes until top of cake becomes firm. Remove cake from oven and cover with a damp cloth. Refrigerate until cool. Remove cloth.

Sprinkle sifted cocoa evenly over a sheet of wax paper that is 1 inch larger than cake at both short ends. Invert cake onto cocoa and carefully peel off greased wax paper.

Cover cake generously with whipped cream flavored with vanilla sugar or vanilla bean. Roll very gently, jelly-roll style, by keeping paper slightly lifted until pastry is completely rolled up. Keep wax paper wrapped around chocolate roll so that it will not lose its shape. Keep refrigerated 1–2 hours before decorating.

Spread chocolate icing over top of roll and refrigerate. When icing is firm, sprinkle ground pistachio nuts over top.

Note: Don't be alarmed if the roll breaks. With the help of cocoa and icing you can cover the little damage and nobody will notice.

HAZELNUT CHESTNUT SQUARES

Very good, a real treat.

About 20 servings

4 egg yolks
1 cup sugar (scant)
2 Tbs. sweet butter, melted
2 bars or squares semisweet
  chocolate, grated
2 cups finely ground hazelnuts
¼ cup bread crumbs (scant)
3 Tbs. cognac or rum
4 egg whites

1 cup heavy cream, whipped
Chocolate curls

CHESTNUT CREAM FILLING:

3 cups cooked, riced chestnuts
1 cup finely ground walnuts
¾ bar sweet butter, soft
¾ cup confectioners' sugar
½ tsp. vanilla extract
¼ cup cognac

9 x 13-inch baking pan

Beat egg yolks with half the sugar until pale and creamy. Gradually add cooled, melted butter. Mix. Add grated chocolate. Blend well. Moisten bread crumbs with rum or cognac and stir into batter. Beat egg whites to soft peaks. Gradually spoon remaining sugar into egg whites, beating until very stiff. Gently fold ground hazelnuts with beaten egg whites into batter. Combine until no white lumps show. Pour into a buttered, flour-dusted 9 × 13-inch baking pan.

Place in preheated oven (375° F.), immediately reducing heat to 350° F. Bake for about 30 minutes or until cake shrinks from sides of pan.

Next day or day after, spread chestnut paste evenly over cake. Keep refrigerated.

Several hours before serving, cut cake into squares about 2½ × 2½ inches.

Cover chestnut cream with lightly sweetened whipped cream. Scatter chocolate curls over whipped cream.

Chestnut Cream Filling: Prepare chestnuts according to directions on p. 20. After chestnuts are peeled, rice them through a food mill. Cream together butter and sugar. Add vanilla. Combine riced chestnuts with ground walnuts and gradually stir into butter alternately with cognac. Mix until well blended and creamy. If necessary add some spoons of warm milk.

HAZELNUT CHOCOLATE STRIPS

12 servings

1 bar sweet butter, soft
⅓ cup sugar (generous)
4 egg yolks
3 bars or squares semisweet
  chocolate, grated
2 Tbs. rum
1½ cups finely ground, roasted,
  blanched hazelnuts
¼ cup sifted bread crumbs (scant)
4 egg whites
½ cup apricot jam
Chocolate Icing

CHOCOLATE CREAM FILLING:

2½ bars or squares semisweet
  chocolate, melted
1 bar sweet butter, soft
¼ cup sugar
½ inch vanilla bean or ½ tsp.
  vanilla extract
1 egg
1 Tbs. instant coffee
6 hazelnuts, split in half, plain or
  blanched, roasted

9 x 13-inch baking pan

Cream butter and sugar until smooth. Add one egg yolk at a time, beating well after each addition. Add chocolate. Mix. Spoon rum into batter. Combine ground hazelnuts with bread crumbs. Fold into batter with stiffly beaten egg whites, mixing gently but thoroughly. Pour into a buttered 9 × 13-inch baking pan.

Bake in preheated oven (350° F.) for about 30 minutes or until inserted cake tester or toothpick comes out dry.

When completely cool, cut cake down the middle lengthwise so that each half measures 4½ × 13 inches. Spread one thinly with jam, cover with chocolate cream, top with second half of cake. Refrigerate.

A few hours before serving, cover cake with chocolate icing. Chill. When icing is firm, slice cake into 1 × 4½-inch strips with a sharp knife. To get clean cuts, wipe knife after each slice.

Place a plain or blanched roasted hazelnut half in center of each strip.

Chocolate Cream: Melt chocolate in double boiler. Cream butter, sugar, and vanilla until fluffy. Add egg and instant coffee. Stir well. Combine with cooled, melted chocolate. Mix. If cream should be too soft, chill to spreading consistency.

Note: If you so desire, chocolate cream can be replaced with chocolate whipped cream.

WALNUT SQUARES

16 servings

3 egg yolks
½ cup sugar
2 Tbs. sifted bread crumbs
2 Tbs. rum
2 cups finely ground walnuts
3 egg whites
Coffee Icing

CHOCOLATE WALNUT BUTTERCREAM FILLING:

2 bars or squares semisweet chocolate, melted
3-4 Tbs. water
½ bar sweet butter, room temperature
2 Tbs. verifine sugar
1 tsp. instant coffee (optional)
1 cup finely ground walnuts
16 quartered walnuts

Two 8 x 8 x 2-inch square baking pans

Beat egg yolks and sugar well until pale and creamy. Add bread crumbs and mix. Spoon in rum and blend. Gently fold ground walnuts and stiffly beaten egg whites into batter. Pour into two buttered, floured 8 × 8 × 2-inch square baking pans.

Bake in preheated oven (350° F.) for about 15 minutes until test done or until cake shrinks from sides. Let cool.

Same day or next, spread one layer generously with cream. Top with second layer. Refrigerate.

Several hours before serving, spread coffee icing over top of cake. Cut into squares. Refrigerate.

When icing has set, place a quartered walnut in center of each square.

Chocolate Walnut Buttercream Filling: In a small pan melt chocolate, combined with water, over low flame. Stir until smooth. In a separate bowl, cream butter and sugar together. Add instant coffee (optional). Fold cooled melted chocolate into mixture. Stir until fluffy. Add ground walnuts. Combine.

7. Yeast Pastries

Introduction

Are you one of those home bakers who tries to avoid yeast baking? What makes you shy away? Why does yeast scare so many, even experienced, bakers? There is nothing to be scared of. The risk of not succeeding is minimal—no reason to give up yeast baking altogether. In my opinion, not to bake with yeast is an unforgivable loss to your culinary enjoyment.

Very early, almost from the start of my baking venture, I became acquainted with and interested in working with yeast, and until this day not once have I been unsuccessful.

You will be fascinated by the fermentation (leavening) process, and you will love to handle this very soft, warm, silklike dough, the touch of which you will enjoy so much that you may find it hard to let go.

There are two kinds of yeast available, fresh and dry (granulated). Always use fresh yeast if you have the choice. It is perhaps a little harder to obtain in New York, where, to my knowledge, it can be found in the listed specialty food stores, food stores in the German section (Yorkville), or in some supermarkets in your neighborhood; there you will find fresh yeast in small 2-oz. blocks on the dairy shelf.

In other parts of the country fresh yeast is generally available; if not, a friendly local baker will surely be willing to help you out. Or you can use active dry yeast, and follow directions on p. 223.

The rising of the yeast sponge (*Dampferl*) is the first step of preparation. It takes only a very short time and will assure you of the freshness and the good working condition of your yeast. Once risen, there should be no doubt in your mind that you are on the way to success.

Yeast contains living bacteria. They will spread and multiply throughout the ingredients with the help of the proper preparations. The amount of air that is beaten or kneaded into the dough is of greatest importance; it will help to make the dough come alive. The right surrounding, a cozy, warm, but not hot place in your kitchen will further support the yeast action, and then you will witness a small miracle: the development of a fruitful activity in your dough.

Rules for Using

Always keep in mind the following simple rules that apply to yeast baking.

Fresh yeast is recognizable by its clean, light bisque-like color and moist brittleness. If brown spots are developing, break them off. Yeast can still be used, but it is a sign that it is beginning to lose its freshness.

Always keep fresh yeast wrapped and under refrigeration. It will keep from four to six weeks, if not longer.

All ingredients used with yeast should be kept at room temperature.

Milk for yeast sponge should be heated to lukewarm, if not otherwise indicated.

Yeast sponge, when risen, should always be thoroughly blended with the ingredients to be used by stirring, kneading, or beating.

Dough should rise at an even temperature.

Bowl or pan should be slightly warmer than room temperature.

Always keep rising (leavening) dough covered with a towel.

Let dough rise to at least double its volume.

Sponge or dough should never be exposed to draft. If a great deal of traffic goes on in your kitchen, an unheated oven will give your dough the best protection against draft.

Do not open oven for the first 15 minutes during baking time.

Close window before opening oven or removing cake; the sudden temperature change could make your cake fall or droop.

Finished baked goods should be removed from pan after a short cooling period to keep the crust crisp.

Fresh Yeast

If fresh yeast is used for sponge, it should be added, finely crumbled, to the ingredients (milk, flour, sugar) to obtain a medium soft crêpe batter.

Dry Yeast

If active dry yeast is used, it must be dissolved in water, but always remember that the minimum amount of water to be used to dissolve the dry yeast is ¼ cup (2 oz.) and must be heated to lukewarm. The amount of water (¼ cup) must then be subtracted from the total amount of liquid in recipe.

Yeast Syrup

Place crumbled fresh yeast on a small plate, sprinkle with 1 tsp. sugar, and mash with a fork until creamy and syrup has formed. Combine with ingredients as indicated in recipes.

CARNIVAL JELLY DOUGHNUTS	*Faschingskrapfen*
CHRISTMAS LOAF	*Weihnachts Striezel*
COFFEE CRESCENTS (DANISH PASTRY)	*Kaffee Kipferl (Plunderteig)*
COFFEE CRESCENTS WITH ALMOND FILLING (DANISH PASTRY)	*Kaffee Kipferl mit Mandelfüllung (Plunderteig)*
DANISH PASTRIES (YEAST BUTTER DOUGH)	*Plunderteig (Germbutterteig)*
EASTER LOAF	*Osterlaberl*
OPEN-FACED CHEESE PASTRY (DANISH PASTRY)	*Topfen Gebäck (Plunderteig)*
OPEN-FACED PRUNE BUTTER PASTRY (DANISH PASTRY)	*Powidl Gebäck (Plunderteig)*
OPEN PRUNE BUTTER KOLATCHEN	*Offene Powidl Kolatschen*
PLUM CAKE (YEAST DOUGH)	*Zwetschgenkuchen (Germteig)*
POPPYSEED STRUDEL (YEAST SHORT DOUGH)	*Pressburger Mohn Strudel (Mürber Germteig)*
POT CHEESE KOLATCHEN	*Topfen Kolatschen*
PRUNE BUTTER CRESCENTS	*Powidl Kipferl*
SAVARIN I	*Savarin*
SAVARIN II	*Savarin*
STIRRED YEAST DOUGH GUGELHUPF	*Abgerührter Germteig Gugelhupf*
WASPS' NESTS	*Wespennester*
YEAST BUNS FILLED WITH PRUNE BUTTER	*Powidl Buchteln*
YEAST GUGELHUPF	*Germ Gugelhupf*
YEAST NUTCAKE	*Germ Nusskuchen*
YEAST NUT CRESCENTS	*Germ Nuss Kipferl*
YEAST NUT STRUDEL (YEAST SHORT DOUGH)	*Pressburger Nuss Strudel (Mürber Germteig)*
YEAST POPPYSEED CRESCENTS	*Germ Mohn Kipferl*

CARNIVAL JELLY DOUGHNUTS

The perfect doughnut is recognized by its lightness.

30 pieces

½ bar sweet butter, melted
⅓ cup sugar
6 egg yolks
Rind of 1 lemon, grated
¾ tsp. salt

3½–3¾ cups flour
1 oz. fresh yeast
2 Tbs. rum
1 cup milk
1 cup apricot jam (approx.)

From the above ingredients, use the following to prepare Yeast Sponge:

YEAST SPONGE

1 cup milk, lukewarm
2 Tbs. sugar

10–12 Tbs. flour
1 oz. fresh yeast (or 2 packages dry yeast)

Heat milk to lukewarm. Add sugar and flour. Stir. Add finely crumbled fresh yeast. Combine. Cover with a kitchen towel. Let rise in a draft-free place until bubbles appear on the surface. If dry yeast is used, follow directions on p. 223.

While sponge is rising, stir cooled butter and sugar until creamy. Add egg yolks, lemon rind, and salt. Add several spoons of flour and yeast sponge. Beat well with wooden spoon. Add rum and gradually beat in remaining flour. If necessary, add more flour. Keep dough on the soft side. Beat for about 10 minutes until satiny, shiny, and blisters form. Cover. Let rise in a draft-free place to more than double its bulk. Punch dough down. Beat a few strokes. Let rise again for about 15 minutes.

Turn dough over on a well-floured pastry board. With a lightly floured rolling pin, roll out to less than ¼-inch thickness. With a biscuit cutter (or a glass) 2½ inches in diameter, mark (but do not cut) rounds into dough, placed closely together.

Place ½–¾ teaspoon of apricot jam in centers of one-half of the rounds. Cut out the other rounds and top the ones filled with apricot jam. Press edges together. Then cut out the whole dough-nut with a slightly smaller cutter (or glass).

Leave to rise on lightly floured board or cloth, covered, for about 15 minutes in a draft-free place.

While doughnuts are rising, heat shortening in a large kettle or a deep (10-inch) frying pan to 375° F. (Shortening will burn less if combined with corn oil. Use 2 parts shortening to 1 part corn oil.)

Place 4 or 5 doughnuts in hot fat, leaving enough room for them to expand. They have to "swim" in deep, hot fat to get a light band around their middle, the distinctive mark of the "*Faschingskrapfen.*"

Cover kettle or frying pan for about 1 minute. Remove cover and let doughnuts fry until golden brown on one side, then turn over to fry other side. Remove with a slotted spoon. Transfer to absorbent paper.

Doughnuts are at their best when eaten fresh, still lukewarm. Before serving, sprinkle generously with confectioners' sugar.

Note: My mother used to prepare doughnuts in a quicker and easier way and I prefer her method. The only difference is that the doughnuts will not be exactly the same size.

Place one tablespoon of dough on floured pastry board. Pat with lightly floured hands into a 2½-inch round. Place apricot jam in center. Lift up and pull edges of dough toward center to envelop apricot jam. Twist edges and pinch tightly together to seal. Place doughnuts, closed side down, on floured board. Cover. Let rise for about 15 minutes and follow above frying directions.

CHRISTMAS LOAF

The Striezel belongs to Christmas. A part of every Christmas celebration is the serving of outstanding, extraordinary food that differs from everyday fare. Bread is no exception. On Christmas the Striezel, a sweet bread, at one time called "The Holy Bread" (*Das Heilige Brot*), was born.

It is a bread made of white flour, milk, and is rich in butter, ground almonds, dried raisins, and nuts. It was indeed festive and different from everyday bread, since white flour in earlier times was considered a great luxury, besides all the other fine ingredients that went into the Christmas loaf.

For many generations it was the custom to bake this festive bread, into which so much love and effort went, only once a year, at Christmastime. But tradition and customs change. The Striezel you buy today is no longer the Striezel of yesteryear—less butter, no ground almonds, fewer nuts and raisins—but I still believe in the good old Christmas Striezel from my own cherished recipe.

A Striezel should be baked several days in advance. If well wrapped and kept in a cool place, it will keep its freshness for many weeks.

All ingredients should be kept at room temperature.

4 bars sweet butter, soft
1¼ cups sugar
2 whole eggs
1 egg yolk
1 tsp. salt (generous)
Rinds of 2-3 lemons, grated
Rind of 1 large orange, grated
10½-12½ cups flour
1½ cups milk
5 ozs. fresh yeast

3 cups finely ground, blanched almonds
1⅓ cups blond raisins
⅔ cup currants
3 Tbs. dark rum
1 cup coarsely chopped or sliced blanched almonds
1¼ cups coarsely chopped or sliced walnuts
1 whole egg (for brushing)

From the above ingredients, use the following to prepare Yeast Sponge:

YEAST SPONGE

1½ cups milk, lukewarm

2–3 Tbs. sugar

1½ cups flour (approx.)

5 ozs. fresh yeast (or 9 packages dry yeast)

Two or three 10 x 16 x 2-inch baking pans

Heat milk to lukewarm. Add sugar and flour. Blend. Add finely crumbled yeast. Combine. Cover with a kitchen towel and let rise in a draft-free place until bubbles appear on the surface.

If dry yeast is used, follow directions on p. 223.

While sponge is rising, cream together butter and sugar in a very large mixing bowl or large kettle (about 5 quarts). Add whole eggs, egg yolk, salt, grated lemon rind and orange rind, and a cup of flour. Mix. Add yeast sponge and with a wooden spoon beat in more flour. Fold ground almonds into mixture. Keep beating, gradually adding more flour until dough is firm enough and cannot be beaten any longer with wooden spoon. Beat by hand until about 10–11 cups of flour have been added and dough becomes very smooth, elastic, and shiny.

Transfer dough to a floured board and knead in more of the remaining flour if necessary (since some flour absorbs more liquid than others) to obtain a rather firm dough; keep kneading until smooth and elastic.

Gradually work in fruits, soaked in rum, alternately with three-fourths of the nuts until evenly blended without overworking dough.

Return dough to mixing bowl or kettle for rising. (If two bowls or kettles are available, divide dough, which will shorten the rising time). Cover with kitchen towel and let rise in a draft-free, warm place to at least double in size. Punch down and fold risen dough over, working remaining nuts into it. Cover and let rest for 30–45 minutes.

If dough has risen in one large bowl or kettle, divide in half. Place one half on pastry board, divide into 6 parts, 3 large and 3 medium pieces of even sizes. Roll each large piece into a roll approximately 15 inches long and 1½ inches thick. Plait the 3 rolls into a tress (it will be easier if you start to plait from the center toward both ends), pinching ends securely together.

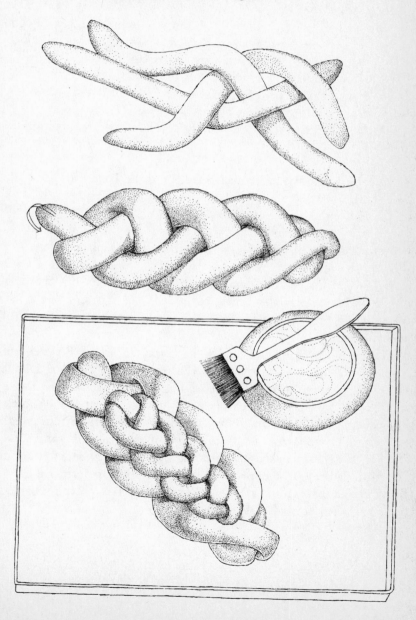

Transfer tress to a generously, evenly flour-dusted baking pan. Roll the 3 remaining medium-sized pieces to about 14 inches long and 1 inch thick. Plait into a second tress. Brush first tress with lightly beaten egg before placing second tress on top. Cover with a kitchen towel and let rise to not quite double in size. Proceed same way with other half of dough. Brush top with remaining beaten egg.

Place in preheated warm oven (400° F.) for 10 minutes. Reduce to 350° F. and bake 35–45 minutes longer until brown and cake tester, inserted into center, comes out dry.

Let cool on baking pans for at least 6–8 hours or overnight. Wrap well and store in a dry, cool place.

Cut into slices and serve generously sprinkled with confectioners' sugar.

Note: A medium and a small Striezel can be baked on the same baking pan, but you must leave ample space between them. It is up to you to decide the size of the Striezel.

In our house in Vienna, the Striezel was made the authentic way— first from a tress plaited of 4–5 rolls, topped by a plaited tress of 3 rolls, crowned by a 2-roll tress, twisted together. It was a very beautiful and impressive "construction job," but I am not that ambitious and therefore take a short cut, using only 2 tresses, one above the other, plaited of 3 rolls each. More modest, but still beautiful and impressive.

There is an even quicker and simpler way to bake a Striezel, but it is not plaited. It is an oval loaf that resembles a Stollen: Divide dough evenly into 3–6 pieces, depending on the sizes of the loaves you wish to obtain. Roll each piece into an oval about ½ inch thick. Fold dough lengthwise about two-thirds over, so that bottom dough will extend beyond top. With the edge of the palm of your hand, form a light indentation by pressing down on extended bottom dough toward edge of upper part; pat upper part to form a mound. Brush whole loaf with beaten egg. Bake as directed, reducing baking time according to size of loaves.

COFFEE CRESCENTS

(Danish Pastry)

This is a simple Danish pastry made from the Yeast Butter Dough recipe on p. 233.

Roll dough out to about ⅛ inch thick. Trim edges straight. Cut into 5-inch-wide strips and cut the strips into squares, then squares into triangles. Roll up lightly and bend into crescents. Place on 11 × 17-inch baking pan. Cover. Let rise.

Brush crescents with lightly beaten egg before placing into preheated oven (425° F.). Bake for 10 minutes, then reduce heat to 350° F. and bake for another 10 minutes until golden brown.

COFFEE CRESCENTS WITH ALMOND FILLING

(Danish Pastry)

This Danish pastry uses the recipe for Yeast Butter Dough on p. 233 and the following filling.

ALMOND FILLING:
2 cups finely ground blanched almonds

½ cup sugar (scant)
Rind of I lemon, grated
1 whole egg

11 x 17-inch baking pan

Roll dough out to about ⅛-inch thickness. Trim edges straight. Cut into 5-inch-wide strips and cut the strips into squares, then squares into triangles. Place a generous teaspoonful of filling close to long side of triangles and roll up. Bend into crescents, pressing edges together. Place on baking pan. Cover. Let rise.

Brush crescents with lightly beaten egg before placing into preheated oven (425° F.). Bake for 10 minutes, then reduce heat to 350° F. and bake for another 10 minutes until golden brown.

Almond Filling: Combine almonds with sugar and grated lemon rind. Break in egg and stir until you obtain a smooth paste.

DANISH PASTRIES (Yeast Butter Dough)

PLUNDERTEIG (GERMBUTTERTEIG)

This Yeast Butter Dough is the basis for Danish pastries. It is used in the recipes for plain Coffee Crescents (p. 231), Coffee Crescents with Almond Filling (p. 232), Open-Faced Cheese Pastry (p. 237), and Open-Faced Prune Butter Pastry (p. 238).

About 20 pieces

PUFF PASTE:
¾ cup flour
1½ bars sweet butter, cold

YEAST SPONGE:
¼ cup milk
1 Tbs. sugar
2–3 Tbs. flour
1 oz. fresh yeast (or 2 packages dry yeast)

DOUGH
½ bar sweet butter
¼ cup sugar
Rind of 1 lemon, grated
2 whole eggs
1 egg yolk
¼ tsp. salt
3½ cups flour (approx.)
Yeast sponge
¼ cup milk
1 whole egg for brushing

Puff Paste: Place half of flour on pastry board. Cut butter into it. Cover with remaining flour and quickly roll out with rolling pin. Form into a brick about ½ inch thick. Cover brick with wax paper. Chill. Brick should be cold but not too firm; it has to be pliable.

Yeast Sponge: Heat ¼ cup of milk to lukewarm. Add sugar, flour, and finely crumbled yeast and blend. Cover. Let rise in a draft-free place until bubbles appear on the surface. If dry yeast is used, see directions on p. 223.

Dough: Cream butter and sugar until smooth. Add lemon rind, whole egg, egg yolk, and salt. Mix. Fold several spoons of flour into mixture, then add yeast sponge and more flour alternately with milk, working about 3 cups flour in to obtain a medium-soft dough. Save remaining flour for rolling. Beat with wooden spoon for about 5 minutes until smooth. Cover. Refrigerate for about 15 minutes.

On a generously floured pastry board or cloth, with a floured roller, roll dough into a long rectangle about ½ inch thick. Place half of refrigerated butter brick in center and fold one-third of dough over brick. Place remaining half brick on top of dough, and cover with remaining dough. Seal ends.

Turn dough so that the short side is toward you. Quickly but gently roll dough into a rectangle about the same size as the first rectangle, always keeping enough flour on the board to prevent sticking. Fold over one-third of dough from short end. Brush excess flour from surface before folding remaining third of dough over (as though folding a business letter). Cover with kitchen towel. Refrigerate for about 15 minutes.

Repeat rolling and folding of dough two more times, refrigerating for about 15 minutes after each time. Before rolling, always place the dough with the short side toward you.

After final rolling and folding, cover and keep refrigerated for 1–2 hours.

Divide dough in half, keeping unused part chilled. Roll and form into desired pastries according to recipe and place well apart on a lightly buttered 11 × 17-inch baking pan. Cover with towel and let rise. Repeat all steps with second part of refrigerated dough.

Brush pastries with lightly beaten egg before placing into preheated oven (425° F.). Bake for 10 minutes, then reduce heat to 350° F. and bake for another 10 minutes until golden brown.

EASTER LOAF

1¼ bars sweet butter, soft
½–⅔ cup sugar
4 egg yolks, room temperature
½ tsp. salt
2 Tbs. rum
3¾–4¼ cups flour
¾ cup milk

1 oz. fresh yeast
½ cup raisins (optional)
⅓ cup slivered blanched almonds
  (optional)
1 whole egg, beaten
3–4 Tbs. slivered blanched almonds

From the above ingredients, use the following to prepare Yeast Sponge:

YEAST SPONGE

¾ cup milk, lukewarm
1 Tbs. sugar

10–12 Tbs. flour
1 oz. fresh yeast (or 2 packages dry yeast)

10 x 16 x 2-inch baking pan

Heat milk to lukewarm. Add sugar, flour, and stir. Add finely crumbled yeast. Combine. Cover with kitchen towel and let rise in draft-free, warm place until bubbles appear on the surface. If dry yeast is used, follow directions on p. 223.

While yeast sponge is rising, cream butter with sugar. Add egg yolks, salt, rum, and spoonfuls of flour. Combine. Fold yeast sponge into mixture, and with a wooden spoon gradually beat in more flour to obtain a shiny dough that no longer sticks to bowl and spoon. In bowl or on a floured pastry board, knead into an elastic, almost firm dough. If necessary, add more flour. Work raisins and almonds into dough (both optional). Let dough rise in bowl, covered with a kitchen towel, to at least double its size in a warm, draft-free place.

After rising, push dough down, turn over, and let rise once more for about 30 minutes.

On a floured pastry board form one big or two small round loaves. Place on a 10 × 16 × 2-inch baking pan, cover, and let rise for about another 30 minutes.

Before placing into preheated oven (400° F.), brush top with lightly beaten egg and sprinkle with slivered almonds. Bake for 10 minutes, then reduce heat to 350° F. and bake 20–30 minutes longer, according to size, until golden brown or test done.

Note: Dough can also be formed into a braid (or two) instead of a round loaf. Such a braid looks very attractive if there is a raw egg embedded in the center of it, as is the custom of farmers in many European countries at Eastertime.

Make 3 long rolls of dough of equal size and place close together. Embed an egg in the center of the middle roll and braid the rolls extending on either end of the egg, pressing ends firmly together. Proceed with baking as indicated above.

Dust with confectioners' sugar.

OPEN-FACED CHEESE PASTRY (Danish Pastry)

TOPFEN GEBÄCK (PLUNDERTEIG)

This cheese Danish pastry uses the Yeast Butter Dough recipe on page 233 and the following filling.

POT CHEESE FILLING:

½ lb. pot cheese
2 Tbs. sweet butter, melted
¼ cup sugar

1 egg yolk
Rind of 1 lemon, grated
1 egg white

11 x 17-inch baking pan

Divide yeast butter dough in half, keeping unused part refrigerated. Roll dough out to less than ¼ inch thick. Trim edges straight. Cut into 4-inch strips and cut the strips into squares. Place a teaspoon of cheese filling in center of each square, spreading filling toward two opposite corners, then fold the other two corners toward center, overlapping slightly. Place well apart on a lightly buttered 11 × 17-inch baking pan. Cover with towel and let rise. Repeat with second part of dough.

Brush pastries with lightly beaten egg before placing into pre-heated oven (425° F.). Bake for 10 minutes, then reduce heat to 350° F. and bake for another 10 minutes until golden brown.

Pot Cheese Filling: Strain pot cheese or mash with a fork until all lumps have disappeared. Add melted butter, sugar, and egg yolk. Combine thoroughly. Add lemon rind and fold mixture together with beaten egg white.

Note: Pot cheese can be replaced with farmer cheese. If too dry, add some milk.

OPEN-FACED PRUNE BUTTER PASTRY

POWIDL GEBÄCK (PLUNDERTEIG)

(Danish Pastry)

Follow recipe for Open-Faced Pot Cheese Pastry, replacing the pot cheese filling with 1½ cups prune butter (lekvar). See p. 233. Sprinkle with sliced almonds.

OPEN PRUNE BUTTER KOLATCHEN

OFFENE POWIDL KOLATSCHEN

Follow same recipe and all steps as for Pot Cheese Kolatchen, substituting 1 cup (approx.) prune butter (lekvar) for the pot cheese filling. See p. 244.

PLUM CAKE (Yeast Dough)   ZWETSCHGENKUCHEN (GERMTEIG)

16–20 servings

¾ bar sweet butter, melted
⅓–½ cup sugar
1 whole egg, room temperature
2¾–3¼ cups flour
Rind of 1 lemon, grated
½ tsp. salt

¾ cup milk
1 oz. fresh yeast
1 whole egg (for brushing)
3–4 lbs. fresh plums, pitted and
    quartered

From the above ingredients, use the following to prepare Yeast Sponge:

YEAST SPONGE

¾ cup milk, lukewarm
2 Tbs. sugar

10–12 Tbs. flour
1 oz. fresh yeast (or 2 packages
    dry yeast)

11 x 17-inch jelly-roll pan or baking pan

Heat milk in one-quart saucepan to lukewarm. Add sugar, flour, and crumbled fresh yeast to the mixture and blend. Place in a draft-free place, covered with a kitchen towel, and let rise until bubbles have formed on the surface. If dry yeast is used, follow directions on p. 223.

In a large bowl, while the yeast sponge is rising, combine cooled melted butter, remaining sugar, the whole egg, 4–5 tablespoons flour, grated lemon rind, and salt. Stir with wooden spoon until smooth. Add yeast sponge. Mix well. Gradually beat in remaining flour. Begin with 2¾ cups (generous) of flour, then, if necessary, add more, depending on the dryness of the flour. The dough should be medium firm. Keep beating and pulling dough away from sides of bowl for about 10 minutes until dough is smooth and satiny and no longer sticks to sides of bowl. Cover with kitchen towel, and in a draft-free warm (but not hot) place, let dough rise to at least double in size. Then punch dough down and let it rise again for a short time.

Place risen dough on a buttered 11 × 17-inch jelly-roll pan, patting it with lightly floured hands to fit pan. Brush top with beaten egg, then arrange the plums.

Create a border along the short sides of the pan by pressing the pointed ends of quartered plums lightly into dough and lifting the dough slightly. On the long sides of the jelly-roll pan, press the cut edge of the plum quarters into dough in the same manner. After borders are completed, place the remaining plums, slightly overlapping, closely together over whole surface. Let rise. Cover. Brush border with beaten egg.

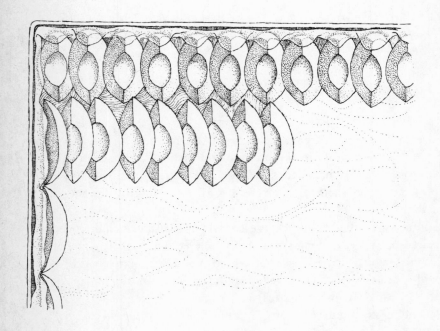

Preheat oven to 350° F. Bake on lowest rack for 30 minutes, then transfer to center rack, raise heat to 375° F. and bake for another 30 minutes or longer, until golden brown. When cooled, sprinkle plums with granulated sugar.

Before serving, cut into oblong or square pieces and serve sprinkled with confectioners' sugar.

Note: During the time the dough is rising, pit and cut plums in quarters, keeping them as dry as possible, then cover and place in refrigerator. Shortly before using, remove plums from refrigerator to bring them back to room temperature.

POPPYSEED STRUDEL

(Yeast Short Dough)

This particular recipe can only be made with fresh yeast.

8–10 servings

2 cups flour (approx.)
¼ cup sugar (scant)
1 bar less 1 Tbs. sweet butter
2 egg yolks
2 Tbs. milk, cold
¼ tsp. salt
¾ oz. fresh yeast
1 egg white

POPPYSEED FILLING:
¾ cup milk
½ cup sugar
3 cups ground poppyseeds
⅛–¼ bar sweet butter, melted
Rind of 1 lemon, grated
½–¾ cup raisins
2 bars or squares semisweet
   chocolate, grated (optional)

10 x 16 x 2-inch baking pan

Form yeast syrup by creaming crumbled yeast with one tablespoon sugar. See direction on page 223.

Mix flour and remaining sugar on pastry board. Make a deep well in center, cut in butter, and add egg yolks, tablespoons of cold milk, salt, and yeast syrup. With a table knife, fold flour mixture toward center to cover well. Combine. With fingertips, work ingredients together, then knead until flour is absorbed, and you obtain a smooth, dry dough that no longer clings to pastry board; if dough sticks to board, remove with knife. If necessary, add more flour.

Cover dough with a kitchen towel and let rest on pastry board in a cool place for about ½ hour.

Place dough between two sheets of wax paper and roll into 1 or 2 rectangular pieces less than ¼ inch thick. Remove top wax paper. Cut short sides straight, patch up if necessary. Spread poppyseed filling evenly over surface, leaving margins of about 1 inch at top and bottom and ¼ inch on both sides. Scatter raisins over top of filling.

With the help of the wax paper, fold over dough lengthwise in wide folds, jelly-roll style. Seal edges tightly. Use wax paper to transfer Strudel to a lightly buttered, floured, 10 × 16-inch baking pan, placing Strudel seam side down. Cover with kitchen towel and let rise in a draft-free place for about 1 hour.

Brush top of Strudel with lightly beaten egg white.

Cut several slits, about 1 inch long, crosswise to allow steam to escape so that top of Strudel won't burst.

Place Strudel into oven preheated to 400° F., then reduce heat immediately to 350° F. and bake for 35–45 minutes or until brown.

Strudel is best served a day or two later. Slice diagonally before serving and dust with vanilla confectioners' sugar.

Poppyseed Filling: In a small pan bring milk and sugar to boiling point. Add ground poppyseeds and let simmer so that poppyseeds can quill (expand), stirring constantly for about two minutes. Remove from heat. Add melted butter and grated lemon rind. Blend. If necessary, add a little more milk to obtain a spreading consistency.

Note: I would like to suggest you include grated semisweet chocolate in the filling. Perhaps a bit richer in texture, but very good in taste.

POT CHEESE KOLATCHEN

About 14 pieces

¾ bar sweet butter, soft
¼ cup sugar
2 egg yolks, room temperature
2 cups flour (approx.)
½ cup milk
½ oz. fresh yeast

POT CHEESE FILLING:
½ lb. pot cheese
2 Tbs. sweet butter, melted
¼ cup sugar
1 egg yolk
Rind of 1 lemon, grated
¼ cup blond raisins
1 egg white
½ cup prune butter (lekvar)

From the above ingredients, use the following to prepare Yeast Sponge:

YEAST SPONGE
½ cup milk, lukewarm
1 Tbs. sugar

6–8 Tbs. flour
½ oz. fresh yeast (or 1 package dry yeast)

10 x 16 x 2-inch baking pan

Heat milk in saucepan. Add sugar and flour and stir. Add finely crumbled yeast. Blend. Cover and let rise in a draft-free place until bubbles appear on the surface. If dry yeast is used, follow directions on p. 223.

In a large bowl, cream butter and sugar until smooth. Beat in egg yolks. Add a few tablespoons of flour. Stir. Add yeast sponge, then gradually add remaining flour, beating well with a wooden spoon about 10 minutes until dough is shiny, satiny, and no longer clings to the sides of the bowl. If necessary, add more flour, depending on the dryness of your flour, to obtain a semi-soft, smooth dough. Cover bowl. Let dough rise in a warm, but not hot, draft-free place to at least double its size. Push dough down, beat with a few strokes, and let rise again for a short while.

You can make two different kinds of Kolatchen, open or closed.

To make open Kolatchen, form balls of dough, about 2 inches in diameter, and place on a greased baking pan, two inches apart. Make a depression in center of each Kolatche so that the edges of dough are raised. Place about a teaspoon of cheese filling into each depression. Cover, let rise for a short while. Brush edges lightly with beaten egg. Bake. Before serving, sprinkle edges with confectioners' sugar.

To make closed Kolatchen, form balls of dough, about 2 inches in diameter, and place on a lightly floured pastry board. With your fingers, hollow out the center of each Kolatche and fill with a teaspoon of cheese filling. Pull edges of dough from all sides toward center, close firmly by pinching or twisting dough. Round out the Kolatchen and place them, seam side down, two inches apart, on a buttered 10 × 16 × 2½-inch baking pan. On top of each, make a small depression and fill with half a teaspoon of prune butter (lekvar). Brush edges all around with lightly beaten egg.

Bake for 20 minutes in preheated oven (400° F.). Reduce heat to 350° F. and bake for another 10 minutes or until golden brown.

Pot Cheese Filling: Strain pot cheese or mash with a fork until all lumps disappear. Add melted butter, sugar, and egg yolk. Combine well. Fold raisins, grated lemon rind, and well-beaten egg white into cheese mixture.

PRUNE BUTTER CRESCENTS

Follow recipe for Yeast Poppyseed Crescents on p. 260. For each crescent use ¾–1 teaspoon of Prune Butter (lekvar) in place of poppyseed filling.

20–22 pieces

½–¾ cup prune butter (lekvar)

11 x 17-inch baking pan

SAVARIN I

12–14 servings

2 whole eggs
1 egg yolk
⅓ cup sugar
½ tsp. salt
2–2¼ cups flour

½ oz. fresh yeast
½ cup half & half or milk
1 bar sweet butter, soft
1 cup Apricot Glaze II
1 Tbs. finely ground pistachio nuts

From the above ingredients, use the following to prepare Yeast Sponge:

YEAST SPONGE

½ cup half & half or milk
2 Tbs. sugar
6–8 Tbs. flour
½ oz. fresh yeast (or 1 package dry yeast)

RUM SYRUP

1¼ cups tea, medium strong
½–⅔ cup sugar
½ cup fresh orange juice, strained
⅓ cup dark rum

10-inch Gugelhupf form (Turk's head) or 9–10-inch Savarin ring

Heat milk to lukewarm. Add sugar and flour. Stir. Add finely crumbled fresh yeast. Mix. Cover with a kitchen towel and let rise in a draft-free place until bubbles appear on the surface. If dry yeast is used, follow directions on p. 223.

While yeast sponge is rising, mix eggs and egg yolk with remaining sugar and salt. Stir in several tablespoons of flour and the yeast sponge. Gradually beat in remaining flour with wooden spoon. If necessary, add 1–2 tablespoons more flour (depending on the size of the eggs and the dryness of the flour), keeping batter on the medium soft side. Beat vigorously for 8–10 minutes. Cover and let rise in a draft-free place until double in size.

Push dough down. Gradually beat soft butter into it and keep beating for a few more minutes.

Butter a 10–inch Gugelhupf form (Turk's head) generously. Pour batter evenly into it. Cover and let dough rise once more to three-fourths of capacity of form. Bake in preheated oven (400° F.) for 30–35 minutes until test done or golden brown. If baked in a Savarin ring, reduce baking time.

Let Savarin settle for about 5 minutes. Invert very gently onto a large plate. Prick top with cake tester (or trussing needle) in several places. Immediately spoon about half of cooled syrup gradually over Savarin and let set for a few minutes. When Savarin has absorbed syrup from bottom of plate, add more. Carefully return Savarin to Gugelhupf form (Turk's head). Spoon remaining syrup over until well soaked.

A few hours before serving, turn Savarin over on a plate and brush with hot apricot glaze. Refrigerate.

When glaze is firm, sprinkle top with ground pistachio nuts.

Rum Syrup: Prepare a medium-strong tea. Combine tea with sugar. Bring to a boil, let simmer for a few minutes. Remove from heat. Add orange juice and rum.

Note: A Savarin can also be served hot. Gradually spoon warm syrup over until well drenched. Apply hot apricot glaze. Best served with sliced strawberries, or any fruit of your choice, placed into center opening and with whipped cream on the side—a real delight.

With a hot Savarin you will have one of the most uncommon desserts for dinner.

SAVARIN II

12 servings

2¼ cups flour
½ cup sugar
3 whole eggs, room temperature
½ cup milk
½ Tbs. salt
¾ oz. fresh yeast (or 1½ packages dry yeast)

1¼ bars sweet butter, soft
1 cup Apricot Glaze II

RUM SYRUP:
1¼ cups tea, medium strong
½–⅔ cup sugar
⅓ cup dark rum
½ cup fresh orange juice, strained

10-inch Gugelhupf form (Turk's head) or 9- or 10-inch Savarin ring

If dry yeast is used, follow directions on p. 223.

Heat milk to lukewarm. Cream crumbled fresh yeast and 1 table-spoon sugar to obtain yeast syrup. See directions on p. 223. Combine flour and salt in a bowl, make well in center, and add yeast mixture, lukewarm milk, and whole eggs. Beat dough well with a wooden spoon, gradually adding half of soft butter in small pieces. Keep beating vigorously for about 10 minutes. Cover bowl with kitchen towel and let rise in a draft-free, warm (but not hot) place until double in size. After rising, push dough down and gradually blend in remaining butter until smooth, beating once more for about 5 minutes.

Butter a 10-inch Gugelhupf form (Turk's head) or Savarin ring generously. Spread batter evenly into form and let it rise to almost double its size or, even better, close to rim of form.

Bake in preheated oven (400° F.) for 30–35 minutes until medium brown or until inserted tester comes out dry. If baked in Savarin ring, reduce baking time.

Let cake settle for about five minutes. Invert Savarin with greatest care onto plate. Prick top with cake tester in several places.

Immediately spoon half of cooled syrup gradually over Savarin until it is well drenched. Return Savarin to form in which it was baked and pour on remaining syrup evenly until well soaked. Let cool.

Before serving, brush top and sides of Savarin with hot apricot glaze. Decorate with red glazed cherries or brandy-soaked strawberries. Decoration is optional.

Rum Syrup: Prepare a medium-strong tea. Combine with sugar in a small pan and let rapidly boil for good 5 minutes. Remove from heat and add strained orange juice and rum.

STIRRED YEAST DOUGH
GUGELHUPF

ABGERÜHRTER GERMTEIG
GUGELHUPF

All ingredients should be at *room temperature*.

About 12 servings

1 bar sweet butter, soft
½ cup sugar (scant)
1 Tbs. vanilla sugar or ½ tsp. vanilla extract
4 egg yolks
2¾ cups flour
¼ cup heavy cream, lukewarm
¼ cup milk
1 oz. fresh yeast
½ tsp. salt
2 egg whites
½ cup blond raisins (optional)

¼ bar sweet butter (for Gugelhupf form)
15–20 blanched almonds, split in half
1 egg white

YEAST SPONGE

¼ cup milk, lukewarm
1 Tbs. sugar
3–4 Tbs. flour
1 oz. fresh yeast (or 2 packages dry yeast)

10-inch Gugelhupf form (Turk's head)

Heat milk to lukewarm in saucepan. Add sugar, flour, and finely crumbled yeast. Combine. Cover with a towel and keep out of draft in a warm place. Let rise until bubbles appear on the surface. If dry yeast is used, follow directions on p. 223.

While yeast is rising, cream butter and sugar. Add one egg yolk at a time, stirring well after each addition. Gradually add flour alternately with heavy cream. Keep stirring until all cream and about half of the flour have been added. Add yeast sponge, mix well, then add salt and gradually the remaining flour, saving 2–3 spoons of flour. Stir batter with wooden spoon until it becomes shiny and satiny and no longer clings to sides of bowl. Gently but thoroughly fold in beaten egg white, the last 2–3 spoonfuls of flour, and raisins (optional).

Pour batter into a generously buttered, lightly floured, 10-inch Gugelhupf form that is decorated with split almonds around bottom and fluted sides of form. Even out batter. Cover with kitchen towel and leave in a warm (but not hot), draft-free place until batter has risen to more than double its size.

Brush top with lightly beaten egg white, combined with 1–2 tablespoons of water. Bake in preheated oven (400° F.) for 10 minutes. Reduce temperature to 350° F. and bake about 30 minutes longer. Do not open oven for the first 20 minutes. If inserted cake tester or toothpick comes out dry, the Gugelhupf is done. Allow to settle for at least 5 minutes, then invert gently on plate. When completely cool, return to Gugelhupf form and cover tightly with foil while storing.

Gugelhupf is best when baked one to two days before serving. Before serving, sprinkle with confectioners' sugar.

WASPS' NESTS

These are yeast buns with chocolate, ground nuts, and raisin filling.

24 pieces

WALNUT CHOCOLATE
FILLING:

¼ bar sweet butter, melted (for
  brushing of dough)

2–2½ cups finely ground walnuts

1½–2 bars or squares semisweet
  chocolate, grated

2 Tbs. sugar

Rind of 1 lemon, grated

¼ cup milk

1 Tbs. rum

1 Tbs. sweet butter, melted

½ cup dried raisins

Follow recipe for Yeast Buns Filled with Prune Butter, p. 253, omitting prune butter (lekvar).

Place risen dough, divided in half, on a floured pastry board. With a floured rolling pin, roll each part into a rectangular piece about ¼ inch thick and brush generously with melted butter. Spread walnut chocolate filling thinly over surface, starting at long edge closest to you, leaving 1-inch margin at top and narrow margins on both sides. Sprinkle with raisins. Roll up lengthwise, neatly, jelly-roll style.

Cut roll into pieces about 1½ inches wide. Close both open ends of each piece by pulling dough over openings and pinching dough slightly together. Pat each piece into a short, rectangular form.

Dip each bun lightly in melted butter, place in a well-buttered pan, closed sides facing and lightly touching one another. Cover and let rise in draft-free, warm, but not hot, place. Brush tops with melted butter before placing in preheated oven (400° F.). Reduce heat to 350° F. and bake for 25–30 minutes until medium brown.

After slightly cooled, carefully invert buns on pastry rack. Before serving, dust generously with confectioners' sugar. Don't cut Wasps' Nests; they can easily be torn apart.

Walnut Chocolate Filling: Combine nuts, chocolate, and sugar. Add grated lemon rind, milk, rum, and tablespoon of melted butter. Mix well together.

YEAST BUNS FILLED WITH
PRUNE BUTTER

20–24 buns

¾ bar sweet butter, melted
¼–⅓ cup sugar
1 whole egg plus 1 egg yolk
¼ tsp. salt
Rind of 1 lemon, grated
2¾–3¼ cups flour

1 oz. fresh yeast
¾ cup milk
1 cup prune butter (lekvar)
½ bar sweet butter, for pan and
   buns

From the above ingredients, use the following to prepare Yeast Sponge:

YEAST SPONGE
¾ cup milk
1 Tbs. sugar

10–12 Tbs. flour
1 oz. fresh yeast (or 2 packages
   dry yeast)

9-inch square baking pan or 9- or 10-inch frying pan or 10-inch loaf pan

Heat milk in saucepan to lukewarm. Add sugar and flour. Mix. Add crumbled fresh yeast and stir. Cover and let rise until bubbles appear on the surface. If dry yeast is used, follow directions on p. 223.

While yeast is rising, combine melted, cooled butter, sugar, egg, salt, and grated lemon rind in a bowl. Add 3–5 tablespoons flour and mix well. Add yeast sponge, combine, and gradually beat in flour to obtain a medium-soft dough. Sometimes you may have to add a little more flour, depending on its dryness. With a wooden spoon or by hand, beat until dough is smooth and elastic and no longer clings to bowl or spoon. Cover with a towel and let rise in a draft-free, warm place until it at least doubles in size. Punch dough down. Let rise again for about 30 minutes.

Place tablespoons of risen dough on a floured pastry board, one next to another, in intervals of about 2 inches. With fingertips pat into 2½-inch rounds and place about one teaspoon of prune butter in each center. With lightly floured fingertips, pull edges of each round toward its center and pinch edges firmly together so that the buns will be tightly closed. Pat lightly into a rectangular shape. Dip buns in melted butter and place them next to one another in a generously buttered 9-inch baking pan or 9- or 10-inch frying pan or 10-inch loaf pan, with dipped and closed sides down.

Cover with towel and let rise for a good 30 minutes. Brush tops with melted butter before placing in preheated oven (350° F.).

It is an old saying that buns have to swim in butter so you will be able to tear them apart easily. Never cut them!

Bake for 35–45 minutes or until buns are medium brown and shrink from sides of pan.

Let settle for 5 minutes, then place gently on pastry rack. Let cool.

Before serving, dust generously with confectioners' or vanilla confectioners' sugar.

Break apart only at the table.

YEAST GUGELHUPF

Keep all ingredients at room temperature.

10–12 servings

1 bar sweet butter, soft
½ cup sugar (scant)
Rind of 1 lemon, grated
4 egg yolks
3 cups flour (approx.)
¼ tsp. salt
⅓ cup chopped blanched almonds

½ cup blond raisins
1 cup milk
1 oz. fresh yeast
¼ bar sweet butter, for Gugelhupf form
2–3 Tbs. bread crumbs, finely grated

From the above ingredients, use the following to prepare Yeast Sponge:

YEAST SPONGE

1 cup milk, lukewarm
1 Tbs. sugar

10–12 Tbs. flour
1 oz. fresh yeast (or 2 packages dry yeast)

10-inch Gugelhupf form (Turk's head)

Heat milk in saucepan to lukewarm. Add sugar, flour, and finely crumbled yeast. Stir. Cover pan with a kitchen towel and set aside in a draft-free place. Let rise until bubbles appear on surface. If dry yeast is used, follow directions on p. 223.

While yeast sponge is rising, cream butter and sugar until fluffy. Add grated lemon rind, stir in egg yolks (one at a time), several spoonfuls of flour, and salt. Mix well. Fold in yeast sponge and gradually add remaining flour. With wooden spoon beat dough from all sides for 5–10 minutes until satiny and blisters are forming. Add finely chopped almonds and raisins. Beat with a few more strokes until well blended.

Pour batter into a generously buttered, lightly breadcrumb-dusted 10-inch Gugelhupf form (shake out any excess crumbs). Cover with kitchen towel and leave in warm, but not hot, draft-free place. Let rise to at least double in size or, even better, almost to the rim.

Bake in preheated oven (400° F.) for 10–15 minutes, then reduce heat to 350° and continue baking for 40–45 minutes more, until top is well browned. Avoid opening oven for the first 15–20 minutes. When an inserted toothpick or cake tester comes out dry, Gugelhupf is done. Allow Gugelhupf to set for 5 minutes, then place a large plate on top of form and turn over very gently. Remove form and let cool.

Gugelhupf will be tastiest if served one or two days after it is baked. Store Gugelhupf by returning it to its form when completely cool. Cover with foil or plastic wrap.

Dust generously with vanilla confectioners' sugar before serving.

YEAST NUTCAKE

About 12–15 servings

¾ bar sweet butter, soft
¼ cup sugar
2 egg yolks
3¼–3⅔ cups flour
1 cup milk, lukewarm
½ tsp. salt
1 oz. fresh yeast
⅓ cup slivered almonds, finely sliced
½ cup blond raisins
⅓ cup diced, candied lemon peel
¼ bar sweet butter, melted (for brushing)
1 egg white

WALNUT FILLING:

3 cups finely ground walnuts
¼ cup sugar
Rind of 1 lemon, grated
3 Tbs. rum

STREUSEL TOPPING:

¾–1 cup flour
¼–⅓ cup sugar
½ bar sweet butter, soft
1 cup coarsely chopped walnuts

From the above ingredients, use the following to prepare Yeast Sponge:

YEAST SPONGE

1 cup milk, lukewarm
1 Tbs. sugar

10–12 Tbs. flour
1 oz. fresh yeast (or 2 packages dry yeast)

10 x 16 x 2-inch baking pan

Heat milk to lukewarm in saucepan. Add sugar, flour, and finely crumbled yeast. Combine. Cover pan with kitchen towel and let rise in a draft-free, warm but not hot, place until bubbles appear on surface. If dry yeast is used, follow directions on p. 223.

During the time yeast is rising, cream butter and sugar in a big bowl. Add egg yolks, spoons of flour, and salt. Stir well. Add yeast sponge and gradually work in remaining flour with a wooden spoon, beating dough from all sides. Keep beating dough with spoon or by hand until it no longer clings to sides of bowl, becomes elastic and satiny, and blisters are forming. After dough is well beaten, work in almonds, raisins, and diced candied lemon peel until evenly distributed. Cover bowl with towel and let dough rise to more than double in size in a draft-free place.

After dough has risen, punch it down and let it rise once more to half the size of its first rise. Divide dough into two equal parts.

On a lightly floured pastry board, roll one part into a rectangular piece to make it fit approximately into a generously buttered 10 × 16 × 2-inch baking pan. Transfer rolled-out dough to pan and pat to fit. Brush dough with melted butter. Scatter nut filling evenly over dough. Sprinkle with rum.

Roll second part of dough out (stretch by hand, if necessary) to make it fit over first part, pinching seams together slightly. Cover. Let rise once more, just to the point where it becomes puffy.

Brush top with egg white and scatter Streusel topping evenly over surface.

Place in preheated oven (400° F.). Reduce heat to 350° F. and bake for about 35 minutes or until Streusel topping becomes lightly browned and cake shrinks from sides of pan.

Walnut Filling: Mix ground walnuts with sugar; add grated lemon rind. Combine well.

Streusel Topping: Mix flour and sugar in a bowl or on a wooden board. Combine with soft butter. Work by hand into coarse crumbs. Combine with chopped walnuts.

YEAST NUT CRESCENTS

Follow recipe for Yeast Poppyseed Crescents on p. 260. Replace poppyseed filling with ½–¾ teaspoon of nut filling in each crescent.

20–22 pieces

NUT FILLING:
½ cup milk
2 cups finely ground walnuts
Rind of 1 lemon, grated

¼ cup sugar
2–4 Tbs. sweet butter, melted
1 Tbs. rum
⅓–½ cup raisins

11 x 17 x 2-inch baking pan

Nut Filling: Combine hot milk with ground nuts. Let stand for about 15 minutes until nuts are well expanded. Add lemon rind, sugar, and melted butter. Mix well until smooth. Fold in rum and raisins.

YEAST NUT STRUDEL
(Yeast Short Dough)

Follow recipe for Poppyseed Yeast Strudel on p. 242. Substitute walnut filling for poppyseed filling.

8–10 servings

WALNUT FILLING:
¾ cup milk
⅓–½ cup sugar
4 cups finely ground walnuts

½ bar sweet butter, melted
Rind of 1 lemon, grated
1 tsp. rum or ½ tsp. vanilla extract
½ cup blond raisins (generous)

Walnut Filling: In a saucepan, bring milk to boiling point. Add sugar and walnuts. Over low flame, let simmer for about 5 minutes, stirring constantly. Remove from flame, add melted butter, lemon rind, rum or vanilla extract. Combine.

When cool, spread mixture evenly over rolled-out dough. Sprinkle raisins over filling.

This particular recipe can only be made with fresh yeast.

20–22 pieces

1⅓ cups flour (approx.)
Rind of 1 lemon, grated
1 bar less 1 Tbs. sweet butter, cold
1 egg yolk
1 whole egg (2 generous Tbs. use
   for dough, remaining save for
   brushing)
1½ Tbs. milk, cold
⅛ tsp. salt

½ oz. fresh yeast
3 Tbs. sugar

POPPYSEED FILLING:

¾ cup milk
⅓ cup sugar (approx.)
3 cups ground poppyseeds
¼ bar sweet butter, melted
Rind of 1 lemon, grated
½ cup raisins

11 x 17 x 2-inch baking pan

Place flour on pastry board. Add grated lemon rind. Make well in center and cut in butter. Whisk egg yolk, 2 tablespoons of whole egg, milk, and salt into dough. Add finely crumbled fresh yeast and sugar. Fold flour over with knife, working toward well. Combine. Quickly work with fingers until dough holds together. Knead dough briefly into a smooth, dry dough, adding more flour if necessary.

Roll dough out twice, then form a ball. Divide into two parts.

On a floured pastry board with a floured rolling pin, roll each part to about ⅛-inch thickness. Cut into about 4-inch strips and cut each strip into squares. (If you cannot obtain the desired thickness at first, cut strips less wide and roll each square to the required size.)

Spread a teaspoon of poppyseed filling across center of each square. With the help of a table knife, roll squares lightly from corner to corner, jelly-roll style, bending them into crescent shapes and sealing ends firmly. Place crescents on a lightly buttered 11 × 17 × 2-inch baking pan. Brush crescents with beaten egg. Cover and let rise in draft-free place for about 30 minutes.

Brush crescents once more with egg before placing in preheated oven (375° F.). Bake for 20–25 minutes or until medium brown. Serve dusted with confectioners' sugar.

Poppyseed Filling: Bring milk and sugar to boiling point, then add ground poppyseeds. Let simmer for a few moments to let poppyseeds expand. Remove from heat and add melted butter, grated lemon rind, and raisins. Mix well. Let cool.

Note: If you prefer, you can also cream fresh yeast with 1 tablespoon sugar to form a syrup (see p. 223) before adding to flour and prepared ingredients.

8. Desserts Served Hot—
Top of Stove

Introduction

In this chapter we are finally coming to hot desserts, and you will have to try them to realize that you are entering a completely new world of fine desserts.

A hot dessert fulfills two purposes: as a dessert after meals, but also, especially in Austria, as a meal in itself. On a meatless day, to replace the main course or, at lunch, to get away from the monotony of sandwiches, no better substitute can be chosen than, for example, yeast dumplings, fruit dumplings, Salzburger Nockerln, ringlets, or an Emperor's Omelet.

Imagine eating a fruit dumpling in which the fresh fruit is thinly covered with dough made of pot cheese. The dough itself is light and delectable. It happens every so often that acquaintances of ours whom we have not seen or heard from for some time will call when fresh apricots, cherries, and other fruit reappear on the market, to invite themselves to a dinner of the "unforgettable fruit dumplings." During the winter, we use fresh strawberries instead.

APPLE FRITTERS	*Gebackene Apfelspalten*
APPLE FRITTERS DELUXE (WINE BATTER)	*Gebackene Apfelspalten de luxe (Weinteig)*

APRICOT DUMPLINGS (CREAM PUFF DOUGH)	Marillen Knödel (Brandteig)
APRICOT DUMPLINGS (POT CHEESE DOUGH)	Marillen Knödel (Topfenteig)
APRICOT DUMPLINGS (POTATO DOUGH)	Marillen Knödel (Erdäpfelteig)
APRICOT FRITTERS	Gebackene Marillen
BOHEMIAN DALKEN (YEAST DOUGH)	Böhmische Dalken (Germteig)
CHERRY DUMPLINGS (POTATO DOUGH)	Kirschen Knödel (Erdäpfelteig)
CRÊPES WITH JAM	Palatschinken
FARINA RINGLETS	Grieskranzerl
PLUM DUMPLINGS (CREAM PUFF DOUGH)	Zwetschgen Knödel (Brandteig)
PLUM DUMPLINGS (POTATO DOUGH)	Zwetschgen Knödel (Erdäpfelteig)
PLUM DUMPLINGS (POT CHEESE DOUGH)	Zwetschgen Knödel (Topfenteig)
POT CHEESE DUMPLINGS	Topfen Knödel
POT CHEESE FARINA DUMPLINGS	Topfen Gries Knödel
POT CHEESE RINGLETS	Topfenkranzerl
POTATO NOODLES WITH POPPYSEEDS AND SUGAR	Erdäpfel Nudeln mit Mohn und Zucker
PRUNE BUTTER POCKETS (NOODLE DOUGH)	Powidltascherln (Nudelteig)
PRUNE FRITTERS (BATTER WITH WINE)	Schlosserbuben (Backteig mit Wein)
PUFFED BEIGNETS	Spritzkrapfen
RICE PUDDING (STEAMED)	Reis Auflauf (Dunstkoch)
ROSE PETALS	Rosenkrapfen
SNOWBALLS	Schneeballen
SOUR CREAM DALKEN	Rahm Dalken
STEAMED PRUNE BUTTER DUMPLINGS (YEAST DOUGH)	Powidl Knödel über Dunst (Germteig)
YEAST NUT DUMPLING (NAPKIN DUMPLING)	Germ Nuss Knödel (Servietten Knödel)
YEAST POT CHEESE PANCAKES	Germ Topfen Palatschinken (Livansky)

APPLE FRITTERS

GEBACKENE APFELSPALTEN

About 24 pieces

1 cup flour (scant)
¾ cup milk
1 whole egg
1–2 Tbs. sugar

3 apples, medium size
Sugar, verifine
Cinnamon (optional)

Blend flour and milk in a bowl. Add egg and sugar. Mix. Refrigerate batter for a few hours. Stir to remove remaining lumps.

Core and peel apples. Cut into round slices about ¼ inch thick, with hole of core in centers. Drop apple slices into batter. When well coated, fry in hot deep fat (375° F.) over low flame until lightly brown on both sides. Remove with a slotted spoon or fork and drain on absorbent paper.

Keep warm on hot plate. Sprinkle with verifine sugar combined with cinnamon (optional).

Serve at once.

APPLE FRITTERS DELUXE
(In Wine Dough)

GEBACKENE APFELSPALTEN
DE LUXE (IN WEINTEIG)

4-6 servings

1–1¼ cups flour
2 egg yolks
½ cup white wine
¼–⅓ cup sugar
¼ tsp. salt

2 egg whites
3–4 apples, medium size
Sugar, verifine
Cinnamon

Whisk flour and egg yolks together. Add wine, sugar, and salt and mix until all lumps have disappeared. Refrigerate.

Core and peel apples. Cut into slices about ¼ inch thick, with hole of core in centers.

Shortly before frying, fold well-beaten egg whites into batter. Blend gently but thoroughly. Dip apple slices into batter. When coated well, fry in hot deep fat (375° F.) over low flame, several at a time, until medium brown and crisp on both sides.

Remove with slotted spoon and drain on absorbent paper. Keep warm on hot plate. Sprinkle with verifine sugar or sugar mixed with cinnamon.

Serve at once.

APRICOT DUMPLINGS
(Cream Puff Dough)

MARILLEN KNÖDEL (BRANDTEIG)

10–12 servings

Follow recipe for Plum Dumplings (Cream Puff Dough, see p. 276), substituting 10–12 medium-sized, medium ripe apricots for plums.

Remove pits by cutting half through along natural seam, and replace with lumps of sugar. Close apricots tightly.

APRICOT DUMPLINGS
(Pot Cheese Dough)

MARILLEN KNÖDEL (TOPFENTEIG)

Here is a dumpling with very few calories—one of the most delicious, light, refreshing, and easy-to-make desserts.

About 12–14 pieces

½ lb. pot cheese
1 whole egg
⅛ tsp. salt (omit if cheese is salty)
¾ cup flour (approx.)
1–2 Tbs. sweet butter, melted
12–14 fresh, medium-ripe apricots, small to medium size

12–14 cubes of sugar

BREADCRUMB TOPPING:
¾–1 bar sweet butter, melted, golden brown
½ cup bread crumbs
Sugar, to taste

Mash pot cheese with fork until all lumps have disappeared. Add egg, salt, and a few spoonfuls of flour. Blend well. Gradually work remaining flour into mixture. (If necessary, add a little more flour, depending on the dryness of the cheese.) Dough should hold together when lightly patted. Add melted butter and combine well. Refrigerate for at least 2 hours, even overnight—no harm will be done.

Cut apricots along natural seam (just enough to remove pit) and replace pit with a cube of sugar. Close tightly.

Place ½ to ¾ tablespoon of dough on a well-floured board or plate, depending on the size of the apricots, which should be thinly covered with dough. Pat dough *very lightly* with floured fingertips into 2½–3½-inch rounds. Place one apricot in center of each round. With lightly floured fingertips pat dough from all sides toward center to cover apricot completely to assure a well-closed dumpling. Between the floured palms of your hands, roll dumplings into a ball. Place on a floured napkin or plate and cover with a second napkin.

During preparation, bring one or two large kettles of lightly salted water to a boil. Place dumplings carefully into boiling water. Do not overcrowd kettle, since dumplings will expand, and keep kettle three-fourths covered. Bring water once more to boiling point. When dumplings have risen, reduce flame and let boil over medium heat for about 10 minutes. Carefully remove with a slotted spoon.

Serve at once.

It is advisable to cut dumplings into quarters before spooning browned butter and sugar or toasted bread crumbs and sugar over dumplings.

Note: Dumplings can be reheated. Place them in pan with melted butter over low flame. Cover and let brown on both sides. Or reheat in 350° F. oven.

Pot cheese can be replaced by farmer cheese. If too dry, add a small amount of milk.

APRICOT DUMPLINGS
(Potato Dough)

MARILLEN KNÖDEL (ERDÄPFELTEIG)

12–14 pieces

Follow same recipe as for Plum Dumplings (Potato Dough, see p. 277), substituting apricots for plums. Remove pits from medium-sized apricots by cutting along natural seams half through and re-place pits with cubes of sugar, since apricots tend to become tart when cooked. Close apricots tightly.

APRICOT FRITTERS

GEBACKENE MARILLEN

4–6 servings

Follow recipe for Apple Fritters Deluxe (see p. 268), replacing apple slices with 14–16 semi-ripe apricots of medium size.

Cut apricots in half and remove pits. Dip apricot halves into batter. When well coated, fry several at a time slowly in deep shortening (375° F.) for 3–5 minutes until golden brown on both sides.

Gently remove with a slotted spoon and drain on absorbent paper. Keep warm on hot plate. Sprinkle very generously with verifine sugar. (Apricots have a tendency to become tart when cooked.)

Serve at once.

BOHEMIAN DALKEN (Yeast Dough)

Bohemian Dalken are unique among desserts, not only in taste, but also in appearance and preparation. A very good and easy-to-make yeast pastry, baked not in the oven but on top of the stove.

Bohemian Dalken are excellent after a light dinner, a Sunday brunch, or when unexpected visitors drop in. But—it is a small "but" —the pastry can only be made if you have an egg-poaching pan, also called a Danish pancake form (available in specialty stores). The Danish pancake form is a good investment, for it also comes in handy for Sour Cream Dalken and Indian Puffs.

8–10 servings

1 cup milk
½ cup sugar (scant)
2 cups flour (approx.)
2 whole eggs, room temperature
½ oz. fresh yeast (or 1 package dry yeast)

2 Tbs. sweet butter, melted
¼ tsp salt
Rind of 1 lemon, grated
1 cup prune butter (lekvar)

Heat milk in about a 1½-quart pan to lukewarm. Remove from flame. Add sugar and about half the flour. Stir. Break eggs into mixture. Mix well. Crumble fresh yeast very finely into batter and add remaining flour and melted butter. Blend batter well. If necessary, add more flour to obtain a heavier crêpe batter. Cover pan with a kitchen towel and let rise in a draft-free, warm place until bubbles appear on the surface. If dry yeast is used, follow directions on p. 223.

Stir batter down, then add salt and grated lemon rind. Beat batter for a few minutes and let rise to at least double in size.

Place about ½ teaspoon melted butter in each cavity of Dalken form. When butter is heated, pour ¾ scoop or a large serving spoon of batter into each cavity. Bake on both sides over low flame until medium brown, turning Dalken over with a table knife.

Transfer Dalken to a hot plate and keep warm until all the batter is used up. During baking time start putting two Dalken together, with ¾ tablespoon of prune butter (lekvar) spread between.

Sprinkle tops generously with confectioners' sugar.

Serve immediately.

Note: Dough can be prepared a day in advance. After it has risen, push dough down, cover with towel, and place in refrigerator. Remove from refrigerator 20–30 minutes before baking.

CHERRY DUMPLINGS
(Potato Dough)

KIRSCHEN KNÖDEL (ERDÄPFELTEIG)

12–14 pieces

Follow recipe for Plum Dumplings (Potato Dough, see p. 277), substituting 3–4 black cherries for each plum.

It is a little more tricky to roll dough with cherries into an even ball, but with a little patience I am sure you will be successful.

CRÊPES WITH JAM

PALATSCHINKEN

About 12 Crêpes

¾ cup flour
¾ cup milk
1 whole egg

Butter for frying
Apricot jam

One or two 7-inch frying pans or skillets

Beat flour and milk until well blended. Break egg into batter and stir. Refrigerate. (For best results, let rest for several hours.) Stir until all remaining lumps have disappeared. If batter is too thick, add a small amount of milk; if too thin, sprinkle more flour in to obtain a thin crêpe batter.

Over a low flame, melt a small piece of butter in a 7-inch frying pan or skillet. Cover surface by tilting pan. Pour half a scoop or a large serving spoon of batter into pan. Spread batter quickly and evenly, covering bottom of pan thinly. Cook until golden brown on both sides by flipping crêpe over with a table knife or spatula.

Place a large plate (if possible, ovenware) on a food warmer or over a pot or kettle of simmering water. Transfer crêpe to plate. Butter pan again and repeat all steps until batter is used up.

While cooking, spread finished crêpes thinly with apricot jam. Roll loosely.

Serve dusted with confectioners' sugar. It will look attractive if you stack the crêpes closely together.

FARINA RINGLETS

36–40 pieces

1½ cups milk
1 cup farina (approx.)
¼ tsp. salt

Rind of 1 lemon, grated
½ cup sugar (scant)
3–4 egg yolks

One or two 10-inch skillets

In a saucepan, bring milk to boiling point and add farina and salt. Cook over low flame, stirring from time to time. When mixture becomes almost too thick to be stirred any longer, remove from flame and stir until cool. Add grated lemon rind and sugar. Mix. Beat egg yolks into the mixture, one at a time, blending well after each addition. (Omit one egg yolk if mixture loses its firmness). Refrigerate for about 30 minutes. Divide into two to four parts.

With floured hands, on a lightly floured pastry board, shape mixture into a long roll (or into several small ones) about ½ inch thick. Cut off about 6-inch long pieces and form doughnut-shaped ringlets. Place ringlets on a lightly floured plate or wax paper and refrigerate for a short time.

In one or two 10-inch skillets, heat shortening to 375° F. Place ringlets in skillets and reduce to low or medium heat. Fry ringlets on both sides until golden brown. Remove them with a slotted spoon and drain on absorbent paper. Then transfer them to a hot plate.

Pour Wine Chaudeau (see p. 326) over ringlets and serve immediately. This can also be served with any fruit syrup of your choice, or stewed fruit.

PLUM DUMPLINGS
(Cream Puff Dough)

ZWETSCHGEN KNÖDEL (BRANDTEIG)

10–12 pieces

1 cup water
1½ Tbs. sweet butter, soft
1 cup flour
½ tsp. salt
1 whole egg
Fresh plums, medium size

BREADCRUMB TOPPING:
½–¾ bar sweet butter
⅔–1 cup bread crumbs, unsalted
3–4 tsps. sugar

Wipe plums clean and dry. If you pit the plums (which is not absolutely necessary), cut them along their natural seam, just enough to remove pits, and replace pits with lumps of sugar (optional). In a saucepan combine water and butter and bring to a boil. Quickly add flour, mixed with salt, all at once, stirring vigorously until smooth. Over low flame cook paste, stirring constantly until it leaves the sides of the pan. Remove from heat and let cool.

Add egg, beating hard until batter becomes smooth. At first it will not be easy since the batter will be slippery, but with some strong strokes you will get a very workable dough. Refrigerate for about 30 minutes.

Place ¾ tablespoon of dough on floured pastry board or plate. With floured fingertips pat lightly into a round about 3½ inches in diameter. Place a plum in center. Bring edges of dough toward center and pinch together well. Roll between the palms of your hands into a tightly closed ball. (Don't leave any openings in the dough.)

Bring a large kettle, three-quarters filled with salt water, to a boil. Since dumplings are expanding, use two kettles if necessary. Carefully place dumplings into boiling water, a few at a time. After they have risen to the surface, let boil, with kettle three-quarters covered, for about 10 minutes over medium flame. Remove with slotted spoon.

Serve immediately, rolled in buttered, toasted breadcrumbs combined with sugar.

Note: Dumplings can easily be reheated in butter over low flame. Brown on both sides and serve with buttered, toasted bread crumbs.

PLUM DUMPLINGS
(Potato Dough)

ZWETSCHGEN KNÖDEL

(ERDÄPFELTEIG)

12–14 pieces

2 medium-sized potatoes (about ½ lb.)

1–1¼ cups flour

¼ tsp. salt

1 egg

1 Tbs. sweet butter, melted

12–14 fresh plums

12–14 sugar cubes

BREADCRUMB TOPPING:

¾ cup bread crumbs

½–¾ bar sweet butter, melted

Wipe plums clean and dry. If you pit the plums (which is not absolutely necessary), cut them along their natural seam, just enough to remove pits, and replace pits with lumps of sugar (optional).

Cook unpeeled potatoes, preferably on previous day, then peel. Grate them on a floured pastry board and combine with flour and salt. Make a well in center and break in egg and butter. (Amount of flour depends on the mealiness of the potatoes.) Start with a small amount of flour and work ingredients together; if necessary, add more flour until you achieve a medium-soft dough.

Work dough with floured hands into a roll about 2 inches thick. Cut into ¾-inch slices. On a generously floured board and with floured fingertips, pat slices lightly into rounds about ¼ inch thick.

Place a plum on each round. With floured fingertips bring edges of dough toward center, pinching together firmly. In palms of lightly floured hands or on a pastry board, roll to an even ball. It is important that each dumpling be tightly closed to prevent opening during cooking. Transfer rolled dumplings to a floured napkin.

Lower dumplings gently into a large kettle of slightly salted, boiling water. Reduce flame after water resumes boiling, and with a wooden spoon loosen dumplings gently from bottom of kettle. After they have risen to surface, let boil for about 10 minutes. Keep kettle three-quarters covered. Remove dumplings with slotted spoon. While hot, roll in browned, hot bread crumbs and sprinkle with granulated sugar.

Serve immediately, with browned butter on the side.

Topping: Toast bread crumbs in melted butter, stirring until brown. Sugar to taste.

Note: Dumplings are delicious the next day when reheated over low flame in melted butter to medium brown on both sides.

Use mealy potatoes, otherwise you may have to add increasingly more flour.

PLUM DUMPLINGS (Pot Cheese Dough)

ZWETSCHGEN KNÖDEL

(TOPFENTEIG)

About 12–14 pieces

Follow recipe for Apricot Dumplings (Pot Cheese, see p. 269), substituting plums for apricots. You may remove pits, although it is not absolutely necessary. Pits, if removed, do not need to be replaced by sugar since plums do not turn as tart as apricots when cooked. Therefore sugar is optional.

POT CHEESE DUMPLINGS

8–10 dumplings

½ lb. pot cheese, dry
1 whole egg
⅛ Tbs. salt (omit if cheese is salty)
⅔–¾ cup flour
2 Tbs. sweet butter, melted

BREADCRUMB TOPPING:
¾–1 bar sweet butter, melted
⅔–1 cup plain bread crumbs
3–4 tsps. sugar

One or two deep, wide kettles

Strain pot cheese through a food mill. Add egg, salt, and flour. Mix together well, then stir in melted butter.

Make a sample dumpling by rolling a piece of dough between the palms of your hands into a 1½–2-inch ball. If dough is still sticky (it is caused by the moisture of the pot cheese), add a little more flour.

Keep refrigerated for at least 1 hour. With lightly floured hands, roll pieces of dough into 1½–2-inch balls to form dumplings. Place on floured towel.

Lower dumplings into one or two big kettles of salted boiling water. Do not crowd, since they will expand. After dumplings have risen to surface, reduce flame and let boil gently for about 10 minutes. Remove carefully with skimmer or slotted spoon.

Serve with butter-browned bread crumbs combined with sugar and, if you like, with melted browned butter on the side.

Topping (butter-browned bread crumbs): Melt butter in a small frying pan. Add bread crumbs. Keep stirring until they are toasted to medium brown. Remove from fire. Combine with sugar.

POT CHEESE FARINA DUMPLINGS

8 dumplings

½ lb. pot cheese, dry
½ bar sweet butter, soft
2 egg yolks
⅛ tsp. salt (omit if cheese is salty)
½ cup farina (approx.)
2 egg whites

BREADCRUMB TOPPING:
½–¾ bar sweet butter, melted
⅔–1 cup plain bread crumbs
3–4 Tbs. sugar

Deep, wide kettle

Strain pot cheese through a food mill.

Cream together butter, egg yolks, and salt. Add pot cheese and farina. Mix well. Refrigerate for about 1 hour to give farina time to expand. Beat egg whites until very stiff and fold into mixture. Roll dough into about 1½-inch balls to form dumplings.

It is advisable to boil a sample dumpling to make sure dumplings will hold together during cooking. If dough is not firm enough, add 1 tablespoon farina. If too firm, add 1 tablespoon milk. It all depends on the moisture in the pot cheese.

Bring a deep, wide kettle of salted water to boiling point. Lower dumplings into it. When dumplings have risen to surface, let boil gently for 12–15 minutes, with kettle partly covered. Drain.

Serve immediately with butter-browned bread crumbs combined with sugar.

POT CHEESE RINGLETS

About 30 pieces

½ lb. pot cheese, room
  temperature
⅓ cup sugar
Rind of 1 lemon, grated
2 egg yolks, room temperature
1 whole egg, room temperature
¼ tsp. salt
2½–2¾ cups flour

½ cup milk
½ oz. fresh yeast

APRICOT SAUCE:

1½–2 cups apricot jam
4–6 Tbs. white wine or liqueur of
  your choice (optional)

From the above ingredients, use the following to prepare Yeast
Sponge:

YEAST SPONGE

½ cup milk, lukewarm
1 Tbs. sugar

6–8 Tbs. flour
½ oz. fresh yeast (or 1 package dry
  yeast)

Heat milk in a pan to lukewarm. Add sugar and flour and combine.
Add finely crumbled yeast and blend. Place in a draft-free place,
covered with a kitchen towel. Let rise until bubbles appear on the
surface. If dry yeast is used, follow directions on p. 223.

Strain pot cheese through a food mill. Add sugar, lemon rind, egg
yolks, whole eggs, salt, and several spoons of flour. Stir. Add yeast
sponge. Blend. Gradually add remaining flour. Beat with a wooden
spoon about 5 minutes and blisters will form. Cover with a kitchen
towel and let rise in a draft-free, warm (but not hot) place to more
than double in size. After rising, push dough down, beat with a few
more strokes and let rise for about 20 minutes more.

Place tablespoons of dough on a lightly floured pastry board or
pastry cloth. With floured hands roll dough into about 7-inch long
rolls. Form doughnut-shaped rings and seal by pinching ends together. Cover ringlets with kitchen towel and let rise once more for
about 10 minutes.

While ringlets are rising, heat shortening in a wide kettle or in a deep frying pan to 375° F. Place several ringlets in hot fat—allowing room for them to expand. Keep covered for the first 2 minutes, and fry slowly on both sides to medium brown. Remove to absorbent paper to drain. Keep warm.

When ringlets are done, spoon apricot sauce over them.

Serve at once.

Apricot Sauce: Heat apricot jam until simmering. Serve plain or, according to taste, combined with sweet wine or liqueur of your choice.

Note: Dough will keep very well for one or two days, if refrigerated and covered. Remove from refrigerator 30 minutes before using.

Leftovers can be eaten cold and still be enjoyable.

POTATO NOODLES WITH
POPPYSEEDS AND SUGAR

4–6 servings

GARNISH
½ cup poppyseeds, ground, or
browned breadcrumbs

½ cup sugar
1 bar sweet butter, melted

Follow recipe for potato dough in the Plum Dumpling recipe (p. 277).

Work dough with floured hands into a roll about 2 inches thick and cut into ½–¾-inch slices. Roll each slice in palms of lightly floured hands into noodles 1½–2 inches long and ¾ inch thick, tapering them off at both ends.

Cook, half covered, in lightly salted water for about 15 minutes. Drain well.

Serve sprinkled with mixture of poppyseeds and sugar, with lightly browned butter on the side, or brown them in butter or roll in breadcrumbs browned in butter.

PRUNE BUTTER POCKETS
(Noodle Dough)

POWIDLTASCHERLN (NUDELTEIG)

About 24 pieces

1 whole egg, room temperature
1–2 Tbs. lukewarm water
⅛ tsp. salt
¾–1 cup flour
1 cup thick prune butter (lekvar)

TOPPING:
½–¾ cup ground poppyseeds
⅓ cup sugar
¾ bar sweet butter, melted

Whisk whole egg, 1 tablespoon water, salt, and one-quarter of flour into a thin batter. Place remaining flour on pastry board, forming a mound, and make a well in center. Pour mixture into well, fold flour over it, and blend and then knead ingredients into a smooth and elastic dough that no longer sticks to hands or board. If dough is too dry, gradually add a little more water; if too moist, add more flour. Dough should stay slightly moist, without being sticky.

Form a ball and cover with an inverted heated saucepan. Let rest for 5–10 minutes.

Divide dough. Keep one half covered. With a lightly floured rolling pin on a lightly floured board, roll other half out as thin as possible. Cut into strips about 2½ inches wide. Handle only one strip at a time. Keep remaining ones well covered to prevent drying out of dough.

Cut each strip into squares and place ¾ teaspoon of thick lekvar on each square. Brush edges with egg white before folding squares over into triangles, closing edges tightly. Press tines of fork around edges to seal them securely. Keep pockets covered with a kitchen towel until you are ready to cook them.

Lower pockets into a large kettle of lightly salted, lively boiling water. Bring water once more to a boiling point, keeping kettle three-quarters covered.

When pockets have risen to surface, reduce flame and cook for 15–25 minutes, depending on the thickness of the dough. Drain.

Serve immediately, topped with mixture of poppyseeds and sugar, with lightly browned, melted butter on the side.

Note: Pockets can be reheated. Place them in melted butter over low flame. Cover. Brown lightly on both sides. Serve with poppy-seed mixture.

PRUNE FRITTERS (Batter With Wine)

SCHLOSSERBUBEN (BACKTEIG MIT WEIN)

About 30 pieces

½ cup white wine
1 cup flour
⅛ tsp. salt
Rind of ½ lemon, grated
1 egg white

30 extra-large, dried prunes
30 blanched almonds
4 bars or squares semisweet
   chocolate, grated
¼ cup sugar

Use precooked, extra-large prunes or cook prunes until they are almost done.

Remove pits by cutting lengthwise but not completely through. Replace pits with blanched almonds. Close well.

Combine wine, sugar, flour, and salt. Beat until smooth. Add lemon rind. Let batter rest for about 30 minutes. Fold in stiffly beaten egg whites. Blend.

Dip prunes into batter. Fry at once in deep fat (375° F.) until golden brown on both sides.

Remove with a slotted spoon and drain on absorbent paper.

Roll in grated chocolate, combined with sugar, or in mixture of half unsweetened cocoa and sugar.

Serve on party picks.

PUFFED BEIGNETS

4–6 servings

1 cup milk
½ bar sweet butter
1⅓ cups flour

4 whole eggs
1 tsp. rum
Raspberry syrup or Wine Chaudeau

Heat milk in a medium-large pan. Place butter in hot milk. When melted and milk starts to simmer, remove from heat and pour flour, all at once, into the hot liquid, stirring quickly and vigorously.

Return pan with paste to a low flame and keep stirring without cooking until paste leaves sides of pan and a fine, dry dough develops.

Remove dough from flame and put into a bowl. After it has cooled somewhat but is still warm, add one egg at a time, beating thoroughly after each addition, until dough becomes smooth and glossy. When well blended, add 1 teaspoon of rum. Mix well.

Into a kettle of hot fat (375° F.) drop walnut-sized rounds through a pastry bag with a large opening, or simply drop tablespoons of batter into hot fat.

Fry beignets over low flame, keeping covered for the first 2 minutes. When golden brown, turn beignets over on other side. (If properly prepared, beignets should rise to double their size and crack open slightly.)

Remove beignets with a slotted spoon and drain on absorbent paper.

Serve hot, slightly dusted with confectioners' sugar and topped with raspberry syrup or with lightly cooled Wine Chaudeau (p. 326).

RICE PUDDING (Steamed)

REIS AUFLAUF (DUNSTKOCH)

6–8 servings

½ cup rice
1½ cups milk
½ bar sweet butter, soft
⅓ cup sugar
4 egg yolks
⅓ cup blond raisins
⅓ cup currants
⅓–½ cup finely chopped pistachios

Rind of 1 lemon, grated
⅓ cup diced candied orange peel
1 Tbs. rum
4 egg whites
Bread crumbs
2–3 Tbs. finely ground pistachio nuts
Raspberry syrup or Wine Chaudeau

1½–2-quart fluted steam pudding mold with tube

Cover rice with cold water and bring to a boil. Cook for 5 minutes over low flame. Drain off remaining water. Combine rice with milk and bring to a boil. Let simmer, three-quarters covered, stirring from time to time until all milk is absorbed and rice becomes tender and thick. (If necessary, add more boiling milk.) Let cool.

Cream soft butter and sugar until light and fluffy. Gradually stir in egg yolks and rice. Add raisins, currants, pistachios, lemon rind, and candied orange peel. Combine well and add rum. Fold in stiffly beaten egg whites. Mix thoroughly.

Pour mixture into a generously buttered, lightly breadcrumb-dusted, fluted steam pudding mold. (Remove excess crumbs.) Place cover securely on top. Set mold in a kettle two-thirds filled with boiling water. Cover kettle. Steam pudding for about 1 hour. Cover with serving plate, invert, and carefully remove pudding from mold by gently tapping top of mold. Sprinkle top with ground pistachio nuts.

Serve at once.

Especially good when served with raspberry syrup or Wine Chaudeau.

Note: This rice pudding can also be baked for about 45 minutes in the oven (350° F.) in a well-buttered, bread-crumb-dusted ring mold or in a 2-quart oven-proof dish.

Serve at once with raspberry syrup or Wine Chaudeau (p. 326).

ROSE PETALS

30–40 pieces

2 cups flour (scant)
⅛ tsp. salt
¾ bar sweet butter
¼ cup sugar

3 egg yolks
2 Tbs. sour cream
Jam of your choice

Combine flour and salt on pastry board. Cut butter into it, then crumble between fingers into coarse pieces. Make well in center, add sugar, egg yolks, and sour cream, and blend quickly with table knife. Work ingredients together, first with fingertips, then with hands. If dough sticks to board, add a little more flour. Shape into a ball. Cover and let rest, refrigerated, for at least 30 minutes.

Place dough on a lightly floured board. Roll out to less than ⅛-inch thickness by turning dough over several times, each time dusting pastry board lightly with flour before turning and rolling, until desired thickness is obtained.

Cut out rounds with three crinkled cooky cutters of different sizes (1, 1½, 2 inches, or larger). In each round, make five short incisions on surface toward center to give it a rose-petal-like appearance. Re-use scraps.

Take three rounds, one of each size. Brush center of largest with egg white and top with medium-sized round; brush with egg white and top with smallest round.

Fry several rose petals at a time in deep fat (375° F.) for about 5 minutes until golden brown. Drain on absorbent paper.

Crown with a drop of jam. Dust lightly with confectioners' sugar. Serve either hot or cold.

SNOWBALLS

About 36 pieces

2–2⅓ cups flour
2 Tbs. sugar
½ bar sweet butter, cold
4 egg yolks

4 Tbs. sour cream
1 Tbs. rum
Raspberry syrup (optional)

Mix flour and sugar on pastry board; make well in center and cut butter into it. Add egg yolks, sour cream, and rum. With a table knife, fold flour and sugar mixture over ingredients, then knead with hands into a medium-soft, smooth dough. From time to time, scrape sticky dough off board. Knead until board is clean of all ingredients. Refrigerate for about 1 hour.

Divide dough into three parts. On lightly floured board, roll each part out to less than ⅛-inch thickness, with a pastry wheel or a knife, cut into 1½–2 × 4-inch strips. Make a diagonal slit in center of each strip, about ¾ inch long, then pull one end of dough through the slit as far as it goes.

Fry several snowballs at a time in deep fat (375° F.) until golden brown on both sides. Immediately place to drain on absorbent paper. While still hot, sprinkle with vanilla confectioners' sugar.

Note: Can be served warm or cold. When served after dinner, top individual servings with raspberry syrup.

SOUR CREAM DALKEN

RAHM DALKEN

Sour Cream Dalken and Bohemian Dalken are closely related. Sour Cream Dalken are lighter and daintier, but equally easy and quick to prepare.

Once more the Dalken form (Danish pancake form) must be used.

6 servings

½ cup sour cream
¾ cup flour
¼ bar sweet butter, melted
2 Tbs. sugar

2 egg yolks
⅛ tsp. salt
2 egg whites
1 cup prune butter (lekvar)

Dalken form or Danish pancake form with 4–6 cavities

Whisk sour cream, flour, and slightly cooled butter together. Add sugar, egg yolks, and salt. Blend well. Shortly before baking, fold together with stiffly beaten egg whites.

Place a dot of butter into each cavity of a Dalken form or Danish pancake form. When melted, put 1 serving spoon or ½ scoop of batter into each cavity. Bake over low flame until bottom is medium brown and top of Dalken starts to get firm. Flip over with a knife and let brown on other side.

Transfer to a hot plate to keep warm until whole batter is used up.

Put two Dalken together, with prune butter (lekvar) spread between.

Serve immediately, sprinkled with confectioners sugar.

STEAMED PRUNE BUTTER DUMPLINGS (Yeast Dough)

POWIDL KNÖDEL ÜBER DUNST (GERMTEIG)

16–18 pieces

¼ bar sweet butter
¼ cup sugar
1 whole egg
¼ tsp. salt
2¾–3 cups flour
¾ oz. fresh yeast

¾ cup milk
¾ cup thick prune butter (lekvar)
GARNISH:
¾ cup ground poppyseeds
½ cup sugar
¾–1 bar sweet butter, melted

From the above ingredients, use the following to prepare Yeast Sponge:

YEAST SPONGE
¾ cup milk
1 Tbs. sugar

6–8 Tbs. flour
¾ oz. fresh yeast (or 1½ packages dry yeast)

One or two roasting pans with high covers

In a small saucepan, heat milk to lukewarm. Add sugar and flour, and stir. Add finely crumbled yeast. Blend. Cover with kitchen towel. In a draft-free place, let rise until bubbles appear on the surface. If dry yeast is used, follow directions on p. 223.

While yeast sponge is rising, cream butter and sugar. Add whole egg, salt, several tablespoons of flour, and stir. Blend in yeast sponge. Gradually beat remaining flour into dough. Keep beating with wooden spoon or by hand until satiny and bubbles appear on surface. Let rise, covered, in a draft-free warm (but not hot) place until at least doubled in size. Punch dough down and knead it very lightly (just to let air escape). Let rise again for 10–15 minutes.

Place a heaping tablespoon of risen dough on a well-floured pastry board. With lightly floured fingertips flatten each mound into rounds about 2½–3 inches in diameter and about ¼ inch thick.

In center of each round, place ½–¾ teaspoon of prune butter (lekvar). Lift edges of dough, pulling them from all sides toward center, and pinch ends tightly together, closing with a little twist. Roll, in the palms of your lightly floured hands, into a ball. Place, seam side down, on floured board and cover with towel. Let rise.

During rising time, fill a large roasting pan ¾ full of water. Stretch a piece of cheesecloth, folded twice, over top of pan. Tie a string around outside edge of pan and tighten securely so that cheesecloth won't give in when dumplings are placed on it. Cover pan with high cover.

When water is boiling, place dumplings on cheesecloth, at least 2 inches apart (since they will expand considerably). Cover. Steam dumplings over medium flame for about 30 minutes.

Remove to deep platter. Prick each dumpling several times with a fork to let steam escape.

Garnish individual servings with teaspoons of poppyseed combined with sugar mixture. Spoon melted, lightly browned butter over.

Serve immediately.

Note: Leftover dumplings can be refrigerated and are equally delicious when reheated. In a skillet, melt a generous portion of butter, and heat dumplings, covered, over low flame until both sides are browned. Sprinkle with poppyseed mixture and pour melted butter from skillet over dumplings.

YEAST NUT DUMPLING
(Napkin Dumpling)

GERM NUSS KNÖDEL (SERVIETTEN KNÖDEL)

6–8 servings

2 cups flour (approx.)
¼ cup sugar
1 whole egg
1 egg yolk
¼ tsp. salt
½ cup milk
½ oz. fresh yeast

¼ cup sugar (approx.)
2½ cups ground nuts
½ cup raisins (optional)

TOPPING:
½–¾ bar sweet butter
1 cup bread crumbs (unsalted)
⅓ cup sugar (approx.)

NUT FILLING:
¼ bar sweet butter, melted

From the above ingredients, use the following to prepare Yeast Sponge:

YEAST SPONGE
½ cup milk (lukewarm)
1 Tbs. sugar

5–6 Tbs. flour
½ oz. fresh yeast
  (or 1 package dry yeast)

Deep, wide kettle

Heat milk in a small pan to lukewarm and add sugar, flour, and finely crumbled yeast. Combine ingredients well. Cover pan with kitchen towel. Let rise in a draft-free place until bubbles appear on the surface. If dry yeast is used, follow directions on p. 223.

While yeast is rising, blend whole egg, egg yolk, sugar, salt, and several spoons of flour together. Combine yeast sponge with batter, gradually adding more flour. With a wooden spoon, beat dough well for about 10 minutes until it no longer sticks to bowl or spoon, adding more flour if necessary to get a firm, elastic, satiny dough. Place dough, covered, in a draft-free warm (but not hot) place. Let rise to at least double in size. After rising, punch dough down and let rise for additional 15–20 minutes.

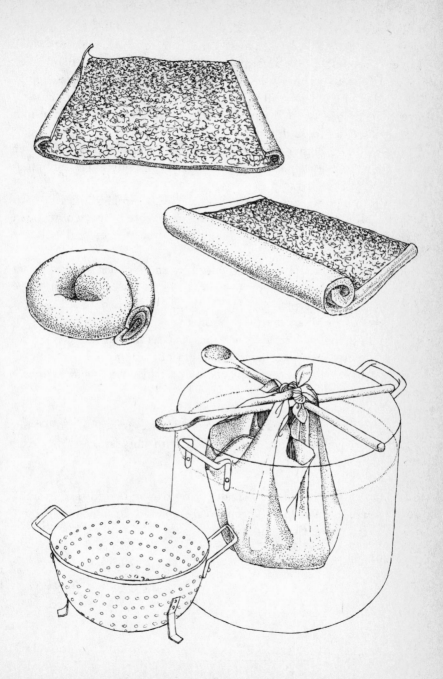

Transfer dough to well-floured pastry board, roll out to an oblong piece about 15 × 18 inches. Brush surface with melted butter. Cover with nut filling and scatter dry raisins over top. Bend over edges of the two short sides slightly to keep filling from escaping, then roll dough, jelly-roll style, into the shape of a long sausage, stretching it gently to about 18 inches long. Twist into a snail-like shape to form a large dumpling.

Flour a large dinner napkin generously. Place dumpling in center of napkin and tie opposite corners together loosely since dumpling will expand considerably.

While dumpling is again rising, fill a wide, deep kettle ¾ full with salted water and bring to boiling point. Secured by two wooden spoons, suspend napkin with dough in water. Cover and boil for about 1 hour.

Place bundle in a sieve, still secured by the wooden spoons, to let the water escape. When you are able to untie the hot napkin, place dumpling on a hot platter. Have buttered, browned bread crumbs ready and pour them over the dumpling.

Cut dumpling into serving portions and serve immediately.

Some guests may like more bread-crumb topping; therefore prepare a generous portion and place on the table with melted, lightly browned butter.

Nut Filling: Mix nuts with sugar. Brush surface of rolled-out dough with melted butter and sprinkle with nuts and sugar. Scatter raisins on top. (Optional)

Topping: Melt butter in a small frying pan and add bread crumbs. Keep stirring until bread crumbs are toasted to medium brown. Remove from fire. Combine with sugar.

YEAST POT CHEESE PANCAKES

8–10 pieces

¾ cup milk, lukewarm
2 Tbs. sugar
¾ cup flour (scant)
1 whole egg, room temperature
½ oz. fresh yeast (or 1 package dry yeast)
Pinch of salt

POT CHEESE FILLING:
½ lb. pot cheese
2–4 Tbs. sugar
2 Tbs. sweet butter, melted
1 egg yolk
Rind of 1 lemon, grated
⅓–½ cup blond raisins

One or two 7- or 8-inch frying or crêpe pans

Cream crumbled fresh yeast with 1 teaspoon of sugar until syrup forms. (If dry yeast is used, follow directions on p. 223.)

In a bowl of lukewarm milk combine remaining sugar, flour, and salt, blending well. Add egg and yeast syrup. Stir until smooth. Cover and let rise in draft-free place until bubbles appear on the surface. Stir down, beat lightly, and let rise again.

Place a 7- or 8-inch frying pan over medium heat. Melt enough butter to cover bottom of pan thinly.

With a 2-oz. ladle or a scoop, pour batter into hot butter, quickly tilt pan to spread batter evenly to make a thin pancake. Brown on both sides by turning over with a table knife or spatula.

Immediately spread pot cheese filling over pancake, roll, and keep warm on hot plate until remaining pancakes are done.

Sprinkle generously with vanilla confectioners' sugar.

Pot Cheese Filling: Strain pot cheese through a food mill or mash with a fork. Add sugar, melted butter, and egg yolk. Combine. Add lemon rind and raisins. Blend.

Note: Dough can be prepared hours in advance. After it has risen and is ready for use, push dough down, cover with towel, and place in refrigerator. Remove from refrigerator 20–30 minutes before baking time.

Pot cheese can be replaced with prune butter as a filling. Pancakes can also be reheated with the filling.

9. *Desserts Served Hot—*
Baked in Oven

Introduction

Surprise, surprise—or maybe you suspected it—but there are more hot desserts to come, though they are not baked on top of the stove, but in the oven. The great advantage of desserts made on top of the stove is that you won't be exposed to the heat of the oven, but you can still produce fine desserts. Most of the desserts baked in the oven take a relatively short time to prepare.

DAY AND NIGHT RICE PUDDING

6–8 servings

¾ cup rice (generous)
2–3 cups milk
¼ tsp. salt
½ bar sweet butter, soft
½ cup sugar
1 tsp. vanilla extract
3 egg yolks

½ cup raisins (optional)
2 bars or squares semisweet
    chocolate, melted
3 egg whites
3–4 Tbs. plain, fine bread crumbs
Raspberry syrup

2-quart shallow oven-proof dish, square or rectangular

Cook rice, covered with cold water, over medium flame for about 5 minutes. Drain off any remaining water. Add milk and salt and bring to boiling point. Let simmer, stirring from time to time, until milk is absorbed and rice becomes tender and thick.

Cream butter and sugar until smooth. Gradually stir in completely cooled rice and egg yolks. Add vanilla extract and raisins (optional).

Divide mixture. Combine one half thoroughly with melted chocolate. Beat egg whites until very stiff, fold evenly divided into both mixtures. Pour chocolate rice mixture (saving about 3 tablespoons) into a generously buttered, bread-crumb-dusted, oven-proof dish (remove excess crumbs). Top with white rice mixture. Spoon remaining chocolate rice mixture in a straight line down the center.

Bake in preheated oven (325° F.) for about 35 minutes.

Serve hot. Sprinkle with sugar or top with raspberry syrup—very delicious!

EMPEROR'S OMELET
(In Bits)

3-4 servings

¾ cup milk
2 egg yolks
2 Tbs. sugar
⅛ tsp. salt
1 cup flour (scant)
3 Tbs. heavy cream (or half &
half)

2 egg whites
¼ bar sweet butter for
skillet (approx.)
½ cup raisins (Sultana)
Raspberry syrup

Two 10-inch frying pans or skillets

Stir milk and egg yolks in a bowl, adding sugar, salt, and gradually flour; keep stirring until batter is well mixed. Add heavy cream. Combine.

Refrigerate for about 1 hour. Blend until all lumps have disappeared. Fold in stiffly beaten egg whites.

Pour batter into two 10-inch frying pans with hot melted butter and drop raisins into it.

Place on bottom of preheated oven (350° F.) until bottom of omelet becomes golden brown, turn over, place on center rack for about 10 minutes longer to brown other side. With two forks tear omelet into small pieces and return to oven for 2-3 minutes longer.

Sprinkle with granulated sugar and serve hot immediately. Spoon raspberry syrup over individual servings or serve with stewed fruit.

Note: Can be reheated the next day. Sauté pieces thoroughly in butter and dust with confectioners' sugar. Spoon raspberry syrup over. (Optional)

FARINA DUMPLINGS IN MILK

About 30 pieces

¾ bar sweet butter, soft
2 whole eggs
¾ cup farina
¼ tsp. salt

3–4 cups milk
2 cups water
2 bars or squares semisweet
   chocolate, grated

Deep, wide kettle
Two 10-inch frying pans or one large oven-proof dish

Cream soft butter and stir in whole eggs. Add farina and salt and blend thoroughly. Let mixture rest for about 30 minutes in refrigerator to let it swell.

In a deep, wide kettle (since dumplings will expand) bring milk, combined with water, to boiling point. Reduce flame. Take about ½ teaspoon of the mixture, pat quickly into oblong shape, and lower into boiling milk. Repeat until all of the mixture is used up. Bring to a boil, reduce flame, and cook for 2–3 minutes.

Pour entire contents of kettle without delay into two 10-inch frying pans, spreading dumplings out so that they lie flat on bottom of pans. Place immediately into preheated oven (350° F.) and bake for 15–20 minutes on lowest rack until dumplings turn yellow in color. By then they should be light and fluffy. With a slotted spoon, remove dumplings to a plate.

Serve at once, sprinkled with grated chocolate and sugar.

GENUINE SALZBURGER NOCKERL

ECHTE SALZBURGER NOCKERL

The often asked question comes up once again: which is the authentic recipe for Salzburger Nockerl? Every Austrian housewife defends her recipe as the genuine one, and I am defending mine as the authentic, delectable, easy, and quick-to-make Salzburger Nockerl.

6–8 servings

1 bar less 1 Tbs. sweet butter, soft
¾ cup sugar
10 egg yolks
½ cup flour (scant)
10 egg whites
1 cup milk

Two 10-inch skillets or one large oven-proof dish

Cream together butter and sugar. Add 2 or 3 egg yolks at a time, beating well after each addition until light and fluffy. Fold flour and very stiffly beaten egg whites into batter. (The success of this recipe depends mostly on the stiffness of your egg whites.)

Cover bottoms of two 10-inch skillets with milk. Bring to a boil and immediately pour batter into hot milk.

Place skillets in preheated oven (450° F.). Reduce heat to 400° F. and bake for 6–8 minutes until golden. Nockerln should be firm outside, but light and fluffy inside. With a serving spoon, quickly cut off large pieces, place on a preheated plate, and dust with verifine vanilla sugar.

Serve at once, since Nockerln do not tolerate waiting; they will collapse.

NOODLE DISH

4–6 servings

½ lb. noodles

½ bar sweet butter

1–1¼ cups ground poppyseeds

¼–⅓ cup confectioners' sugar

½–¾ cup thick prune butter

(lekvar)

7–8-inch oven-proof dish

Boil noodles in a large kettle of salt water for about 8 minutes until barely done. Drain. Rinse for a moment under cold water. Divide noodles into three parts.

On a generously buttered 7–8-inch oven-proof dish arrange a layer of noodles and cover with ground poppyseeds combined with sugar. Arrange second layer of noodles, spread evenly with prune butter, and top with third layer of noodles.

Place dots of butter all over top and bake in preheated oven (350° F.) for about 30 minutes or until golden brown.

OMELET SURPRISE

OMELETT SURPRISE

4–5 servings

4 egg whites
⅓ cup sugar
4 egg yolks

½ cup sifted flour
½ bar sweet butter for skillets
⅓–½ cup apricot jam

Two 10-inch frying pans or skillets

Beat egg whites until firm. Gradually add sugar and beat until very stiff. Gently fold in egg yolks and flour. Blend. Divide batter in half and spread into two 10-inch frying pans or skillets with melted, but not hot, butter.

Bake in preheated oven (375° F.) for 4–6 minutes on bottom of oven or on lowest rack until top becomes just firm.

Quickly but gently spread lightly heated apricot jam over half of omelet (if jam is too thick, thin with 1 tablespoon of water). Fold unfilled part over until ends meet. Remove to a hot plate.

Serve immediately, sprinkled with confectioners' sugar.

Note: This is a very dainty, feather-light omelet; accordingly it has to be treated very gently. A delight for every palate.

PANCAKE TORTE

6–8 servings

1¼ cups milk
2 whole eggs
1⅔–2 cups flour (scant)
¼ tsp. salt
¼ cup soda water
Milk or butter for oven-proof dish

FILLING:
1½ bars or squares semisweet
  chocolate, grated
½ cup apricot jam
1½ cups finely ground walnuts
⅓ cup blond raisins

8-inch frying pan or skillet
9-inch oven-proof dish or baking pan without removable bottom

Stir one-third of milk, eggs, and several tablespoons of flour until smooth. Alternately add more milk and flour and keep stirring until all lumps have disappeared. Combine with soda water. If batter is too thick, add more milk; if too thin, more flour, to obtain a medium-thin crêpe batter.

Coat 8-inch frying pan or skillet lightly with melted butter, pour about half a scoop of batter into it and quickly cover bottom by tilting pan to all sides. Crêpes must be thin to obtain 15–16 layers. Brown on both sides over medium flame.

Place finished crêpes on a plate, separating them with sheets of wax paper to prevent them from sticking together.

Pancakes can be baked several hours in advance.

Stack pancakes in a 9-inch oven-proof dish or baking pan. Barely cover bottom with milk or coat it generously with butter before placing first pancake in dish. Cover first pancake with grated chocolate, second pancake thinly with lightly heated apricot jam, third generously with ground walnuts combined with raisins. Repeat alternately with remaining layers. Brush top with melted butter.

Place torte in preheated oven (325° F.). Cover and heat for about 15 minutes. Remove cover and bake in oven for another 15 minutes.

Serve immediately, generously sprinkled with confectioners' sugar.

PLAIN YEAST BUNS WITH WINE CHAUDEAU

Follow recipe for Yeast Buns Filled with Prune Butter (see p. 253). The only difference is that Plain Yeast Buns are prepared without filling and differ in size.

40–50 small buns

WINE CHAUDEAU:
1 cup white wine

2–3 Tbs. sugar (to taste)
4 egg yolks

9- or 10-inch square baking pan or frying pan

Pat teaspoons of risen dough into plump, short rectangles. Dip each lightly in melted butter and place, one next to another, on a generously buttered 9- or 10-inch baking pan. Cover with kitchen towel and let rise again.

Brush tops of buns with melted butter. Bake in preheated oven (350° F.) for 15–20 minutes until brown. Invert on pastry rack. Serve lukewarm, with hot Wine Chaudeau on the side.

Wine Chaudeau: In a double boiler whisk ingredients together. Beat with a rotary beater steadily over gently boiling water until mixture becomes light and fluffy and has risen considerably. Serve at once. If wine is too strong for your taste, dilute with ¼ cup of water.

POT CHEESE OMELET

(In Bits)

4–6 servings

12 ozs. (¾ lb.) pot cheese
¼ cup sugar
½ cup sour cream
2 egg yolks
Rind of 1 lemon, grated

½ cup blond raisins (scant)
1 cup flour (scant)
2–3 egg whites
½ bar sweet butter for skillet

Two 10-inch skillets or frying pans

Strain pot cheese through food mill.

Mix pot cheese with sugar, sour cream, egg yolks, lemon rind, and raisins. Gradually add flour and fold stiffly beaten egg whites into mixture.

Over medium flame, melt butter in a 10-inch skillet or frying pan. Pour mixture into hot butter and immediately place in preheated oven (350° F.) for 20–25 minutes until bottom is brown and top is firm and lightly colored.

With two forks, tear into small pieces.

Serve hot, sprinkled with sugar. May also be served with stewed fruit.

SPONGE OMELET

4–6 servings

4 egg yolks
⅓ cup sugar
¾ cup flour (scant)

4 egg whites
½ bar sweet butter, melted
½ cup apricot jam

Two 10–12-inch frying pans or skillets

Beat egg yolks and sugar until very light and fluffy. Gently fold in flour and stiffly beaten, but not dry, egg whites. Pour batter, evenly divided, into two 10-inch frying pans, with hot melted butter.

Place pans into a preheated oven (375° F.) and bake for 12–15 minutes or until bottom of omelet becomes golden brown. Quickly spread half of omelet generously with lightly heated apricot jam (or with stewed fruit). Fold unfilled half over until edges meet, and remove to warm plate.

Serve immediately, sprinkled with confectioners' sugar.

10. Icings and Fillings

Introduction

The decorations of your tortes or pastries are as important as trimmings or accessories are to your dress. They should be attractive but simple. A single nut in the center of your cake can be as impressive as a grandiosely mounted decoration. Simplicity is what counts.

When it comes to fillings and icings, we would, of course, not dare to work against tradition or alter the specific character of a torte such as Dobos Torte or Sachertorte. Can you imagine changing the icing and still calling it Sachertorte? There is no need for doing it, since there are so many other pastries on which your imagination can work freely and change; for instance, from a chocolate to a coffee filling, from a cream topping to a lemon icing, or use a delicious flavored whipped cream as a filling, to suit your own personal taste.

What is of great importance is that the filling does not overshadow the cake's flavor so that you can savor both filling *and* cake.

Almond Filling

Apricot Glaze I

Apricot Glaze II

Caramel Icing

Chocolate Cream Filling I

Chocolate Cream Filling II

Chocolate Cream Filling and Frosting

Chocolate Icing I

Chocolate Icing II

Chocolate Icing III

Chocolate Whipped Cream Filling

Coffee Buttercream Filling

Coffee Cream Filling

Coffee Icing I

Coffee Icing II

Currant Glaze

Lemon Icing

Orange Buttercream Filling

Parisian Cream Filling and Frosting

Punch Icing

Vanilla Cream Filling

Walnut Butter Filling

Walnut Orange Filling

Whipped Cream

White Icing with Cooked Sugar

Wine Chaudeau

ALMOND FILLING

1½ cups finely ground blanched
  almonds
⅓ cup sugar

1 egg yolk
2 egg whites
1 tsp. cognac or rum

Combine ground blanched almonds with sugar.

Fold egg yolk into beaten egg whites, gradually stir almond mixture into it. Spoon 1 teaspoon of cognac or rum into mixture. Combine.

APRICOT GLAZE I

½ cup apricot jam

2–3 Tbs. rum

Heat apricot jam in a saucepan over low flame. Stir jam until it thickens. Remove from fire. Add rum by tablespoons. Mix. Coat top of torte while glaze is still hot.

APRICOT GLAZE II

Heat apricot jam in a saucepan over low flame until slightly thick. Stir until smooth. Use while still hot.

CARAMEL ICING

¾ cup sugar

½ tsp. sweet butter

Place sugar into a small saucepan over low flame. Stir constantly. When melted and liquid turns golden brown, add butter. Combine. Spread caramel icing quickly over pastry.

CHOCOLATE CREAM FILLING I

1½ bars sweet butter, soft
4 Tbs. verifine sugar
2 egg yolks

2–3 bars or squares semisweet
chocolate, grated
1 Tbs. instant coffee
2 Tbs. hot water

Blend butter and sugar well. Add egg yolks and beat until very creamy. Stir in grated chocolate, then add instant coffee. Mix until fluffy.

CHOCOLATE CREAM FILLING II

2 bars or squares semisweet
chocolate, melted
1 bar sweet butter
2–4 Tbs. sugar

1 whole egg
1 tsp. instant coffee
1 inch vanilla bean or ½ tsp.
vanilla extract

Melt chocolate in double boiler.

Cream butter and sugar well. Add lightly beaten egg. Stir. Add cool, melted chocolate, coffee, and vanilla. Combine until fluffy. If cream is too soft, chill to spreading consistency.

CHOCOLATE CREAM FILLING AND FROSTING

4 bars or squares semisweet
chocolate
⅓ cup water
2 Tbs. flour

2–3 egg yolks
½ inch vanilla bean or ½ tsp.
vanilla extract
1 cup heavy cream, whipped

Melt chocolate with water in double boiler. Remove from double boiler. Stir flour into melted chocolate. Combine with egg yolks. Return to double boiler, keep stirring over low flame until thick. Add vanilla. Combine. When cool, blend thoroughly with whipped cream. Refrigerate before using.

CHOCOLATE ICING I

¾–1 bar sweet butter, soft

4 bars or squares semisweet
chocolate

Melt chocolate in double boiler. When soft, add butter. Stir from time to time until dissolved and all lumps have disappeared.

CHOCOLATE ICING II

This is a less rich but very good and more economical chocolate icing. Especially suitable for icing of small pastries or decorating.

4 bars or squares semisweet
chocolate
2 Tbs. sugar

6–8 Tbs. water
1 Tbs. sweet butter

Melt chocolate in double boiler until soft.

Combine sugar and water and bring to a boil over low flame. Pour into soft chocolate in double boiler. When smooth, after all lumps have disappeared, remove from flame. Stir butter into chocolate sauce; when lukewarm, spread over pastry. Let dry.

CHOCOLATE ICING III

1 bar or square bitter chocolate
3 bars or squares semisweet
chocolate

1 cup water
½ cup sugar (scant)
1 Tbs. butter

Heat chocolate with ¼ cup of water over low flame until soft. Add remaining water and sugar. Blend. Stir until completely dissolved and let mixture boil until it reaches 200°–220° F. on a candy thermometer or it spins a very fine thread. Remove from heat, add butter. Stir occasionally until lukewarm, then pour over pastry.

CHOCOLATE WHIPPED CREAM FILLING

3 bars or squares semisweet
chocolate

2–4 Tbs. water
1 cup heavy cream, whipped

Place chocolate and water into a small pan. Let simmer over low flame. Keep stirring until you have a smooth chocolate sauce and all lumps have disappeared. If necessary, add some more spoons of water. Let cool without refrigeration to keep in liquid form. Only when chocolate sauce is completely cool, combine gradually with whipped cream.

COFFEE BUTTERCREAM FILLING

2 tsps. instant coffee
3 Tbs. hot water
1 bar less 1 Tbs. sweet butter, soft

3 egg yolks
⅓ cup sugar

Combine instant coffee with water. Stir butter until creamy.

In a double boiler, mix egg yolks, sugar, and coffee. Over low flame, beat mixture without stopping until very thick. Remove from flame. Place pan into ice water and keep beating until cool. Spoon mixture gradually into creamed butter, stirring well after each addition.

COFFEE CREAM FILLING

1½ bars sweet butter, soft
⅓ cup sugar
2 egg yolks

2–3 tsps. instant coffee
2 Tbs. hot water

Cream butter and sugar together. Add 2 egg yolks and stir. Combine coffee with 2 tablespoons hot water. Spoon into mixture, and beat until light and very fluffy.

COFFEE ICING I
(With Cooked Sugar)

¾ cup extra strong coffee   1¼ cups sifted confectioners' sugar
⅔ cup granulated sugar

Combine coffee with sugar. Let boil and stir over low flame until syrup is formed and spins a fine thread or until mixture coats the spoon. Gradually pour into confectioners' sugar, stirring continuously with a wooden spoon until icing is very smooth and small sugar lumps are no longer visible. Quickly spread icing thinly over pastry.

COFFEE ICING II

1¾ cups confectioners' sugar   ¼–⅓ cup extra strong coffee
½ egg white

Place sugar with egg white in a glass or porcelain bowl, gradually combine and stir coffee into mixture until you obtain a coating consistency. Several hours before serving, spread icing over pastry.

CURRANT GLAZE

1 envelope unflavored gelatin   1 cup currant jelly or raspberry
2–3 Tbs. water   and currant jelly

Place 1 envelope of gelatin into a small saucepan, sprinkle with water, and add ¼ cup currant jelly. Dissolve completely over low flame. Remove from fire, combine with remaining jelly, and blend until smooth.

Use when nearly firm.

LEMON ICING

1½ cups confectioners' sugar   1 Tbs. boiling water
4–5 Tbs. lemon juice, strained

Place sugar and lemon juice into a glass or porcelain bowl. Add boiling water. Stir with wooden spoon until very smooth and shiny. When mixture covers back of spoon, the icing has the right consistency.

If too thin, add more sugar; if too thick, more boiling water.

ORANGE BUTTERCREAM FILLING

1½ bars sweet butter, soft   Rind of 1½ oranges, grated
⅓–½ cup verifine sugar   Juice of 1 orange, strained

Cream together butter and sugar. Add grated orange rind, then gradually orange juice. Beat until fluffy and well combined.

PARISIAN CREAM FILLING AND FROSTING

Considered one of the finest creams.

4 bars or squares semisweet   1 cup heavy cream
  chocolate

Place heavy cream with small pieces of chocolate over medium low flame. Stir constantly until chocolate dissolves completely, simmers, and starts to thicken. Remove and place pan in cold water, or even better over ice cubes. Stir by hand or beat using only one attachment of electric beater.

Refrigerate for several hours or overnight, and then stir once more until you obtain a very firm cream.

PUNCH ICING

Red food color
1 Tbs. boiled water
2 cups confectioners' sugar

3 Tbs. lemon juice, strained
3 Tbs. dark rum

Boil ¼ cup water and add 3 drops of red food color to it. In a porcelain or glass bowl combine sugar, lemon juice, rum, and colored boiling water. With a wooden spoon stir until smooth and shiny. When the back of the wooden spoon is well covered with mixture, the icing has the right consistency.

If too thick, add more boiling water; if too thin, more sugar.

VANILLA CREAM FILLING

1 cup milk
3 egg yolks
¼ cup sugar

1½–2 Tbs. cornstarch
½ tsp. vanilla extract

Whisk ¼ cup cold milk, egg yolks, sugar, and flour together. Gradually add remaining milk (warmed) and whisk until smooth. Place in a double boiler over medium heat, beating until cream becomes thick. Remove from fire and combine with vanilla extract. Cool by placing pan in cold water, stirring from time to time to prevent forming of skin on top of cream.

WALNUT BUTTER FILLING

¾ bar sweet butter, soft
⅓ cup verifine sugar
1 cup finely ground walnuts

1 Tbs. rum
1 Tbs. milk

Cream butter and sugar until fluffy, then fold together with walnuts. Blend well. Combine with rum and milk.

WALNUT ORANGE FILLING

¼ cup milk
¼–⅓ cup sugar
1½ cups finely ground walnuts
½ tsp. vanilla extract or ½ inch
  vanilla bean

¼ cup candied orange peel,
  grated
1 Tbs. dark rum

Bring milk and sugar to boiling point. Add walnuts, stir, then remove from flame. Add vanilla, orange peel, and rum. Blend. Use when completely cool.

WHIPPED CREAM

Whipped cream is to the Austrians what ice cream is to the Americans. It seems to have a magnetic power for many people who enjoy it daily and, apparently, cannot live without it.

Whipped cream can be served with coffee or hot chocolate or as a topping, filling, or decoration for pastry. It can be lightly sweetened, unsweetened, or combined with almost any flavor of your choice.

Heavy cream is best beaten when one or two days old and well refrigerated. During the hot season it is advisable also to chill bowl and beater. Beat heavy cream until it starts to thicken; gradually add tablespoons of sugar. Keep beating until stiff and only then add the flavor of your choice.

PLAIN WHIPPED CREAM:

1 cup heavy cream
2–3 Tbs. confectioners' sugar

COFFEE WHIPPED CREAM:

1 cup heavy cream
2–3 Tbs. confectioners' sugar
1–2 tsps. powdered instant coffee

VANILLA WHIPPED CREAM:

1 cup heavy cream
2–3 Tbs. confectioners' sugar
½–1 inches vanilla bean or vanilla
  sugar (If vanilla sugar is used,
  omit plain sugar.)

COCOA WHIPPED CREAM:

1 cup heavy cream
2–4 Tbs. confectioners' sugar
2–4 tsps. sifted, dark, unsweetened
  cocoa

CHOCOLATE WHIPPED
CREAM:

1 cup heavy cream
1–2 Tbs. confectioners' sugar
1½–2 bars or squares semisweet
  chocolate, grated

WALNUT WHIPPED CREAM:

1 cup heavy cream
2–4 Tbs. confectioners' sugar
¾–1 cup finely ground walnuts
1 Tbs. rum

STRAWBERRY WHIPPED
CREAM:

1 cup heavy cream
2–4 Tbs. confectioners' sugar
1 pint sliced strawberries

CHESTNUT WHIPPED
CREAM:

1 cup heavy cream
2–4 Tbs. confectioners' sugar
1 Tbs. vanilla sugar or 1 Tbs. dark
  rum
¾–1 cup mashed chestnuts

LIQUEUR WHIPPED CREAM:

1 cup heavy cream
2–4 Tbs. confectioners' sugar
2–3 Tbs. rum or maraschino or any
  liqueur of your choice

WHITE ICING WITH COOKED SUGAR

½ cup granulated sugar
¼ cup water
1 cup confectioners' sugar, sifted

1 Tbs. liqueur of your choice or
  strained lemon juice or coffee

Stir sugar and water over medium flame until completely dissolved. Reduce to low flame and keep boiling until sugar reaches 200°–220° F. on a candy thermometer or, when placed between thumb and finger, sugar feels very sticky.

Gradually pour into confectioners' sugar and stir with a wooden spoon continuously until smooth.

Use as is or add a tablespoon of liqueur of your choice or a tablespoon of very strong coffee or strained lemon juice.

Spread icing on pastry. Let dry before serving.

WINE CHAUDEAU

1 cup white wine
2–3 Tbs. sugar (to taste)

4 egg yolks

In a double boiler, whisk ingredients together. Beat with a rotary beater steadily over gently boiling water until mixture becomes light and fluffy and has risen considerably. Serve at once.

If wine is too strong for your taste, dilute with ¼ cup of water.

SPECIALTY STORES

Unusual Ingredients and Baking Accessories:

H. Roth & Son, "Lekvar by the Barrel," 1577 First Avenue, New York, N. Y. 10028

Paprika Weiss, Importers, 1546 Second Avenue, New York, N. Y. 10028

Heidi's Around the World Foods, 1149 South Brentwood Blvd., St. Louis, Mo. 63117

Old Europe Fine Foods, 3855 Lawrence Blvd., Montreal, Canada

Zabar's Gourmet Foods, 2245 Broadway, New York, N. Y. 10024

Baking Accessories:

Bazar Francais, 666 Avenue of the Americas, New York, N. Y. 10010

The Bridge Company, 212 East 52nd Street, New York, N. Y. 10022

Cross Imports, 210 Hanover St., Boston, Mass. 02113

Kitchen Glamour, Inc., 26770 Grand River, Detroit, Michigan 48240

Maid of Scandinavia, 3244 Raleigh Avenue, Minneapolis, Minn. 55416

Williams-Sonoma, 576 Sutter Street, San Francisco, California 94102

Index